"This remarkable book reveals the seldom-discussed connection between Autism Spectrum Disorder (ASD) and cybercrime. The book illustrates that predatory tactics by online exploiters target vulnerable characteristics of individuals with ASD, who then become criminal defendants. The authors leverage substantial experience to provide new insights for potential forensic expert witnesses. The related phenomena they discuss, in 14 outstanding chapters, provide a new framework for professionals to educate attorneys, prosecutors, and juries on matters previously unexplored. I regard this book as essential reading for all attorneys and mental health professionals involved in criminal cases with defendants on the autism spectrum."

Kenneth J. Weiss, MD, *Clinical Professor of Psychiatry at the Perelman School of Medicine University of Pennsylvania, Philadelphia*

"I recommend *Cybercrime and the Autism Spectrum* to all judges. Not only does it describe the challenges people on the spectrum face in the criminal legal system, but it details the reasons for their behavior and why they are vulnerable to committing online offenses."

Judge Bernice Donald, *Retired Judge of the U.S. Court of Appeals for the Sixth Circuit*

"*Cybercrime and the Autism Spectrum: How the Online World Creates Victims and Offenders* is an essential, powerful and comprehensive resource on cybercrime and autism spectrum disorder written by world-leading experts in the field. This groundbreaking book will be an invaluable addition to the bookshelves of academics, mental health and legal professionals, teachers, caregivers and other professionals working with individuals on the spectrum. The potential real-world impact the knowledge and guidance this book will give is priceless."

Clare Allely, *Professor of Forensic Psychology at the University of Salford, United Kingdom*

I0025272

Cybercrime and the Autism Spectrum

Cybercrime and the Autism Spectrum explores the intersection of cybercrime and the autism spectrum, offering a multidimensional perspective from a clinician, an attorney, and a technical forensic expert. With a focus on real-life anonymized cases, discover how the online world impacts autistic individuals as both victim and offender.

This book provides strategies on how to detect and prevent autistic individuals engaging in criminal behavior online, such as communication with minors, child pornography, stalking, and online radicalization. Current research and clinical case studies provide a sympathetic and non-pathologizing insight into recognizing problematic behavior, creating online safety, and treatment for autistic individuals.

This is essential reading for mental health professionals working with neurodiverse individuals and their families, attorneys working with autistic clients, judges, law enforcement officers, those in training, and anyone seeking to understand the challenges and vulnerabilities facing autistic people in the digital age will have renewed compassion for the difficulties they face.

Mary Riggs Cohen, PhD, is a clinical psychologist with 30 years of experience in autism diagnosis, treatment, and advocacy. She has been conducting forensic evaluations of autistic individuals and providing expert testimony since 2009.

Elizabeth Kelley is a criminal defense lawyer with a nationwide practice focused on representing people with mental disabilities. She is the editor of several books published by the American Bar Association, including Representing People with Autism Spectrum Disorders, Representing People with Dementia, and Representing People with Mental Disabilities.

Michele Bush is a digital forensics expert, a private investigator, and the owner of digital forensics firm Loehrs Forensics. She has been a certified digital forensic examiner since 2013, worked on hundreds of criminal investigations, and testified as an expert in state and federal courts throughout the United States.

MARY RIGGS COHEN, ELIZABETH KELLEY, AND MICHELE BUSH

Cybercrime and the Autism Spectrum

How the Online World Creates Victims and Offenders

Routledge
Taylor & Francis Group

NEW YORK AND LONDON

Designed cover image: © Getty Images

First published 2026
by Routledge
605 Third Avenue, New York, NY 10158

and by Routledge
4 Park Square, Milton Park, Abingdon, Oxon, OX14 4RN

Routledge is an imprint of the Taylor & Francis Group, an informa business

For Product Safety Concerns and Information please contact our EU representative
GPSR@taylorandfrancis.com. Taylor & Francis Verlag GmbH, Kaufingerstraße 24,
80331 München, Germany.

ISBN: 9781032889689 (hbk)
ISBN: 9781032878119 (pbk)
ISBN: 9781003540571 (ebk)

DOI: 10.4324/9781003540571

Typeset in Joanna
by Newgen Publishing UK

Contents

Individuals on the autism spectrum are particularly vulnerable to committing online offenses, in many instances unwittingly. They are also victimized by online predators, financial scams, and extremist groups. Consequently, they are increasingly interacting with the criminal justice system as either offenders or victims. The authors examine this phenomenon from a clinical, legal, and technological perspective. The book addresses current legal issues in the United States criminal justice system with regard to dealing with persons with autism. It describes the characteristics of autism spectrum disorder (ASD) that create a risk of offending or of being victimized: social isolation, trauma, lack of social awareness, insufficient sexuality education and support, immersion in fantasy, rigidity of thinking, and the need for community.

The online world is a unique space where conventional boundaries are often blurred and misunderstood. Chatrooms, online forums, and social media sites can provide a sense of belonging; however, fake identities and deception are common. Autistic individuals have difficulty detecting this deception or the underlying agendas of others during these online interactions. Autistic individuals are especially vulnerable to manipulation by those with radical agendas or criminal intent. The book presents how these vulnerabilities can, over time, result in criminal activities such as communication with minors, sexual exploitation, stalking, and online radicalization. It discusses instances when individuals on the spectrum were manipulated into participating in illegal activities without their full knowledge or comprehension. The emerging issues of AI-generated images, deepfakes, voice cloning, fraudulent scams, and the susceptibility of autistic individuals are explored. Throughout the book, current research and clinical case studies (altered to preserve confidentiality) are provided for illustration. Recommendations from those in the field are presented regarding how to recognize online problematic behavior, create online safety, and obtain appropriate treatment for autistic individuals. It presents current data on autistic individuals' experiences in all phases of the justice system as offenders and victims. In the case of arrest, the book explains the processes involved in obtaining an attorney, an evaluation, and appropriate trauma-informed support. It explores the legal issues of competency and criminal responsibility, mitigation, and sentencing as it relates to autistic defendants. It examines current issues in the US prison environment and the matter of access to appropriate mental health support. The book contrasts other international models for diversion and addressing the mental health needs of those on the autism spectrum against the US.

*In the autism community, there is a debate around the use of person- and identity- first language (Botha et al., 2023). The authors acknowledge that there are many other terms used in this community (autist, neurodivergent, Aspie) and always ask for an individual's preference. Both identity-first "autistic" and person-first "individuals on the autism spectrum" and "individuals with autism" will be used throughout this book. In the chapters related to legal matters, the diagnostic term autism spectrum disorder (ASD) will be used. This is because an autistic offender or victim will need to be identified in court proceedings.

*All cases presented in this book are composites, created from multiple forensic cases and modified to preserve confidentiality.

I would like to thank the entire team at Elizabeth Kelley Law and especially Lisa Johnson for her capable, efficient, and good-humored assistance. I also would like to acknowledge Attorney Robert Herz and the Forensic Computer Examiner with whom I have worked on digital cases and from whom I have learned a good deal.

My sincere appreciation goes to Dr. Brittany Lyman and Dr. Reginald Candio for their support, insightful feedback and contributions to the clinical content of this book. I am grateful to the autistic individuals who shared their personal experiences of online victimization and offending, as well as their interactions with the criminal justice system.

Mary Riggs Cohen

I extend my deepest gratitude to the autistic community, whose insight, resilience, and experiences have shaped this book. Your voices challenge assumptions, enrich understanding, and continue to inspire meaningful change. To the investigators, attorneys, judges, and representatives of the legal community—thank you for your dedication to truth, fairness, and protecting the vulnerable.

Michele Bush

Introduction

Mary Riggs Cohen, Elizabeth Kelley, and Michele Bush

NEURODIVERSITY

In today's society, individuals are frequently categorized as either neurodivergent or neurotypical. Neurodiverse describes those who process information differently from most of the population, who are neurotypical. Along with autism spectrum disorder (ASD), attention deficit hyperactivity disorder (ADHD), intellectual disability (ID), and dyslexia are all now recognized as neurodiverse conditions with a distinct neurobiology (Fung, 2021). Human minds are wonderfully diverse, each offering unique perspectives and interpretations of the world around us (Armstrong, 2015). In psychology and psychiatry, individuals with similar neurodiverse thinking styles are grouped into conditions like autism or ADHD. These diagnoses describe a cluster of characteristics in individuals who process information similarly. Even within these neurodiverse conditions, there is great variation. This is conceptualized as a spectrum of behaviors, present to different degrees in each person.

The neurodiversity movement emphasizes the societal benefits of these diverse ways of thinking. It encourages us to re-examine what is seen as the norm and to appreciate the contributions of these different "out-of-the-box" thinkers. Those of us who work with autistic individuals or have autistic friends or family members appreciate the many ways they enhance our communities with their creativity, distinctive observations, and humor. Their uniqueness enriches many aspects of our lives. Accordingly, enhanced awareness of neurodiversity in our societal institutions is essential for equity and inclusion for those who experience the world differently. The objective of this book is to improve the criminal justice system's understanding and treatment of autistic individuals who may become offenders or victims online.

DOI: 10.4324/9781003540571-1

THE AUTISM SPECTRUM

Autism is characterized by narrow repetitive behaviors and difficulties with social interaction, communication, and adjusting to change. It is a neurodevelopmental condition that is present from birth. Life outcomes are highly variable depending on environmental factors, age at diagnosis and intervention, and individual personality factors. Each autistic person is unique and will present differently from others. Dr. Stephen Shore, an autism advocate and frequent speaker who is himself on the autism spectrum, has remarked, "Once you have met one person with autism, you have met one person with autism" (Shore, 2016). People on the autism spectrum process the world in an exceptional way. They have a very distinctive lens with which they perceive and understand their experiences. Autistic individuals often attend to details in their environment that neurotypicals miss. They have a distinctive thinking style that promotes new perspectives and creative expression. These different approaches can be valuable with regard to finding unique and unconventional solutions to problems. Conversely, autistic people are often at a great disadvantage when they encounter complex social situations. They take in social information (both verbal and non-verbal) differently from neurotypicals. Some do not look at faces and instead attend to other aspects of the situation. As a result, they often struggle with real-time communications involving rapid, simultaneous social processing. Autistic people are challenged by less formal social language and may interpret idioms, sarcasm, or slang literally. Many individuals struggle with non-verbal communication, including facial expressions, gestures, and various forms of body language. As a result, face-to-face social interactions can be especially challenging for them. The neurotypical world appears to be speaking a foreign language that they cannot decipher. Some individuals on the autism spectrum also have a limited ability to understand others' perspectives. This ability is often referred to as "theory of mind" (ToM). It is essentially the capacity to understand that other people have their own thoughts, beliefs, intentions, desires, and emotions which are different from one's own. Understanding others' beliefs and desires is crucial for social success and helps us navigate social situations and build relationships. Without Theory of Mind, it is difficult to respond appropriately to others' behavior. Although Theory of Mind deficits are associated with autism, this ability exists to varying degrees in autistic individuals.

Autistic individuals are detail-oriented and sometimes do not see "the bigger picture," They may seem socially and emotionally immature compared to their neurotypical peers. Some individuals on the autism spectrum have difficulty understanding why their conduct is at times socially off-putting. This, combined with their naivety, lack of social experience, and social awkwardness, can produce inappropriate behaviors. As a result, many experience repeated social rejection and isolation. Most autistic people are seeking a social connection and are not loners by choice. Their social avoidance emanates from their intense social anxiety, which is often misunderstood by neurotypicals.

For many years, autism was thought to be a rare condition and was narrowly defined. It is now understood to be more prevalent, with current estimates of 1 in 36, or 2.8 percent of the population (CDC, 2023). The range of behaviors has also expanded from non-verbal or intellectually limited individuals, to those functioning in highly qualified professions in education, science, technology, law, medicine, and the arts. Accordingly, it is essential that society develops a greater understanding of these neurodivergent individuals, so as to create an inclusive, empathic, and just world.

AUTISM AND THE CRIMINAL JUSTICE SYSTEM

Individuals on the autism spectrum are particularly vulnerable to committing online offenses, in many instances unwittingly. They are also victimized by online predators, financial frauds, and extremist groups. Consequently, they are increasingly interacting with the criminal justice system as either offenders or victims (Cooper et al., 2022). Currently, our system often marginalizes autistic individuals who are not adequately understood, evaluated, represented, or receiving appropriate support (Clasby et al, 2021). In this book, we will focus on the factors that bring those on the autism spectrum into the criminal justice system and examine how to improve outcomes for autistic offenders and victims of cybercrime.

It is estimated that 25 percent of the autistic population aged 16 and older have had contact with the criminal justice system either as a victim or as an offender (Miller et al, 2022). According to several current studies examining the experiences of autistic persons in the criminal justice system, 75 percent of those did not receive appropriate supports during the process (Slavny-Cross et al., 2022), and age, gender, race, and economic conditions create an increased risk (Koffer Miller et al., 2022).

PROBLEMATIC LAW ENFORCEMENT INTERACTIONS

Many autistic individuals are often proficient with "masking," a term defined as "hiding or disguising oneself in order to better fit in" (Pryke-Hobbes et al., 2023). If they do not self-identify as autistic, their masking may prevent law enforcement from recognizing their communication differences. For an autistic person, unsupported social communication can be discouraging or unsettling and, at times, may constitute a violation of their civil rights. Civil rights violations against autistic individuals are often addressed retroactively through legal proceedings because many people struggle with simultaneous interpretation, particularly in high-stress situations. However, some report they can understand many social concepts after the event, when processing these with a familiar trusted person (Whitney, 2023).

Law enforcement purposely harnesses the power of surprise in arresting accused individuals. This is often the strategy used to make the process less dangerous for everyone involved, but for an autistic individual, this can create exaggerated reactions and effects. When the autistic individual's routine is disrupted by law enforcement, it often causes heightened anxiety. This type of disruption is alarming to non-autistic people, but to an autistic individual, the aftereffects are often felt over the long term. These situations are exacerbated by the fact that many autistic individuals do not do well with novelty, new environments, and new people (Whitney, 2023). Some on the autism spectrum also have extreme sensitivity to being touched and may respond negatively to being patted down or held. They may attempt to flee or strike out against the arresting officers. In some tragic situations, autistic individuals have been injured, tazed, and even shot. These difficulties continue throughout the process and into courtroom settings that are not designed to accommodate their sensory issues and communication differences. These accommodations that are not always identified or understood by law enforcement or court personnel and places the autistic individual at a specific disadvantage during questioning, while in custody, or in court proceedings. Autistic victims and offenders must have access to fair justice through reasonable accommodations and autism-informed approaches, evaluation, and treatment.

AUTISM AND ONLINE BEHAVIOR

Information and communications technology are increasingly integrated into almost all aspects of our daily activities (Hruska & Maresova, 2020). Online communications and social media are qualitatively different from in-person or phone communication. The online environment produces behavioral changes such as harassment, trolling, cyberbullying, and the tendency to engage in inappropriate behaviors that would normally be inhibited. This is referred to as "online disinhibition" (Suler, 2004). Disinhibited behavior while online is attributed to the unique characteristics of the internet. The online world is a unique space where conventional boundaries are often blurred and misunderstood. Most prominent is the fact that online communication provides the ability to hide or change one's identity, and a sense of invisibility is further enhanced when a person is not physically seen by others. In addition, online communication enables delayed responses, which eliminates social anxiety. Many individuals perceive the online environment as an imaginary world with no connection to reality. There is also a perception of the online world as something unregulated by any authority. The perception is that everyone is equal in the online environment, and therefore, the rules that dictate appropriate interactions between different groups (adults and children) do not apply. The tendency for people to feel less restrained in cyberspace and behave in a way they never would in the real world is often evident in online communications. The ability to hide one's identity online causes many to experience a dissociation from their online behavior. In essence, the online self is compartmentalized. This psychological effect is often observed in autistics due to the large amounts of time they spend online.

The propensity to engage in certain negative behaviors online without inhibition has produced a toxic and sometimes dangerous online environment for many. Autistic individuals are operating in this environment without the social understanding and societal guardrails necessary for their personal safety (Sallafranque-St.-Louis

& Normand, 2017). The uninhibited world of the internet and social media can create a perfect storm for those on the autism spectrum that may result in offending behaviors or victimization.

Autistic individuals are often described as "systematizers" because they are interested in systems and how things work. Their attention to detail and facility with understanding systems can develop into advanced computer and technological skills (Lim et al., 2023). It has been hypothesized that autistic people have a "predisposition to engage in technology" (Ruzich et al., 2015), and they are frequently found in STEM professions. Naturally, they are drawn to online activities and spend much of their time on electronic devices. Some of these activities involve research on their specific areas of interest. They will exhaustively research topics and become experts on these subjects. Autistic people are also often avid collectors, and some have an obsessive need to possess all the items required to complete their collection (i.e., graphic novels or comics in a series). They may not fully understand how their online behavior when amassing collections may be an infringement of copyright and related rights.

The distinctive worldview of those with autism can be viewed as a strength; conversely, it can also be a cause of confusion, social misunderstanding, and social rejection. Many autistic individuals go online to seek the social acceptance that they cannot find in their daily in-person interactions. The online world eliminates the need for real-time interactions and allows the person to respond in their own timeframe. It also does not demand the simultaneous processing of verbal and non-verbal social cues which is so difficult for those on the spectrum. They can communicate in chatrooms and on social media easily without exposing their social awkwardness. As a result, the online world has become almost their exclusive source of social contact. The online world is a fast, fluid situation; specific and unpredictable. It requires the ability to think flexibly and relies heavily on social pragmatic language. These are the very issues that individuals with autism find extremely challenging. We see that online situations are often misinterpreted by neurotypicals. Accordingly, this type of social contact is even more taxing for someone on the autism spectrum. They are extremely vulnerable to bullying, cyber scams, inappropriate sexual behavior, and even radicalization and cult recruitment.

In this book, we will explore the susceptibility of those with autism to becoming cybercrime victims or offenders. Cybercrime is defined as "any illegal activity involving the use of computers or information technology" (Donalds & Osei-Bryson, 2019). The following are specific areas of vulnerability we have encountered as a mental health clinician, a defense attorney, and a forensic technologist. We will present case examples from experience, altered to protect privacy, that are illustrative of each of these areas of concern.

INTERNET ADDICTION

Many individuals on the spectrum have a great facility for computers and fluency with web-based resources. They may enjoy web surfing and gathering information online as a way to reduce their anxiety (Woodbury-Smith et al., 2022). The repetitive nature of this activity is often calming; however, it can also lead to internet addiction. Various aspects of the internet (surfing, chatrooms, and video games) employ variable reward structures similar to those of gambling, making them highly addictive to some. Some people report spending multiple hours a day online and, consequently, get very little sleep. Many on the spectrum are prone to gaming addiction and become immersed in online role-playing games (RPGs). Many report experiencing pleasure in internet activities that they do not find elsewhere. Intensive prolonged gaming increases dopamine levels, experienced as a reward. Along with sleep deprivation, some suffer from malnutrition, lack of exercise, and inadequate sunlight exposure (Cash et al., 2012). They become victims of the highly addictive nature of certain online behaviors such as pornography viewing, gaming, and online buying. Unfortunately, these addictions may also lead to illegal activities, and they then become offenders. In the case of pornography, it can promote confusing and illegal depictions of sexuality that normalize sexual exploitation of children, rape, incest, and sexual violence.

Case: A 16-year-old male on the autism spectrum spent 12 hours a day playing *World of Warcraft*. He developed a urinary condition, was malnourished, and severely sleep-deprived. He began paying individuals in other time zones to play for him when he was asleep. He could not function at school, had extensive absences, and was failing all his classes. After his family's many attempts to find appropriate treatment, he was sent to a residential treatment program for gaming addiction for 3 months.

Case: An autistic college student, JW, was overwhelmed by the transition to a large university his freshman year. He began compulsively surfing the internet for articles on famous disasters throughout history (Titanic, Pompeii, Hindenburg) and compiling them in online folders. He found this activity calming, and it provided a diversion for him from the intense social anxiety he was experiencing. JW eventually became addicted to the surfing and would stay up most nights, to the point of becoming extremely sleep-deprived. During his first semester, he did not attend classes and rarely left his dorm. At the end of the semester, he received incomplete grades in all classes and received a letter of dismissal from the university.

ONLINE SEXUAL BEHAVIOR

Most autistic people have not had the usual social and sexual experiences which are typical during adolescence/early adulthood. Dr. Tony Attwood, an internationally renowned expert on high-functioning autism, explains the atypical sexual development of autistic individuals to be a result of social isolation (Attwood, Hénault, & Dubin, 2014) and having no ability to discuss sexual thoughts or feelings with their peers. Autistic people are sexually curious and may spend many hours viewing pornography to understand their own sexuality. Much of what they may be viewing online is fetishistic and outside the realm of conventional sexual behavior. Many of their special interests have pornographic versions (Pokemon, My Little Pony). They may be exposed to a variety of pornography that is violent, disturbing, and involves children. This introduction may, over time, develop into an online sexual addiction. Individuals on the spectrum enjoy repeating behaviors and often have specific sexual interests. Several have reported an addictive sequence of compulsive viewing which led to a need for novel stimuli in increasing amounts to achieve sexual satisfaction. These individuals created brain pathways of sexual arousal based on the images viewed. The pornography viewing released dopamine to the brain's pleasure centers, which became a conditioned response. Compulsive viewing of these images can result in arousal being restricted to sexual material such as anime characters (Doidge, 2007). Unfortunately, some report that they do not respond to human images and are only responsive to sexualized animation.

> Case: A 28-year-old autistic male, RM, reported to his therapist that he was addicted to cartoon pornography and had been viewing it since he was 12. He cannot become sexually aroused by pictures of real women and responds only to pornographic cartoon images of females with exaggerated breasts. He was depressed and felt this was a barrier to him ever having a romantic relationship. RM did not know where to get treatment for this type of sexual dysfunction, and his therapist referred him to a residential sexual addiction program.

UNDERAGE COMMUNICATION WITH MINORS

Many autistic individuals are socially isolated and have had few interpersonal relationships. They are intensely lonely and turn to the computer for a connection to the outside world. They have the social and emotional skills of individuals below their chronological age. Their social maturity is closer to that of a much younger person because they are at a similar level to theirs, socially and emotionally (Cutler-Landsman et al., 2013). This is sometimes referred to as the "drop down" phenomenon. They are communicating with an age group that is at their social and emotional maturity level. Autistic individuals often have difficulty with reciprocal conversation, which impacts their ability to be socially successful. They are limited when it comes to the fast-paced social interactions of their peers. Many therefore prefer those who are younger, with whom they find communication easier.

Some people on the autism spectrum do not perceive, understand, or appreciate the feelings of others. It is likely they also find understanding others' intentions and motivations challenging. They may not be able to judge the appropriateness of their responses and may misinterpret others' responses. Many individuals with ASD engage in such behaviors because they cannot consider others' points of view. Referred to as Theory of Mind (ToM), the lack of perspective-taking ability can result in negative outcomes and leaves these individuals vulnerable to abuse and exploitation. Conversely, they may not fully recognize the inappropriateness of having an online relationship with a much younger person or how it could be exploitative and harmful.

> Case: A 23-year-old autistic man was arrested for inappropriately communicating with a 14-year-old girl online. They met on a comic chat app, talked for several months, and exchanged phone numbers to text each other. They never talked on the phone and only communicated through texts. The conversation eventually became sexual, and she began sending him sexually explicit photos, which he did not solicit. The FBI began monitoring these exchanges after her parents discovered their texts on her phone. The FBI came to his family home with a search warrant and confiscated his phone and all other electronic devices he used. He was charged with possession of child sexual abuse material.

GAMING AND FANTASY CHATROOMS

Some individuals on the spectrum are very drawn to fantasy worlds and enjoy comics, role-playing video games (RPGS), live-action roleplay (LARP), science fiction, manga, and anime. They may collect specific books, videos, and other memorabilia online and participate in gaming or anime chats on platforms such as Discord. These intense interests, at times, become obsessions and may come to define their self-identity. This phenomenon may be more pronounced with excessive internet use. Due to their own negative experiences, autistic individuals may relate to genres containing storylines of trauma or victimization. When this level of immersion develops, it is sometimes difficult for them to discern their true self from their fantasy character. They refer to these characters as reference points for their own life and appear to blur fiction and reality. When such impairments in the ability to differentiate the boundaries between fantasy and reality occur, there can be serious mental health implications.

Fantasy role-playing provides the individual "a perfect virtual medium for identifying with, relating to and acting out fantasies" (Higham et al., 2016). As individuals become more immersed in fantasy worlds, they become increasingly detached from the real world. For example, during a forensic evaluation, an individual described himself as a specific anime character and the events of his life as part of this character's story. He could not describe his own life experience. Some on the autism spectrum may identify with superheroes, antiheroes, or villains. Often, the character is marginalized or seen as different. A considerable number of the characters have a backstory containing trauma, which the autistic person relates to. Fortunately, if used as a therapeutic tool, identification with these characters can help autistic persons to feel empowered and to communicate their own feelings. This was illustrated in the 2016 documentary *Life Animated*, which details how an autistic boy understood relationships and how to express himself through his fascination with Disney characters (R. Suskind, 2014).

Case: A 32-year-old male on the autism spectrum, KS, described his life as being the same as that of his favorite anime character Rei, who was severely bullied as a child and could not communicate well with others. He identified strongly with the character and thought his life would play out exactly as this character's. His belief was that this story predicted what would happen in his life, and he had no control of his own destiny. He spoke through the character when talking with others and frequently used Rei's direct quotes. KS was extremely socially isolated and had no outside interaction with peers and minimal contact with his family. He was unemployed and spent his waking hours online. KS's immersion in this character became so intense that his thoughts were not consistently grounded in reality. He was eventually diagnosed with a psychotic disorder.

SEXUAL VICTIMIZATION ONLINE

Lack of sexual experience and social naivety combined with intense loneliness create a perfect storm for those on the spectrum, leading to them becoming victimized by sexual predators. Autistic young people are often easily deceived and manipulated by online pedophiles seeking pictures and videos. Clinicians have heard many of their clients discuss sending sexual pictures online or allowing themselves to be videoed in sexual scenarios. Clearly, this is not just happening to those on the spectrum and is an issue that must be addressed with all adolescents and young adults. Sexting and sexual exploration online are common among teenagers (Madigan et al., 2018). The primary concern is the increased risk of those with autism becoming the object of online sexual solicitation (Wells & Mitchell, 2014; Sallanfranque-St. Louis & Normand, 2017). Those with autism are at risk due to their inability to detect deception or discern the motivations of these predatory individuals. They may not have social maturity or knowledge of the boundaries of appropriate sexual behavior and may be operating with "social scripts" they learned in chatrooms or by texting. Many do not fully understand the social implications of their imitative language.

> Case: An autistic 17-year-old female began communicating with an individual she met in a gaming chatroom. She found this person easy to communicate with, unlike her peer group at school, and began sending pictures of herself. After a week of online chats, the individual asked her to send nude photos. After she complied, she received a threatening message telling her to purchase $500 in gift cards and supply the redemption codes, or her photos would be posted to everyone in her school. She purchased the cards and sent the codes without telling her parents.

PORNOGRAPHY ADDICTION/CHILD SEXUAL ABUSE MATERIAL

Individuals on the autism spectrum are particularly prone to pornography addiction due to their obsessive-compulsive tendencies, perseverative behavior, and social isolation (Hénault, 2005). They are frequently drawn to the computer to explore their sexuality and have no real sexual experience or knowledge. Many have limited peer relationships, and a significant number have been exposed to pornography at a young age (10+ years). This exposure often involves young children portrayed in a highly sexual way, and the distinction between age-appropriate and underaged females and males is intentionally blurred (Mahoney, 2009). This may result in a preference for images of minors even as the individuals become older. If the emotional maturity of the person is that of someone 11 or 12 years of age, their viewing may focus on that age group, which feels less threatening. Autistic individuals may also seek out highly novel sexual content out of curiosity. Some are attracted to pornographic animation such as Japanese hentai, which is sometimes incorporated into anime, manga, and video games.

Dr. Tony Attwood explains the sometimes-atypical sexual development of autistic individuals to be a result of social isolation (Attwood, Hénault, & Dubin, 2014) and not having the ability to discuss sexual thoughts or feelings with peers. Dr. Attwood also stated that the internet is a link to the outside world which becomes a substitute friend for individuals on the autism spectrum. The concept of counterfeit deviance is often used to explain the unusual sexual behavior of those on the autism spectrum. These behaviors are "due to challenges in judgement, social skills or impulse control which are diagnostically different from a paraphilia" (Mahoney, 2009). Dr. Isabelle Hénault has said that "the lack of sociosexual knowledge is always a major issue" contributing to the inappropriate sexual behavior of those diagnosed with autism (2014).

COLLECTING/COMPLETING THE COLLECTION

For many autistic individuals, their activities revolve around a specific interest: finding, collecting, and "completing the collection." This completion is necessary to satisfy their compulsion and results in the amassing of substantial amounts of images or other materials on their computer or phone. At times, this occurs through filesharing software. Filesharing can result in large dumps of computer files to a receiver's computer while it has been left on overnight. Many illegal items may be embedded in these files, and the receiver is unaware of the content. Besides being avid collectors, autistic individuals may also be adept at obtaining copyrighted materials and circumventing security controls.

Collecting is commonly seen in people with autism, and it has been suggested that their extreme collecting is due to a poorly developed sense of self (Skirrow et al., 2014). Skirrow posited they collect and hoard items to provide an "external scaffolding" to their identity. They are defined by their collections and, there-fore, are highly particular about maintaining them. In essence, this collecting is critical to maintaining their self-identity. One autistic individual had a compulsion to collect books both physical and digital. He amassed a vast collection, driven not only by his passion for reading but also by his belief that, as he said, "these books are me." Some autistic collectors carry their collections with them. These items provide comfort and reduce their anxiety. Some have a compulsion to collect everything that exists online and amass large amounts of files in their areas of interest.

ONLINE RADICALIZATION

Individuals on the autism spectrum are particularly at risk of joining cult-like organizations and radicalized groups. As these groups have proliferated online, the instances of radicalization are increasing. Autistic individuals are seeking a community where they will be accepted and are drawn to rigid ideologies that match their "black and white" thinking style. Many have decreased social contact and can be easily drawn into groups that encourage isolation from others. Many on the autism spectrum like the structure and routine that are associated with group affiliation. Some autistic individuals are highly impressionable and do not understand the motives or agendas of the group (Allely, 2022). They are seeking group acceptance and may be easily manipulated by group members. The lack of social judgment is apparent to groups looking to employ them in terroristic plots. Due to their social naivety, individuals on the spectrum are used as pawns by those who deceive them into thinking they are trusted allies. It is common to see autistic individuals "set up" by those more socially savvy to carry out risky or illegal actions for them.

LEGAL ISSUES: COMPETENCY AND CRIMINAL RESPONSIBILITY

The traditional categories available within the criminal justice system—competency and responsibility (sometimes called "insanity")—do not serve people on the autism spectrum well. For example, the legal definition of competency does not mean the same thing as the lay def-inition. The legal definition requires that the accused understand the proceedings and be able to assist counsel. For example, if the accused has been the target of online radicalization, they may sincerely believe in the righteousness of their actions and, thus, not understand why they were charged or insist that counsel put forward their earnest beliefs. Moreover, the way a competency argument plays out in courts is that competency is a low standard. When representing someone on the spectrum who is of high intelligence (and who may not hesitate to demonstrate this), it is often difficult to persuade the court and the prosecutor that this individual is "incompetent." However, ultimately, their state of mind may be used to negate or at least minimize intent, which is sometimes an element of the offense.

While competency is a low standard, insanity is a high standard and, thus, difficult to meet. Different jurisdictions have different definitions of this term, but the concept of insanity is more appropriate to someone with a mental illness, rather than a developmental disability like autism. Aside from the issue that insanity does not fit individuals on the spectrum, persuading them or their families to go forward with an insanity defense is another matter. And even if they did agree, an expert report would use the relevant legal definition of insanity and might be hard put to fit the individual's history and behavior into that definition. Most jurisdictions place the burden of proving insanity on the accused. And merely being on the autism spectrum alone does not constitute an offense.

MITIGATION AND SENTENCING

Given the limitations of competency and sanity, most cases involving people on the spectrum will (or should) result in the autism being used as mitigation in order to negotiate a better plea; a better sentence, such as less time, probation, or diversion to a facility; a more appropriate prison placement; or even dismissal. All of this is largely dependent on the jurisdiction where the individual is charged, the nature of the charges, the individual circumstances of the accused, such as the nature of the autism, and the path forward presented by counsel, which will assure the court that the accused will not be a danger to themselves or the community.

INCARCERATION

For most people on the spectrum, jail or prison could be the worst place in the world. Depending on how they manifest their symptoms, they could be unable to follow the rules or be disruptive. This could result in disciplinary infractions and even solitary confinement, which brings a world of additional trauma. If they have odd behaviors such as stimming, they could be made fun of or even victimized by other inmates. Their naivety could result in them or their families being shaken down for protection. Because of sensory issues, the smells, continual noises such as shouting, and bright lights could be absolute torture. In addition, a common concern for anyone on medication is whether the formulary at the facility offers that particular medication.

TECHNOLOGICAL ABILITY AND ONLINE OFFENSES

The landscape of today's digital age presents significant legal implications involving security and privacy because our data is more accessible than ever before. Our most private information is no longer protected by a deadbolt lock to a physical building or the code to a safe. That information is now stored on electronic devices, connected to the internet, and controlled by centralized electronic service providers like Apple, Google, and Microsoft.

For individuals with greater than average technological abilities, like "systematizers," accessing this data can occur innocently and unintentionally. The stereotype associated with the term "hacking" is that of a highly sophisticated ominous figure in a black hoodie studying lines of code across multiple monitors in a basement to nefariously cause damage. However, the term "hacking" within the industry simply refers to any unauthorized accessing of data or a system. Becoming an "unauthorized user" of electronic information stored online may occur innocently and unwittingly for those who have an inherent technical ability in the new digital age. Yet, the punishment can be substantial.

EFFECTS OF ARTIFICIAL INTELLIGENCE

If the lines between reality and the internet were not blurred enough, the introduction of artificial intelligence has significantly complicated our ability to discern authentic human content from machine learning. Artificial intelligence is designed to provide constructive responses to human input. Artificial online personas may be mistaken for genuine human interaction, which can further influence individuals who are already vulnerable to disinhibited behavior.. This can lead to increased empathy deficits and difficulty perceiving criminal activity, which should be taken into consideration when evaluating the intent of an individual with ASD, who may be eliciting affirmation or responses from machine-generated personas.

The nebulous concept of artificial intelligence has also increased the desensitization to egregious content online due to the assumption that it may not be depicting actual victims of abuse—much like gore in horror films. The proliferation of artificially generated imagery creates a false belief that graphic content discovered on the internet does not violate local and federal laws.

AIM OF THIS BOOK

In summary, there are multiple factors which increase the vulnerability of those on the autism spectrum to committing online offenses or being victimized. These vulnerabilities must be recognized by society and addressed by our current legal system. In this book, we will examine the experiences of autistic victims and offenders from our perspectives as a clinician, a defense attorney, and a forensic technical expert. By reviewing the current research and legal trends, we hope to increase awareness regarding the circumstances in which autistic persons become victimized or ensnared in cybercrime. Our aim is also to provide safety guidelines, effective recommendations for treatment, and alternatives to incarceration that will improve the outcomes for autistic individuals navigating the online world.

Online Behavior and Autism

Mary Riggs Cohen

One

The online environment is often described as a "wild west" due to its lack of real-life authority and oversight. This leads to the proliferation of extreme content, scams, and illegal activities. Social media platforms struggle to protect vulnerable groups from disturbing content and dangerous activities. Autistic individuals, who may have difficulty understanding social norms and boundaries, are particularly vulnerable to online manipulation and deception. They often lack the ability to intuit others' feelings and motivations, what is known as Theory of Mind, making them easy targets for online predators. Cases like that of a 45-year-old autistic man who was financially exploited by someone he met online highlight these risks.

Online disinhibition is another critical factor in the online behavior of autistic individuals. This phenomenon, described by Suler, involves a reduction in psychological barriers due to factors like anonymity, asynchronicity, and invisibility. While these factors can facilitate open communication, they also lead to behaviors that might not occur offline, such as cyberbullying or financial fraud. Autistic individuals may struggle with distinguishing between fantasy and reality online, further complicating their interactions. Their intense interest in specific topics can override their ability to detect fake websites or scams, making them susceptible to spear phishing and other forms of cybercrime.

The online world's impact on autistic individuals is complex, offering both a refuge from social challenges and a source of vulnerability. While it provides a space for creative expression and social interaction, it also exposes them to dangers like cybercrime and manipulation. Efforts to educate autistic individuals about online safety and to improve their understanding of social cues are crucial. Additionally, developing strategies to help them distinguish between fantasy and reality online can mitigate some of these dangers. Despite

DOI: 10.4324/9781003540571-2

these challenges, the internet remains a vital tool for autistic individuals, offering opportunities for connection and self-expression that are not always available in offline environments.

ONLINE BEHAVIOR

Much has been written about the impact of the internet and technology on Millennials and Gen Z. These generations grew up without knowing a time before the internet. Internet-based services create a range of services, including online shopping, banking, gaming, digital data transfer, and participation in chat rooms, bulletin boards, and social media sites. The worldwide web and its associated technology have had a profound influence on human behavior. This has generated a new field of study: cyberpsychology.

The internet has had such an impact on autistic people that it has been compared to the use of sign language for the deaf community (Blume, 1997). It opens new channels of communication for musical and artistic expression and allows autistics to meet, form groups, and provide support to each other. Unfortunately, there is also a downside to online communication which includes cyberbullying, cyberstalking, trolling, and sexual victimization. Autistic females are at risk of online sexual harassment while autistic males are exposed to risks such as phishing (Macmillan et al., 2022). Autistic individuals may become either victims or online offenders due to their lack of social and societal awareness. They may also be vulnerable to compulsive use and addiction (MacMullin et al., 2016).

The internet has profoundly changed social communication for autistic individuals. They frequent online environments, and it has been suggested that they become exceptionally attached to the internet to compensate for their offline social difficulties (Romano et al., 2014). Communication using the internet can be empowering for individuals with ASD because they sense they are communicating "on an equal basis" with other people, unlike their in-person social experiences (Benford & Standen, 2009). This form of communication breaks down perceived barriers created by their social disability. Many feel more confident and comfortable in the online world (Stuart & Scott, 2021). According to many autistics, they feel more relaxed because they do not have to worry about identifying and interpreting others' nonverbal communication or think about their own facial expressions or voice tone. They are looking for a way to have a "level playing field" socially. However, this sense of liberation from traditional forms of socializing also puts them at significant risk of losing control during these exchanges and results in victimization. Many turn to the online world as a refuge from reality, perceiving it as a space free from its limitations. However, this perception is misleading, as their actions within the digital realm carry tangible consequences in the real world.

Due to their social isolation, people on the autism spectrum use the internet as a compensation for the social problems they encounter in-person. These communication challenges stem from fundamental neurological differences in autistic individuals, which profoundly impact their language processing, pragmatic communication, and ability to modulate vocal prosody. First, they have difficulty conveying their emotions due to their limited or unusual inflections or tone of voice. Sometimes they may speak in a monotone or sound "robotic." Consequently, their interactions can seem less natural to neurotypicals. They have difficulty synchronizing their speech patterns to match those of conversational partners, resulting in the exchange feeling odd. They do not detect voice tones well in themselves or others. This causes confusion and misunderstandings when communicating with others. They are particularly challenged by voice tones that reflect sarcasm or playfulness. Research suggests that they also struggle with the reduced nonverbal social cues online. This may further confuse them and make it hard to interpret social network norms (Shane-Simpson et al., 2016).

When reading online social exchanges that are provided for forensic evaluations of an autistic victim of cybercrime, it is often apparent that the individual does not know he is being humiliated or made fun of by others in the chat. Individuals with autism strive to fit in and may adopt online social "scripts" they observe from others. However, this approach can lead to challenges when the scripts are not suitable for specific social contexts.

HOW INTERNET BEHAVIOR DIFFERS: THE ONLINE DISINHIBITION EFFECT

People behave very differently online than they do in the offline world (Suler, 2004; Saunders et al., 2017). Suler posited that certain elements of cyberspace weaken the psychological barriers that block our hidden feelings and needs. He proposed that disinhibited behavior while online is attributable to cyberspace's unique characteristics. Suler termed this phenomenon the online disinhibition effect and identified six different unique qualities contributing to this effect: asynchronicity, anonymity, invisibility, solipsistic introjection, dissociative imagination, and minimization of authority. Because people feel less concerned about their self-presentation or the judgment of others, they may disclose very personal aspects of themselves. This can have positive or negative effects. They may act in a more prosocial way, such as donating generously to someone in need. Other positive behaviors include giving compliments and defending others (Lapidot-Lefler & Barak, 2015). Conversely, some people may be more aggressive, rude, or deceitful and may participate in criminal acts they would not consider otherwise. Reduced social cues and the inability to see others' facial expressions or emotional responses may promote anti-social behaviors. When individuals are not confronted with the aftermath of hurtful comments or actions, they do not experience repercussions or feel shame or remorse. They can depersonalize their victims. As society adapts to these dynamics, there is an ongoing discussion about managing both the benefits and the risks associated with online interactions.

Online communication is qualitatively different from in-person interactions. To begin with, much of internet communication does not occur in real time. This is referred to by Suler as **asynchronicity**. While there are instant messaging, video group chats, and many audiovisual networks which provide real-time exchanges, text-based communication is still widely used. It lacks certain features of person-to-person interactions, such as the ability to view body language reflected by posture, facial expression, eye contact, and voice tone. These features convey emotional context and more nuanced aspects of the words used. The ability to delay responses is a relief to many on the autism spectrum who struggle to process fast-paced real-time interactions. This lack of immediacy can also contribute to uninhibited behaviors because one does not have to deal with an immediate response (Benford & Standen, 2009).

Text-based communication also eliminates social status and physical attractiveness and other personal characteristics from social exchange. In essence, anyone can be anonymous. **Anonymity** can result in reduced social anxiety for those on the autism spectrum. It may encourage them to be more open to communication and social risk-taking (Bareket-Bojmel & Shahar, 2011). Many with autism feel less judged. Anonymity can also lead to more self-disclosure. Unfortunately, the social naivete of autistics may make them extremely vulnerable to manipulation, abuse, and exploitation. Many individuals also feel liberated by a sense of **invisibility** and the ability to not be seen. Suler defined the "online disinhibition effect" as unique to cyber environments, where psychological constraints and behavioral boundaries are often lower or completely absent from the online world. While this freedom has positive elements for autistic people in the form of reducing their anxiety, neurotypicals (and some with ASD) may enjoy the freedom to engage in uncontrolled, provocative, and socially negative behaviors (Wright et al., 2019) Collective trolling, harassment, threats, and other negative group behaviors have also increased (Massanari, 2017) in gaming and social networks.

Case: A 43-year-old autistic man participated in an online group of *Sandman* enthusiasts. He begins talking with someone who he thinks is a 20-ish female. He began having intimate conversations with this woman and revealed a lot of personal details. He said, "I thought she was my soulmate." They exchanged addresses and he began sending her multiple gifts by mail. He later discovers that this person is in fact a man and that the man is older than himself. He felt duped and betrayed by this individual who sent him pictures of a young woman and led him to believe that this was who he was communicating with for 3 years.

This case illustrates both anonymity and **dissociative anonymity.** People are unidentifiable and, therefore, feel an opportunity to detach from their real selves and identity. This attitude leads to unwanted sexual aggression and cyberbullying. For some, their perception is that anonymity frees them from responsibility. Of course, no one is fully anonymous online due to computer identifiers; however, the sense of being dissociated from one's real self persists. Some online groups promote the use of fantasy chats with fictional characters or role-playing characters while others use fictitious names, genders, or age for sexual role playing. There is also an assumption by many that "everyone is using a false name," as has been described by many clients who are charged with communicating with minors. This can also lead to dissociative imagination, relieving them from their responsibility for their actions. This may also explain why people will view cruel and humiliating videos or even torture and violent pornography with a less empathic response. Their belief that people online are not "real" or that the scenes are staged has a desensitizing effect.

Case: A 30-year-old autistic man is arrested for possession of child sexual abuse material. During the forensic evaluation, he tells the psychologist that the children are "paid actors who are also probably being rewarded with candy or gifts." When he is told that many of them are missing or kidnapping victims, he said that "that's impossible because it's a movie that has been produced by a film company in Hollywood."

Another aspect of online desensitization is termed **solipsistic introjection**. This is the degree to which a person creates an image or voice of the other individual while participating in online communication. Does the texter think about how the other individual looks and behaves during their exchange? How does their mental image make this person "real?" Many people create their own versions of the other person they are communicating with, and this may not have any relation to what the other person is feeling or experiencing. This certainly contributes to the phenomenon known as "catfishing," where people are communicating with someone entirely different (in terms of age, gender, etc.) than who they think they are talking with. If there is no visual information available, an online user may create an idealized version of the person they are communicating with. Conversely, if the online user does not create an image or imagined voice, it can cause a desensitization to the individual, which may encourage inappropriate or even abusive interactions. When texting or participating in online chats without video, the lack of visual and vocal information may affect each person's perception of the experience. For autistic individuals, the absence of social cues, which is already an area of weakness, may result in even more confusion. For many, they are creating a version of the interaction that bears little resemblance to how the other person experiences it.

THE ROLE OF FANTASY

Many individuals on the autism spectrum have a heightened interest in fantasy (Fein, 2015; Visuri, 2019). They are highly creative, imaginative, and produce rich fantasy content. Some engage in **immersive daydreaming**, which is more vivid and enduring than what most people experience. Many autistic individuals report daydreams that involve detailed narratives they have been developing over many years. This immersive activity may be an escape from the day-to-day challenges they experience and are a refuge from reality. As such, this immersion into fantasy worlds is compelling for many with autism (West et al., 2023) The online world presents a portal into fantasy worlds that create a sense of control. Autistics frequent fan fiction sites and role-playing video games. They also are drawn to create online fantasy worlds, complete with interactive maps, characters, and storylines. Some also enjoy live-action role playing (LARP) in parks and various other locations during live events. Unfortunately, autistic individuals may become immersed in their characters to an extreme that is unhealthy. Over-identification with cyber personas may promote confusion about one's real-life identity, particularly for individuals experiencing trauma or gender dysphoria (Recupero, 2008).

One young man told his therapist that he spent all his free time developing his online character's storyline and didn't really care about his own life. This level of immersion can result in autistic individuals totally neglecting their real lives, with many negative consequences. Some may struggle with distinguishing between fantasy and reality, leading to impaired functioning in daily life. This addiction can also create a cycle of dependency on fantasy for coping, worsening their mental health outcomes.

Case: A 35-year-old female (HR) with autism spends hours every day on fan fiction websites. She has also created a medieval character that she plays on online live-action role-playing (LARP) sites. She has spent hundreds of dollars creating her costume and spent 3 years writing a diary for her character: a female knight (Sichel). She is more invested in her character than in her real life and leads a very reclusive existence. She becomes obsessed with another LARP character (Gonal) she is attracted to and is eventually banned from the LARP site due to threats she made toward another character because of her intense feelings for Gonal. HR tells a therapist that she feels she has nothing to live for now that she cannot visit this site. In her words, "my real life means nothing to me."

IMMERSION IN FANTASY

Many autistic individuals spend much of their time in online fantasy environments. They have rich fantasy lives and enjoy the fantasy worlds of gaming, scifi, and fan fiction. Some assume the identity of a character or multiple characters online and are immersed in these fantasy scenarios. For some, their excessive involvement in imaginary worlds causes difficulty in transitioning back to real-world tasks. Consequently, some individuals may struggle to differentiate fiction from reality (Ferguson et al., 2019), particularly in immersive environments like video games and virtual reality. This can lead to risky behaviors if the virtual rules are mistakenly applied to real life. This immersion can also lead to an assumption that much of what they encounter online is not real.

Obviously, technological advances enable the creation of deepfakes that blur the line between fantasy and reality. As a consequence, individuals must develop a skepticism about what they encounter online and develop ways to discriminate real from manufactured content and images. This is particularly an issue with child sexual abuse material (CSAM). In several forensic cases involving an autistic individual possessing these images, the offending individual said that they did not think the shocking sexual or violent images they saw were of real children. When someone spends most of their time immersed in fantasy worlds with minimal real-life interaction, it becomes increasingly difficult to distinguish between fiction and reality. It can also lead to a sense of detachment or dissociation from reality.

A 14-year-old autistic boy, Sewell Setzer, developed an intense relationship with an AI chatbot and it gradually became his "closest friend." He became increasingly isolated from his real life and relationships. The chatbot was designed to be a "personalized companion." Sewell's immersion was such that he communicated with the chatbot (Dany) multiple times a day and developed a psychological dependency with this character. During this period, he became increasingly sleep-deprived, lost interest in previous interests, and underwent a decline in his school performance. He had sexualized conversations, and according to reports, he desired a romantic relationship with the chat bot. The company that created the character, Character AI, was sued by Setzer's family after he committed suicide following a conversation where the chatbot allegedly encouraged the young boy to take his own life. The chatbot failed to recognize his metaphor for death ("coming home") and told him to "come home" to her. The lawsuit also expressed concern that Character AI's characters insist that they are real people and not bots, which contributed to the blurring of reality in this case (Roose, 2024). In many ways, this tragedy exemplifies the most extreme example of an immersion into a fantasy character to escape the difficulties of real-life relationships.

THE UNREGULATED ONLINE ENVIRONMENT

Finally, the online world appears to many to **lack any real-life authority** that enforces societal rules. It is a "wild west" environment, with diffuse boundaries, a lack of oversight, and content that is often unconstrained, extreme, or alarming. For example, "Rule 34" of the internet is that if anything exists in the world, there is online pornography involving it. The proliferation of bizarre content, false information, and criminal scams only further illustrates the sense that nothing online is off limits. While there is much creativity in the limitless forms of human expression found online, there is also an unrestrained, "pure id" quality that reveals the darkest facets of humanity. Online disinhibition also contributes to the spread of activities and ideologies that are unacceptable or marginalized by society (Recupero, 2008). These include pro-pedophilia chat rooms, hate groups, pro-suicide factions, and cults. Social media platforms have proved ineffectual at protecting vulnerable groups from disturbing content and the dangerous activities proliferating there (Martilla et al., 2021). In 2024, the founder and CEO of Telegram, Pavel Durov, was arrested in France as part of an investigation into criminal activity on the platform. French authorities accused Telegram of failing to comply with requests to curb illegal content, including child sexual abuse images, drug trafficking, and money laundering. The charges alleged that Telegram did not respond to law enforcement inquiries and allowed its platform to be used for serious criminal activities (Breeden & Satariano, 2024). This case is ongoing.

MEASURING ONLINE DISINHIBITION

People behave quite differently in online environments. Scales have been developed to measure these dimensions of online disinhibition (Febriana & Fajrianthi, 2019; Cheung et al., 2020; Stuart & Scott, 2021). Those who experience anonymity endorse items such as "My actions are unidentifiable in the online environment." Those that experience asynchronicity will endorse items like "I can delay my feedback to others in the online environment." Items that reflect the feeling of invisibility include "I think I can't see other people's facial expressions on social networking forums, and they can't see mine." Solipsistic introjection is measured by items such as "I interpret others' messages with my expectations during online communication." The sense of dissociative imagination is reflected in items like "I feel like people in the online space are just imaginary with no connection to reality." As noted, many online feel there is no authority or rules pertaining to online interactions. These individuals endorse items such as "I am away from real life authorities in the online environment." These statements illustrate the factors that make the online world a vastly different environment for many people.

ONLINE DISINHIBITION AND CYBERCRIME

Cybercrime is a broad term for any illegal activity involving the use of computers or information technology (Donalds & Osei-Bryson, 2019). Cybercrimes are often described as computer-dependent. These types of criminal behavior, such as hacking or virus writing, require a computer. Cyber-deviant is the term used for those negative behaviors that occur online but are not necessarily computer-dependent, such as cyberbullying, harassment, pirating copyrighted materials, and even identity theft. Toxic online disinhibition encompasses behaviors such as making sexually inappropriate comments and viewing or sharing explicit violent or sexual material online (Lapidot-Lefler and Barak, 2012). While not all these types of behavior require the use of a computer, online disinhibition may cause these types of behavior to occur more frequently (Seigfried-Spellar et al., 2015). Once again, the sense of freedom and a perceived lack of consequences cause many to behave in a way they would not in the outside world. The online environment can foster the illusion of a world detached from societal principles or rules. For many on the autism spectrum, who are typically rule-bound, this is a very confusing landscape. Clinicians often hear from their clients statements like "I thought it was legal because it's on the internet." Many autistic individuals are immersed in the online world and have lost connection to societal norms and boundaries. They may have had an incomplete understanding of many of these social rules to begin with and are further perplexed by the behaviors they see occurring online. Many attempt to imitate these behaviors simply to fit in.

Some individuals with autism become targets for those with criminal intentions. Online predatory types can easily identify the socially awkward or trusting by their online communication and then zero in on them. Sometimes, opening an email attachment, following a link in a text message, or making an online purchase can open an individual up to online criminals. Autistic individuals are often prey to online financial frauds and, in some cases, will give money or credit card numbers to people they meet and perceive as "friends." There may be an element of "grooming" to these interactions, where the autistic person believes they can trust this person after several online chats. These predators take full advantage of the autistic individual's naivete, lack of social experience, and poor awareness or understanding of other people's motivations. This ability to intuit or sense others' feelings, needs, and motives is referred to as Theory of Mind (Frith & Frith, 2005). This is also sometimes referred to as mentalizing or mind reading. The ability to mentalize is related to our capacity to empathize with other people. Most neurotypicals can think about another's point of view or take that person's perspective. Having this ability also allows some people to successfully manipulate others. Autistics have differing levels of this ability, and some have little awareness of the thoughts, feelings, and motivations of the other people they encounter. Lack of Theory of Mind (TOM) is why they often do not understand when they are being deceived. This makes them highly vulnerable to manipulation, especially in online environments. Certain spaces in the online world are rife with fraud and deception.

Case: 45-year-old man on the autism spectrum (KB) meets a woman (LS) online and says she is "his soulmate." He gives her all his personal financial information including credit card numbers and pays for all her TV subscriptions and an Amazon account. She purchases over $16,000 in jewelry, clothes, phones, and computers. LS continues to communicate with him online and frequently sends him pictures of herself. KB's father finally learns of this and tells him he must stop sending money and change his credit cards. KB is adamant that this person is his girlfriend and refuses. His father contacts law enforcement and is told there is nothing they can do legally. KB's father was finally able to convince him to cancel his credit cards; however, he continued to purchase additional items for her through his debit card.

PHISHING AND FAKE WEBSITES

In today's world, many people experience phishing attacks that come into their email or lead them to fake websites to gain personal information. It is therefore important to learn how to identify the visual cues indicating a link is fake. A study found that the participants with autism noticed the missing security locks/certificates, logos, and obfuscated URLs in the fake websites (Neupane et al., 2018). These results were attributed to the several distinctive traits commonly found in individuals with autism, such as meticulous attention to detail, a methodical approach, a strong memory for information, and a unique perspective on problem-solving. These skills are essential for cybersecurity positions, where autistic individuals are in high demand (Neupane et al., 2018).

While autistic individuals may be able to outperform non-autistics on visual search tasks (Shirma et al., 2017), this does not necessarily mean they are better at detecting fake from real websites. This is particularly true when the website is related to their specific area of interest (Macmillan et al., 2022). Their intense interest may override their perceptual abilities. For example, an autistic individual may be excited to find anime videos for sale and enter their credit card information without detecting how the website address has been altered to resemble a legitimate site. Some are victims of "spear phishing," in which the autistic individual is targeted due to their interest in electronic devices and promised a reward of an iPhone in exchange for personal information. Many of these types of attacks are directed at autistic males (Grove et al., 2018).

IMPORTANCE OF ONLINE SAFETY TRAINING

The above techniques are often employed in identity theft and financial scams. In addition, fake websites and pop-ups often lure individuals to illegal and inappropriate content. Anyone using the internet and communicating through social media sites must be educated in internet safety to avoid such pitfalls. In addition, individuals can encounter threats, stalking, and cyberbullying when online that create extreme stress and anxiety and may impact an individual's mental health overall. Training must assist users in recognizing phishing emails, spoofing emails (which hide or disguise the origin of the email), or other attempts to obtain personal and financial information. In many instances, the email is disguised as coming from a friend or known organization. The training must also cover how to use web filters to track websites and block inappropriate content. This knowledge can prevent a user from downloading illegal content on their phone or computer. Most importantly, users should be aware that others online may not be who they claim to be. Deception and fantasy are common in virtual environments. Additionally, chat rooms can provide a space where people engage in behaviors they might never consider in real life. Some examples of these training programs are included in the "Concluding Thoughts" chapter.

Case: An 18-year-old autistic woman (JG) answered an email request from a charity to send money for a disaster relief fund for some flood victims in her state. She was asked to provide her bank account information and social security number to make her donation online. She was familiar with the organization, so she filled out the form and sent it back. She did not notice that the URL listed on the email was slightly different from that of the charity's website. Immediately, she received notification from her bank that her account had been emptied just five minutes after she sent in the form.

Risk Factors for Becoming a Victim or Offender

Mary Riggs Cohen

Two

Autistic individuals often possess advanced computer skills and spend extensive time online, which can be both a strength and a risk. Their affinity for technology aligns with their problem-solving abilities and attention to detail, making them adept at coding and systematizing. However, this can lead to compulsive internet use and engagement with unmonitored or dangerous sites. Social media plays a crucial role in their lives, offering easier communication but also exposing them to negative interactions and safety concerns. Autistic individuals may struggle with understanding appropriate social behaviors, leading to misunderstandings or unintended actions such as stalking behaviors, which are often driven by a desire for social connection rather than malice.

The unique characteristics of autistic individuals, such as intense interests and difficulties with social understanding, can lead them into situations where they might engage in or facilitate cybercrimes unintentionally. While they are generally law-abiding, their advanced computer skills can be exploited by others for illicit activities. Autistic individuals may be manipulated into creating tools for cybercrimes without fully understanding the legal implications, making them vulnerable to being targeted and held accountable by law enforcement. Overall, the reliance on virtual communication highlights the need for support and education to ensure that autistic individuals can navigate online environments safely and effectively.

INCREASE IN VIRTUAL COMMUNICATION

The popularity of social media and our increasing dependence on computer-mediated communication have altered the way we connect with each other. We have experienced a dramatic societal shift and are transitioning to a world that relies less on in-person interactions. The COVID-19 pandemic only exacerbated this trend. In many ways, this

DOI: 10.4324/9781003540571-3

transition has positive implications: expanded opportunities to meet a wide variety of people with no geographical boundaries and multiple possibilities to connect to people with similar interests through various platforms. Conversely, there are also adverse effects to our increased dependence on virtual forms of communication. Among these, the loss of interpersonal social skills, particularly among Gen Y and Gen Z, has been a topic of increased concern and discussion (Munderia & Singh, 2019; Hooker, 2016). In the research conducted by Buyanova et al. (2018), it was concluded that virtual communication and internet use significantly impact face-to-face interpersonal communication in real life. Adolescents who prefer virtual interaction to face-to-face interaction have a lower level of sociability and insufficient communication ability, and this interaction method hurts their personality development and interpersonal communication. In addition, computer-mediated communication (CMC) may reduce people's ability to establish face-to-face interactions. If people prefer computer-mediated communication (CMC) to face-to-face communication, they may experience a crisis with regard to knowing themselves and others. It is better to pay attention in face-to-face interactions, where understanding people's emotions and attitudes is more crucial than their words and writings, than to use the internet (Venter et al., 2023).

For autistic people who are already experiencing social challenges, this reliance on virtual communication only exacerbates their lack of social awareness and skills necessary to navigate in-person social situations. It has been suggested that those with autism have been impacted more by these societal changes in communication and that autistic characteristics increase their vulnerability to online offending and victimization. It should be noted that previous studies have never concluded that autistic individuals are more likely to commit computer crimes (Seigfried-Spellar et al., 2015; Ledingham & Mills, 2015). The main concern is their vulnerability due to their autism, as illustrated by the cases presented in this chapter.

There are several traits and characteristic behaviors of autistic individuals that may increase this vulnerability: their advanced computer skills, repetitive behaviors, extensive time spent online, propensity to collect items, a limited ability to discern social cues, and a lack of understanding of others' perspectives. Of these traits, the lack of perspective-taking (also known as Theory of Mind) is a key factor in both victimization and the potential for becoming an offender. The cases presented in this chapter all involve reduced Theory of Mind as a factor in the crimes committed and who was victimized. To the extent that autistic individuals have a high level of engagement online, they may be particularly vulnerable to the grooming activities of others online and have a greater risk of becoming involved in illegal cyber activities (Lim et al., 2024).

ADVANCED COMPUTER SKILLS AND TIME SPENT ONLINE

It is no surprise that computers and online activities strongly resonate with autistic individuals. Technology aligns with their strengths, particularly their aptitude for problem-solving and attention to detail. The structured nature of coding languages and the logical framework of the internet offer a clear, predictable environment, providing opportunities for them to explore their special interests (Ledingham & Mills, 2015).

Baron-Cohen et al. (2007) speculated that there is a specific relationship between having autism and a technical mind. He reasoned that many individuals on the autism spectrum prefer working with objects and systems and choose STEM occupations (Baron-Cohen et al., 2007; Ruzich et al., 2015). The cognitive style of autistic individuals increases the likelihood that they will develop advanced computer skills (Man et al., 2023). Some have superior systematizing abilities and have excellent attention to detail. These studies suggested that many autistics have an innate predisposition toward developing advanced computer skills. While not all autistic people are technological or possess exceptional computer skills, many spend prolonged periods of time online and on social media (Hassrick et al., 2021). Younger autistic individuals are highly active on social media and online gaming sites, where they share interests and find social connections (Grove et al., 2018).

Temple Grandin, the well-known autistic advocate for autism awareness and understanding, has said, "the internet may be the best thing yet for improving an autistic person's social life" (celebsandplaces.com). As discussed in Chapter One, online activities are perceived by autistics as less stressful, and this facilitates their social interactions. A study found that autistic people reported more satisfaction with their online social lives than with their offline social lives (Van der Aa et al., 2016). Another study (Ritzman & Subramanian, 2024) found that young adults on the autism spectrum prefer computer-mediated communication because of the differences of the online environment. They are attracted to the decreased sensory input during conversations, which do not require the simultaneous processing of verbal and visual input (facial expressions) that most autistics find challenging. Many autistic individuals are "masking" their social deficits and find that this is much easier online (Cook et al., 2022).

Research suggests that autistic traits such as social challenges, repetitive behaviors, and intense interests may lead to compulsive internet use (Shane-Simpson et al., 2016). This characterization of their computer use as compulsive may just reflect autistic individuals' need for repetition and sameness. Many report that they repeatedly visit certain sites as part of their daily routine. If those sites are unmonitored and dangerous or illegal activities are happening there, the autistic individual is at significant risk of being subsumed in it. One young man on the spectrum reported to his therapist that he reviewed and revised Wikipedia entries every day for hours as part of his daily routine. Another autistic woman said she spent 5 hours daily researching the origins of first names and recording them in her journal.

The amount of time autistic individuals spend online may be related to their high rates of unemployment and underemployment (Shattuck et al., 2012). Many have reported boredom and a need to fill their time (Wang et al., 2020). Some autistic people have more time to spend online than their peers because they are less involved in outside activities. In many of the cases presented in this chapter, individuals spent between 10 and 12 hours a day online engaged in gaming, web searching, and social media platforms.

INTERNET ADDICTION AND SOCIAL ISOLATION

Internet addiction is highly related to social isolation and depression for those on the autism spectrum (Tateno et al., 2025). In fact, those on the autism spectrum appear to be very susceptible to compulsive gaming and pursuit of their special interests. Dr. Rachel Wurzman (2018), in her TED talk, described how social isolation and loneliness fuel addictive behaviors. Feeling connected to others is fundamental to human well-being, and when this basic need is disrupted, it can trigger significant neurochemical changes in the brain. If we lack the ability to connect socially, our brains become so deprived of social interaction that we will seek to restore balance to our social neuro-chemistry in any way possible. We will engage in addictive behaviors that fulfill our need for the feelings of social reward. This is why social isolation and loneliness can be powerful drivers of addiction (Wurzman, 2018; TED). A study of autistic college students' internet use and addiction found that loneliness was the greatest predictor of internet addiction (Shiri et al., 2024).

For many individuals on the autism spectrum, the online world serves as their primary—sometimes only—source of social inter-action. Many have said that their only friends are online friends. These digital friendships, often formed through shared interests such as gaming, offer much-needed social connection and support. Unfortunately, many autistic individuals lack access to a supportive social network within their local neighborhoods, schools, or com-munities. As a result, they rely heavily on online relationships, which explains their excessive amounts of time spent online. While many of these relationships are positive, relying heavily on socializing with individuals they may never meet in person can also lead to frustra-tion and a sense of disconnection from their immediate environment. Face-to-face interactions are important as they help individuals learn to read body language and develop essential conversation skills.

SOCIAL MEDIA

Social media is a key component in the lives of many autistic indi-viduals, providing them with an easier format for communication. Like with many neurotypicals, it consumes a sizable portion of their daily lives. Many autistics are highly motivated to connect socially (Mazurek, 2013). Social media can help them seek new relationships, maintain existing ones, and reduce boredom. According to a 2020 study of the benefits and challenges autistic people face when using social media, researchers found that the benefits were sometimes overshadowed by negative interactions and safety concerns (Wang et al., 2020). They experienced rejection when attempting to make friends or found the communications confusing and disappointing. These autistic users reported finding social media stressful and some-times needing to take a break from it or leave it completely (Wang et al., 2020). They were disturbed by the drama and harassment present on many social media sites. They reported experiencing increased anxiety when friend requests were not answered quickly, and some reported needing to deactivate their social media accounts completely. Mazurek (2013) also found that social media use did not decrease the loneliness reported by persons on the autism spectrum. Many social media sites emphasize neurotypical standards for socializing, such as one's number of online "friends" or how often an individual initiates chats. Instead, many on the autism spectrum are just looking to build meaningful and long-lasting friendships or to learn strategies to find welcoming social networks.

Social media can help create a social environment that is beneficial for autistic people and even improve their social abilities. The difference in whether it is beneficial or harmful may be mainly how it is used. People's active and passive communication styles on the internet can significantly affect their ability to understand non-verbal information. Individuals who are passively present online—those who primarily read and observe others' posts—tend to develop a stronger ability to interpret non-verbal cues (body language). By quietly observing interactions, they enhance their skills for face-to-face communication. In contrast, those who are actively engaged online—frequently creating and posting their own content—often show weaker abilities in understanding non-verbal information. This active participation may limit their capacity to read and respond effectively to others during in-person interactions (Ruben et al., 2021). In the research conducted by Buyanova et al. (2018), it was concluded that virtual communication and internet use significantly impacted face-to-face interpersonal communication in real life. Adolescents who preferred virtual interaction to face-to-face interaction had a lower level of sociability and insufficient communication ability. Their reliance on this interaction method negatively impacted their personality development and interpersonal communication. For autistic individuals who already face challenges in these areas, relying on virtual communication may make these difficulties even harder to manage.

Social media at times perpetuates bullying and victimizes individuals. For individuals with autism, who are often harassed online, social media can also become an extremely confusing and negative environment. Their innate difficulties, such as poor emotional recognition, a lack of social reciprocity, and limited empathetic understanding, can negatively affect their interactions with online friends and create frequent conflicts with others online. For example, their difficulties in understanding emoji expressions or hidden meanings of words may create misunderstandings. A 2023 study by Leung et al. found that autistic social media users were less able to understand the "internet" culture and were less aware of the harm caused by their cynical online comments than other young adults. Compared with other young adults, the participants were more likely to take these comments seriously and personally, which at times led to frustration and mood fluctuation. These difficulties in making friends through online platforms have been similarly reported by autistic individuals using dating apps (Leung et al., 2023).

The cycle in which victims become victimizers is depicted in the Netflix limited series *Adolescence* (Thorne, Graham, & Barantini, 2025). In the series, an adolescent boy (Jamie) is bullied on social media and then murders a girl (Katie) in his school. Katie has also been victimized by having a topless photo shared around school. Jamie explains to the forensic psychologist that he thought Katie would go out with him due to her lower social status on account of her having been shamed by the photo. Katie then also becomes a victimizer when she humiliates Jamie by calling him an incel. The escalating series of events illustrates the toxicity of social media in a middle-school environment.

STALKING

Today, stalking often takes place online and is commonly called cyber harassment. Individuals on the autism spectrum may be more prone to engaging in stalking behaviors in a misguided attempt to establish close social relationships. This is due to their unique social challenges, feelings of isolation, and difficulties in understanding others' perspectives and the impact of their own actions. Autistic individuals often develop intense interests in or fixations on specific topics or, occasionally, people. This characteristic can increase the likelihood of a person becoming the focus of their circumscribed interest (Sperry et al., 2021). These types of stalking incidents often arise from misunderstanding rather than any malicious intent. However, the continuous messaging and barrage of texts are not experienced that way and are stressful for the victims. The defining characteristic of the "incompetent stalker" type is often attributed to the autistic individual's difficulty recognizing the victim's lack of emotional reciprocity (Dell'Osso et al., 2015). This is further compounded by their confusion or lack of awareness about what constitutes appropriate dating behavior, coupled with their desire for intimate relationships, limited social experiences, and insufficient overall social and sexual understanding (Ventura et al., 2022).

The character of Martha in the Netflix series *Baby Reindeer* has sparked speculation about whether she might be autistic. While her portrayal includes traits such as social challenges and intense interests that align with autism, these interpretations remain speculative and are not confirmed. Media representations like this can perpetuate stereotypes, as they often reduce autism to a narrow set of traits or behaviors, which risks misrepresenting the diversity of the autism spectrum. These portrayals may reinforce harmful misconceptions, emphasizing deficits over strengths and contributing to stigmatization (steadystridesaba.com).

Case: SJ, a 20-year-old autistic woman, was in a politics class during her freshman year and met a male student, MD, whom she found attractive. Due to her intense social anxiety, she did not ever attempt to talk with him in class. The class had a final group project requiring students to work in assigned groups outside of class. Each student provided their email and phone number to the rest of the group so as to be able to work remotely on their respective group projects. MD was in SJ's group, and therefore, she had access to his personal contact information. After the class ended, SJ began to continuously text MD and express her love for him and her feeling that they were destined to be together. She also found him on several social media sites and continued her messages there as well. This behavior eventually led to MD changing his phone number and creating a new email. He blocked her on social media and eventually filed a harassment complaint with the university administrators. SJ was contacted by the university disciplinary council and told that if her harassment did not stop, it could result in her expulsion. She was referred to the campus counseling center and was not allowed to register for any classes where the other student was enrolled.

IMPORTANCE OF SPECIAL INTERESTS

Many autistics are drawn to online searching to gather information related to their specific interests and connect on platforms with others who share their various interests (e.g., famous disasters, Russian history, Civil War battles, types of mushrooms). Autistic adults report that engaging with these special interests is important to their life satisfaction (Grove et al., 2018), and this motivates them to find a community of like-minded people online. Because the online world is so diverse, they have an opportunity to connect with interest groups for even the most obscure topics. They can also unknowingly connect with bizarre, disturbed, or dangerous groups of individuals. Some autistics are just looking for a connection and may not fully understand the motives of the group or how they may be being used by members of these groups. Sometimes their preoccupation with their unique types of interests, combined with their limited knowledge of social and legal consequences, has a profoundly negative outcome. This is exemplified by the case of an autistic man who was interested in Luftwaffe planes and ended up joining a group that promoted Neo-Nazi ideology. The group was being monitored by the FBI as a terroristic threat, and he was seen as a potential terrorist. This man was oblivious to the ideology of the group but was laser-focused on German planes and aerial campaigns.

COMPUTER-DEPENDENT CRIMES VS. CYBER-DEVIANT CRIMES

As mentioned in Chapter One, some crimes can only be committed with a computer, and these are known as cyber-dependent crimes. The motivations for cyber-dependent crimes, such as hacking, can be financial gain or, for many with autism, a sense of challenge or risk that appeals to them. There is also the case of "ethical hacking," in which the hacker believes his/her hacking is justified (Ledingham & Mills, 2015). The determination of "good vs. bad hacking" may appeal to their binary thinking or black-and-white worldview.

Some autistics report a feeling of greater self-esteem or an enhanced reputation with an online community due to their computer skills (Payne et al., 2019). This can be a significant factor for individuals who feel they have had little personal success in the real world. A considerable number are under- or unemployed despite having post-secondary education, and many have few successes in the social realm. For some, it is their intense interest in how systems work which may lead them into hacking to break a security system. In a 2021 study, 20 percent of the autistic respondents self-reported "accessing another person's computer account or files with their knowledge just to look at the information." Another 20 percent self-reported "accessing or using another person's email account without permission" and self-reported "viewing information from a business system they did not have authority to view" (Lim et al., 2024). It is important to note several studies' findings that autistic people are actually less likely to commit a cyber-dependent crime (Payne et al., 2019). This aligns with existing literature indicating that autistic individuals tend to be law-abiding, often even more so than the general population.

Some individuals may create coding that enables a crime. In these situations, it is important to understand that the individual is using their superior computer knowledge to solve a puzzle. In some instances, the autistic individual facilitates online crime unknowingly, just for the thrill, and does not care about any financial reward. In many instances, they never ask for payment, and if they are compensated, they do not use the money. These individuals may be easily manipulated by another party to create coding or malware (Ledingham & Mills, 2015). Underground forums serve as a platform for cybercriminals to engage in various illicit activities. These forums facilitate the exchange of values, attitudes, techniques, and motivations related to criminal behavior, which is believed to play a crucial role in the commission of cybercrimes. By connecting individuals with a shared interest in cybercrime, these forums not only enable the sharing of information and services but also provide opportunities for users to trade and monetize their skills and methods (Man et al., 2023). Autistic individuals can be influenced by these forums and be persuaded to engage in illegal activity. In certain cases, individuals with autism are deliberately targeted and manipulated into taking the blame if a crime is uncovered. For example, they may be coerced into creating a Venmo or Cash App account, which is then used to facilitate payments for illegal goods or illicit online content. This tactic allows criminal organizations to create a layer of separation between themselves and their activities, leaving the autistic person vulnerable to being charged and held accountable by law enforcement when the crime is discovered.

Case: WR was a 26-year-old autistic male who had a great facility with numbers and created an algorithm for stock trading. WR was only interested in the creation of the algorithm and did not use it to make any money for himself. He was active on several stock-trading forums and was contacted by an individual on one of these sites who wanted to use the algorithm with his "clients." After WR provided the algorithm to this person, it was used in a scheme to "hook" investors and defraud them of their investment. WR was arrested for his participation even though he had never contacted the investors or profited personally. WR had never asked the person he provided the algorithm to anything about how he would use it or asked to be paid for it. He was never compensated for the use of his intellectual property. After several stressful months, the charges against him were eventually dropped.

ARE AUTISTIC INDIVIDUALS MORE LIKELY TO ENGAGE IN CYBERCRIME?

There has been a general belief that autistic people may engage in cybercrime to a greater extent than neurotypicals. This stereotype has been largely driven by media portrayals of cybercrime offenders as autistic. While there are some high-profile examples such as Gary McKinnon and Julian Assange, research into underground forums by Man, Siu, and Hutchings (2023) found that while self-autistics post more frequently, they are less likely to discuss cybercrime activities. Underground forums are public online platforms where users can exchange information, express their opinions, and trade tools and services. Analysis of the posts of those who were self-identified as autistic found that they primarily discussed being autistic and the personal issues they faced. These individuals used the forum for social connection and self-expression. Autistic individuals are active on these forums and post frequently; however, they were mostly involved in non-criminal conversations. The primary concern is that some autistic people, due to their trusting nature and challenges with recognizing deception or suspicious behavior online, may become involved in criminal activities. In some cases, autistic offenders later reported that they had not been aware their actions were illegal. Whether acting out of ignorance or curiosity, their actions were deemed criminal. Some who have opened files containing CSAM have even attempted to alert law enforcement. In a particularly unusual criminal case, the autistic offender was writing a paper about the ease of obtaining CSAM and downloaded thousands of images to his computer. He told the officers he wanted to raise awareness about the widespread presence of CSAM online and hoped to persuade authorities to take stronger action to track and crack down on its proliferation. When arrested, he explained this to the skeptical officers and then provided the multi-page document. He thought his actions were completely justified and couldn't comprehend why he was being arrested.

Obtaining illegal materials online does not require sophisticated technical skills. It is easy to arrive at these sites through pop-ups or typing in certain search terms. This is particularly true of words and phrases that have double meanings. An innocent search of words such as kittens, peach, or ATM can produce pornographic material. Users may also be routed to extremist sites by searching for information on weapons, bomb-making, and explosives. Law enforcement and intelligence agencies use open-source intelligence (OSINT) to monitor public websites. They track trends and identify the users of these sites. Individuals who visit these sites out of curiosity may be seen as potentially violent. Because some individuals on the autism spectrum may have developed a focused interest in certain types of guns and enjoy collecting images of various weaponry, their behavior could be misunderstood or subject to scrutiny.

"MATE CRIMES"/COUNTERFEIT FRIENDSHIP

Mate crime is a subtype of hate crime in which the perpetrator is known to the victim. It refers to deliberately abusive actions against a person by someone known to them, often someone considered a friend, although family members and carers can also be perpetrators. A disturbing feature of mate crime is that it encompasses acts of cruelty, humiliation, servitude, exploitation, or theft and is often aimed at autistic people (Forster & Pearson, 2020).

Andrew Landman (2014) acknowledged that autistic people may be particularly vulnerable due to an inability to recognize subtle indicators of exploitation; however, Landman also recognized that other disabilities (e.g., mental illness) and factors (such as age) could put people at higher risk of victimization. One of the participants in the study was able to identify a clear example of having been exploited by a "close friend." This participant also reflected on how outside perceptions of autism influenced their behavior, as they were concerned about being perceived as "rude." This statement was particularly concerning, given the number of interventions that focus on "social skills training" and being "compliant" (Chandler, Russell, & Maras, 2019). This highlights the need for interventions to improve the ability of an autistic person to trust their own judgment or express concern when faced with inappropriate social behaviors from others.

Another consideration is the "double empathy problem" (Milton et al., 2022), which suggests that difficulties in communication and understanding between autistic and non-autistic people are mutual. Both groups struggle to empathize with and understand each other due to the differences in how they experience, interpret, and communicate. Autistic individuals often process requests by focusing on the explicit information provided, which can lead to a different understanding of the situation. This means they might miss subtle cues or unspoken motivations on the part of a "bad actor." They tend to focus on details, which can cause them to overlook the broader context and inadvertently place themselves in compromised or illegal situations.

CYBER-DEVIANT CRIMES

Cyber-deviant crimes can occur without the use of a computer and can involve sexual exploitation of children and other individuals, harassment, extortion, identity theft, and the sale of stolen goods and drugs. Despite these crimes not requiring a computer, the online world provides a fertile environment for criminal behavior. Crime is currently proliferating online. The online world allows more deception through encrypted sites and false identities. This is often not detected by individuals on the autism spectrum due to their naive and trusting nature. They have difficulty discerning bad actors and are easy prey. In some cases, autistic people are specifically targeted by online predators and criminals who are looking for "an easy mark." Some are repeatedly victimized on these sites, and they can become both victims and offenders when using these sites.

Case: A 23-year-old autistic man (CJ) is arrested for inappropriately communicating with a 14-year-old girl (ML) online. He had an average IQ and verbal communication deficits (expressive and receptive) and was in autistic support classes. CJ is currently unemployed and lives with his parents. The two met in an anime chatroom and talked for several months and then exchanged phone numbers to text each other. They never talked on the phone and only communicated through texts.

The conversation quickly became sexual, and she began sending him nude and sexually explicit photos, and then he sent nude pictures of himself. CJ had been introduced to pornography sites by a classmate and had been watching pornography since he was 10 years old. He had also been to sexual chatrooms and copied the explicit sexual language used there as a script to communicate with the girl.

The FBI began monitoring these exchanges after her parents discovered their texts on her phone. The FBI and local police came to his family home when his parents were at work, questioned him, and conducted a search. CJ was frightened and anxious because there were multiple agents and local police in his home. They confiscated his phone and all other electronic devices he or his family members used. He was confused by the interrogation and was not sure why they were asking him about his communication with ML. He cooperated fully and talked about his texts with ML. CJ was never informed of his Miranda rights during his questioning. When asked if he knew ML's age, he said he never asked. CJ was later arrested and charged with possession of child sexual abuse material and exploitation of a minor. His family immigrated from the Dominican Republic and spoke minimal English. They were unaware of his online activities or texting. The parents had difficulty communicating with law enforcement and his attorney to explain his autism even though he had been in autistic support classes. CJ pleaded guilty and received a 6-year sentence despite being a first-time offender with no criminal record.

THEORY OF MIND IN CYBERCRIME DEFENSES AND VICTIMIZATION

When autistic individuals are engaged in cybercrime, diminished Theory of Mind is almost always an essential factor in why the crime occurred. When a person lacks the ability to fully understand the other person's intentions, they can easily be manipulated or make false assumptions about their interaction. Theory of Mind (ToM) is the ability to know what is really happening or to detect deception (Engel et al., 2014). Levels of ToM vary from one individual to another; however, many autistic individuals find understanding other people's perspectives challenging. In typically developing children, this ability is present from the age of 4 (Baron-Cohen, 2000). It should be noted that ToM difficulties are not confined to autistic individuals, and not all autistic individuals demonstrate difficulties (Michael & Brewer, 2024). These differences may be related to the degree of autistic characteristics present in an individual (Michael & Brewer, 2024). It is therefore important that any forensic evaluation of an autistic offender or victim include a measure of ToM ability such as the Adult Theory of Mind Test (A-ToM).

Many of the issues inherent in cybercrime stem from the fact that many autistic people have difficulty understanding others' beliefs and motivations. They tend to expect that people share their perspectives and will behave like them. Some refer to this ability as "mindreading," and it is critical to social communication and understanding social norms. When a mental health professional states that an autistic person lacks empathy, it does not imply that the person is callous or socio-pathic. Rather, it means they face significant challenges with regard to understanding the world from another person's perspective. This can make it difficult for them to recognize emotional distress in others or accurately interpret others' feelings (Mesibov et al., 2005). When an autistic person is communicating online using a computer or texting on their phone, these deficits are often consequential. Neurotypicals have well-developed "mindreading" skills that have been evolving over their lifetime. For many autistic people, their struggles with mindreading are reflected in their gullibility and penchant for inadvertent offensive comments or inappropriate sexual behavior.

THEORY OF MIND DEFICITS AND ONLINE VICTIMIZATION

While autistics prefer online social communication and may feel it masks their social deficits, the lack of Theory of Mind is still evident in some individuals (Engel et al., 2014). Even though the autistic person has more time to process the interaction when online (video chat or text), this does not mean they are fully understanding what is being said. Online predators can ascertain when they have encounterered a naive, easily manipulable potential victim. Many autistics tend toward a literal interpretation of spoken words and text. They may miss obvious signals related to the intent of the other persons in the chat. This can also be seen in their inability to see that certain online actions are unwelcome, inappropriate, or illegal. Many autistic people are naturally trusting and motivated by a genuine desire to form meaningful connections. They may also be eager to please others, hoping to secure relationships they perceive as friendships. They do not question the motivations of those they encounter online. A study by Pearson et al. (2022) examined the victimization of autistic adults by familiars or perceived friends. The findings indicated that many autistic people have difficulty recognizing when someone is acting abusively toward them. They often comply with unreasonable requests out of fear or a desire to avoid confrontation. These individuals are unclear on appropriate boundaries and need to be educated about what constitutes a healthy relationship. Due to their computer skills, they may be asked to provide free services that would normally be compensated.

Case: RV is a 30-year-old autistic man who provided IT support for a large healthcare corporation. He was an excellent employee but had no social connections in his office. He ate lunch at his desk and never conversed with other employees. His social anxiety prevented him from going to any office social gatherings, and he mostly kept to himself. One day, he received an email from a co-worker (TO) asking him if he knew anything about website design and if he would consider helping TO design a website to sell sports memorabilia. RV was excited because he thought this might be a good way to make a friend at his office. He agreed and spent about 10 hours designing the website. TO thanked him but never offered RV any money for his time. He was disappointed but didn't want to confront TO and thought maybe it was just "how things worked." He wanted to keep TO as a friend. Later in the week, they both met for lunch, and TO said he had a friend who would also like to have his website designed by RV. He agreed because he felt that this would make TO like him and want to have lunch with him again. The same scenario played out with three other people, and RV did not ever receive any payment for his design work. He was confused that they didn't offer him anything in return but didn't want to cause trouble. Sometimes, he was able to sit with them at lunch or during breaks, and he felt included.

In many cases, when forensic experts review online transcripts of social media or chatrooms, the confusion of the autistic participant is apparent. In many instances, these records are important in assessing the person's level of Theory of Mind. Also, autistic individuals with limited Theory of Mind have difficulty thinking flexibly and quickly adapting to changes during an online interaction (Diamond, 2013). Some are unaware that they are being bullied or humiliated in an online group, as is illustrated in the following case. In some instances, they endure their mistreatment just to continue to feel like they are part of the group.

Case: JB, a 20-year-old girl on the autism spectrum, had a special interest in My Little Pony and was active in a fan chatroom on Discord. JB had never had friends and was excited to be part of this group. She was happy to meet other young adults who shared her interest and were going to the My Little Pony convention near her hometown. After a few weeks, she began getting requests to post her picture online so the others could meet her at the convention. When she did post her picture, there were several demeaning comments made by members in the chat that JB totally misinterpreted as positive and a sign that she was accepted by the group. She did not detect the sarcasm in their chats. After they made fun of her for several days, the group removed her from the server. JB was emotionally devastated and began talking about suicide. She later ingested 20 tablets of her prescribed anti-depressant medication and was hospitalized. A review of the phone texts indicated that she was being harassed by the group from the beginning but did not seem to realize that she was the target of their bullying.

RESEARCH ON THEORY OF MIND AND DETECTING CRIMINAL INTENT

Brewer et al. (2023) examined the ability of autistic adults to discern suspicious or criminal behavior using 34 professionally written short stories. From these stories, 152 short vignettes were extracted that could stand alone and that appeared to vary in terms of the extent to which they suggested suspicious behavior. One hundred and fifty-two adult participants (half autistic and half non-autistic) read each vignette and indicated whether it signaled "dodgy" or suspicious behavior or not. The results indicate that impaired ToM, or reading the minds of others, is associated with poor detection of "dodginess" in both autistic and non-autistic individuals. This increases their vulnerability to involvement in some form of criminal activity or becoming the victim of a crime (Brewer et al., 2023).

Another study by Michael and Brewer (2024) found that ToM difficulties "heighten criminal vulnerability" for both autistic and non-autistic individuals. While many autistic individuals have challenges understanding other people's perspectives, there are varying degrees of impairment, and being autistic does not always imply that a person has a limited ToM ability. The study asked subjects to respond adaptively to another's criminal intent as they listened to seven audio scenarios. Four of the scenarios depicted an unfolding crime, and three did not. The subjects were asked how they would respond as a character in each scenario, as in the following:

> A man (Aaron) is asked by a friend (Jim) if he can store some files on his computer. Jim says he is out of space on his hard drive and offers to pay him. Jim also says that Aaron can't look at the files or share them with anyone. When Jim transfers the files to Aaron's computer, Aaron notices image thumbnails of young children. When Aaron asks about the pictures, Jim says these are models for a photography class assignment. He indicates these are a surprise for his wife and asks Aaron not to tell her.
>
> About a week later, Aaron hears a knock on the door and when he opens it there are two police officers.

This study supports the importance of ToM as a risk factor for criminal behavior. It further reported that ToM difficulties "may contribute to an individual misreading another's reactions and assuming the interaction partner was accepting of their behavior." In some cases, this might result in inappropriate sexual behavior due to misreading their subtle verbal signs of disapproval. They may reason that the interaction partner tacitly approves of their actions (Michael & Brewer, 2024). In each of these studies, autism does not predispose an individual toward committing online crimes; however, significant ToM difficulties create vulnerability to criminal involvement.

IMPORTANCE OF AN "AUTISM-INFORMED" EVALUATION

Individuals who come into contact with the criminal justice system as either victims or offenders require an evaluation conducted by a clinician trained in the diagnosis and treatment of autism. The evaluator must be familiar with the unique processing and communication styles of autistic persons. When interviewing victims, the evaluator may need to rephrase questions and allow extra time to process the question. The evaluator must avoid using idioms, slang, or abstract terminology. Many autistic individuals are literal thinkers and speak in a formal manner, have odd prosody (intonation), or speak in monotone. Some may have an evasive conversational style when interrogated or appear to not be listening. They may also exhibit little emotion or even appear bored. These behaviors should not be interpreted as callousness or lack of remorse. In the case of those who have been victimized, the lack of emotional expression does not equate to a lack of trauma. Many autistic victims (and offenders) have a significant history of trauma and may be displaying numbing or dissociation as a result. When a victim is interviewed, a family member should provide information regarding the victim's preferred communication style, and the interviewer should plan the questions accordingly. As discussed earlier, an offender may fail to appreciate the impact of his/her behavior due to their diminished "theory of mind" (Baron-Cohen et al., 1985).

If evaluators have access to audio or video of the interrogation of an autistic offender, it can provide valuable insight into his/her social communicative style. Often, there is evidence of their literal/concrete interpretations of the questions posed by law enforcement. Frequently, the autistic individual will display confusion, and they can be easily manipulated into making false confessions. They are particularly anxious in these situations, and some will confess to a myriad of offenses they did not commit when interrogated. Autistic offenders have been known to make these confessions just to terminate the interview and relieve their anxiety. Law enforcement must consider these factors when a suspect is identified as autistic (Bagnall, 2023). When provided as evidence, these issues must be identified and explained to judges and juries. An example is when a 25-year-old autistic male is asked "why is it a problem for you to be talking with a fourteen-year-old girl and exchanging pictures?" and he replies, "because its illegal." Many struggle to understand the abstract concept of exploitation or the imbalance of power intrinsic to online relationships with underage individuals.

An evaluation conducted by an evaluator with training in autism can help elucidate these issues to the court. The evaluation should include the following:

1. A thorough review of the medical, psychiatric, psychological, and school records available. If the individual is currently incarcerated, hospitalized, or in residential or day treatment, progress notes and reports from the facility.
2. Interviews with parents, siblings, or spouse/partner of the individual.
3. A forensic interview of the individual.
4. A diagnostic measure such as the Autism Diagnostic Observation Schedule (ADOS-2).

5. A developmental history completed by a parent, caregiver, or older family member (if parents are deceased).
6. A diagnostic interview with a parent or caregiver, such as the Autism Diagnostic Interview-Revised (ADI-R).
7. A measure of social impairment completed by a parent, spouse, or partner, such as the Social Responsiveness Scale, Second Edition (SRS-2).
8. A measure of Theory of Mind (perspective-taking), such as the Adult Theory of Mind Test (A-ToM).
9. Assessments of emotional functioning, such as the Beck Depression Inventory (BDI) or Depression Anxiety Stress Scale (DASS); assessments of social anxiety, such as the Social Anxiety Scale (SAS); and behavioral rating scales.
10. Cognitive assessments that measure ability for abstract thinking, cognitive flexibility, and executive function, such as the Wechsler Adult Intelligence Scale, Fifth Edition (WAIS-5); Wechsler Abbreviated Scale of Intelligence, Second Edition (WASI-II); Delis-Kaplan Executive Function System (DKEFS); Stroop Color and Word Test; Trail Making Test; Tower of Hanoi; and Wisconsin Card Sorting Test. If an individual is intellectually disabled, a competency evaluation may be appropriate. This would determine whether the individual is mentally capable of understanding the charges against them and able to participate in their own defense.
11. A trauma evaluation such as the Detailed Assessment of Posttraumatic Stress (DAPS) may be appropriate if the individual has a history of trauma. Trauma can affect memory, attention, processing speed, and emotional regulation.

These instruments play a crucial role in confirming an autism diagnosis and assessing the individual's level of communicative and social functioning. A Theory of Mind test evaluates the individual's ability to take others' perspectives and understand others' motivation or intent. Emotional assessments provide valuable insights into the person's current emotional state, while cognitive and executive functioning tests help create a comprehensive profile of how they process and organize information. Additionally, a trauma evaluation, often guided by the individual's history, can shed light on the impact of trauma on their daily functioning, offering a more holistic understanding of their needs and challenges. In cases involving sexual offenses, a risk assessment instrument like the Static-99R may be used to evaluate specific risk factors for reoffending. This is usually conducted by a mental health professional trained for this type of risk assessment.

Autistic individuals are often misunderstood by society as a whole, particularly within the realms of law enforcement and the judicial system. A person on the autism spectrum may present as highly competent due to their intelligence, memory for detail, and expertise in certain subjects. This can obscure their more subtle communication difficulties, Theory of Mind deficits, and lack of social understanding that may have contributed to their victimization or offending. It is imperative that these issues be highlighted when they are in front of a judge or jury. In many instances, intelligence does not always correlate with social judgment or appropriate responses.

Three

The lack of social maturity and difficulty in forming peer relationships can further exacerbate these issues. Autistic individuals may seek connections with younger individuals due to their own social and emotional delays, which can lead to problematic online interactions. The internet, while providing a means of connection, also poses risks such as sextortion, blackmail, and exposure to illegal content. The concept of "counterfeit deviance" highlights that behaviors perceived as deviant may stem from naivete and social misunderstandings rather than paraphilic tendencies.

Inadequate sexuality education and social isolation can lead autistic individuals to develop unhealthy online habits, including pornography addiction. This addiction can be exacerbated by obsessive-compulsive tendencies and the use of the internet as a substitute for social interaction. The legal system often struggles to address these issues appropriately, as autistic offenders may not fit typical profiles of sex offenders. Comprehensive evaluations are necessary to distinguish between genuine deviance and behaviors resulting from social and educational deficits. Treatment programs focusing on cognitive behavioral therapy and social skills are crucial for addressing these challenges effectively.

INADEQUATE SEXUALITY EDUCATION

Clinicians working with autistic adolescents and adults often find that their clients have had very little education regarding their sexuality, sexual orientation, or sexual desires or societal rules surrounding sexual expression. This lack of sexuality education for autistics has been recorded for many years (Brown et al., 2017). Dr. Isabelle Hénault was the first in the field of psychology to write about the need for sexuality education and autism (Hénault, 2006). She described autistic individuals as "intrinsically naive in terms of sexual knowledge

DOI: 10.4324/9781003540571-4

and experience" and explained how this naivete increases their vulnerability to victimization or to engaging in inappropriate behaviors (Dubin et al., 2014). The lack of provision of healthy sexuality education for autistic individuals is well-documented (Mogavero, 2016). Individuals identified as being developmentally disabled or emotionally impaired are often placed in special education classes, where they typically do not receive the same sex education as neurotypical students. If they receive any information at all, it is usually to correct an inappropriate behavior such as masturbation in a public setting (Allely & Dubin, 2018). Much of this stems from the discomfort that teachers and society as a whole feel regarding expressions of sexuality. As a result, many autistic people are not equipped with an understanding of their own sexuality or ways to keep themselves safe. They also often lack clear guidance as to acceptable behaviors, which can increase their vulnerability and risk of offending.

Parents of autistics may erroneously assume their child has no interest in sex and do not consider their sexual development or the need to provide sex education to them in the most effective way. There are few resources for parents or educators attempting to teach this material to autistics (Brown et al., 2017). Parents are often overly protective of their autistic child (or adult child), which puts that individual at greater risk of inappropriate sexual behavior, exploitation, and abuse. Most autistic people are just as sexually curious as neurotypicals. If they have received sex education, it often focuses primarily on the mechanics of reproduction, contraception, and sexually transmitted diseases. There is little or no discussion of the complex social rules regarding sexual expression (i.e., privacy, consent, underage laws). A 2024 study found that most autistic participants shared feelings of intense anxiety about romantic and sexual relationships, in part due to anticipated difficulties in social communication. Issues surrounding romantic relationships and their links to one's current self-concept were prominent themes in many autistic participants' responses. The results suggested that "autism-friendly" sex education programs need to address issues related to romance for adolescents and adults (Au Yeung et al., 2024). In our culture and especially in the online world, autistic individuals receive many mixed messages regarding sexuality. "Autism-friendly" sexuality education is crucial for the safety and personal fulfillment of those with autism. In Canada, a sexuality curriculum was developed for autistic students focusing specifically on puberty, relationships, and gender and sexual diversity (Davies et al., 2024). Autism-specific sexuality education programs address the significant gaps left by traditional sex education by tailoring content to the unique needs of autistic individuals. This includes providing clear practical instruction on abstract concepts like consent, personal boundaries, and safety. Some laws regarding consent are particularly confusing, such as how consensual sexual activity between a 16-year-old and a 17-year-old is legal, but the same activity between a 19-year-old and a 17-year-old is not.

In addition to their inadequate sexuality education, an individual with autism may have a limited understanding of why certain sexual conduct is societally unacceptable. Neurotypical adolescents and young adults often navigate and internalize social norms through peer interactions and social experiences. Most adolescents with autism, however, often struggle to form the close reciprocal friendships that are crucial for sharing and discussing important information about sexuality (Loftin et al., 2021). Consequently, autistic individuals often do not recognize sexual boundaries. Some have obvious social and emotional immaturity. This combined with their naivete and social awkwardness may produce offending behaviors online. In the complex world of online communication, they are particularly vulnerable to committing offenses, in many instances unwittingly. Many autistics have not had the usual social and sexual experiences of typical adolescents and adults despite their sexual drives being the same (Higgs & Carter, 2015). Some parents avoid discussing sexuality with their autistic child or assume they have no sexual interest. One parent commented to their child's therapist, "I thought that was the one thing I wouldn't have to deal with." Individuals with autism are often misperceived as asexual, and their rights are frequently restricted under the pretense of protection (Gougeon, 2010). This harmful mindset led to a lack of action toward providing them with proper sexuality education.

This avoidance can also send a message to the child or adolescent that it is not acceptable to ask their parents about their sexual feelings. This may be especially true for those that are gay, lesbian, or bisexual. Many autistic therapy clients report that they had no discussion of sexuality with their parents. In some cases, their sexual curiosity and confusion regarding appropriate sexual behaviors led them to commit sexual offenses online. This is further complicated by the conflicting messages about sexuality prevalent in our culture.

Lacking an adequate (or any) sexuality education, some autistic individuals use the internet as their primary source for sexual education and to explore their sexual desires. Pornography is not a good resource for sexual education. The abrupt and impersonal sexual encounters depicted fail to offer realistic expectations and do not provide a meaningful understanding of genuine sexual intimacy. Instead, what they find online can be confusing, disturbing, and outside the norm of what is considered healthy sexual expression. Their natural sexual curiosity combined with their propensity for repetition may cause them to repeatedly visit extreme sites. This is compounded by the fact that they have little knowledge of conventional sexual behavior or societal norms (Higgs & Carter, 2015). Some pornography sites bombard them with a variety of sexual material that may include incest scenarios, rape scenarios, violence, fetishes, or bestiality. When these individuals repeatedly visit pornography sites, they may develop online sexual addictions. Many are socially isolated and have had few interpersonal relationships. In the unregulated online world, they will encounter sexual material that they are unable to fully process or respond to appropriately. Some visit sexual sites and chatrooms just to meet people but have had no education regarding internet safety. They may meet sexual sadists and individuals involved in sex trafficking and other sexual crimes.

SEXUAL VICTIMIZATION ONLINE

The combination of limited sexual experience, social naivete, and profound loneliness can create a perfect storm, making individuals on the spectrum particularly vulnerable to sexual predators. Autistic young people are often easily deceived and manipulated by online pedophiles seeking pictures and videos. Sexting, the practice of using social media and the internet to exchange and view sexualized content, is prevalent among students. Snapchat and WhatsApp are the preferred social media for sexting for some students because they perceive that messages sent through these platforms are safe and temporarily stored, without permanent implications (Stone et al., 2025). Clinicians have heard many of their clients discuss sending sexual pictures online or allowing themselves to be videoed in sexual scenarios. This issue is not limited to individuals on the autism spectrum; it affects all adolescents and young adults and must be addressed comprehensively.

Sexting and sexual exploration online are common among teenagers (Madigan et al., 2018). A 2022 study found that sexting among middle schoolers was usually the result of peer pressure and caused greater stress than in older adolescents and adults (Parti et al., 2023). A primary concern is the increased risk of those with autism becoming the object of online sexual solicitation (Mitchell et al., 2014) or blackmail. Sexting can be a gateway to sextortion, online grooming, or cyberbullying. Those with autism are at risk due to their inability to detect deception or discern the motivations of these predatory individuals. They may not possess social maturity or knowledge regarding the boundaries of appropriate sexual behavior and may be operating with "social scripts" they learn in chatrooms or by texting. Many do not fully understand the social implications of their imitative language (Cohen & Candio, 2023). They use sexualized language, which may invite predators. There is a significant need for education among middle and high schoolers about the risks of sexting, as well as effective coping strategies for managing peer pressure. This is especially true for young people on the autism spectrum.

Case: JL, an autistic middle-school student, sent a nude picture of herself to a boy in her class whom she liked but had never talked to due to her social anxiety. She had become obsessed with this boy who sat in front of her in two classes and often fantasized about him. She later explained to her therapist that she thought this would make him like her. The boy never spoke to her but thought it was funny and shared the image with two of his friends. It eventually spread throughout her school, and she was humiliated and bullied continuously by her peers. She was ashamed and therefore did not discuss this with her parents or notify the school administrators. After a month, the proliferation of this picture had become a safety issue as it had been put on an online sexual site. Her parents contacted the FBI to ask them to investigate and, eventually, had to move her to another school.

COMMUNICATION WITH MINORS

Individuals with autism may be attracted to younger individuals because of their social and emotional delays. They are looking to connect with people that they feel comfortable with, and this may be outside of their age group. Some have the social and emotional skills of an individual younger than their chronological age. Their social maturity is closer to that of a much younger person because they are at a similar level to theirs, socially and emotionally (Mogavero, 2016). Many have been rejected by their chronologically aged peers. This often creates problems in online communication because the autistic person will gravitate to younger individuals for their own social comfort. These relationships can become troublesome to the outside world, especially when there is a perceived power imbalance due to the age difference. Autistic individuals do not always perceive age differences or inquire about them. If a conversation involving an underaged individual turns sexual, the older participant of the two will invariably be perceived as the predator, regardless of the younger person's level of aggression. Some autistic individuals may engage in sexual chats online without fully understanding social boundaries. Feelings of loneliness can contribute to this behavior, and the excitement of online sexual interactions may provide them with a sense of stimulation or connection that they otherwise find difficult to experience (Mahoney, 2021).

In some cases, the parents of the underaged person have discovered the conversations and contacted law enforcement. At that point, future conversations are typically monitored by an FBI agent. Sometimes, the conversation will then become a device to entrap the older party. They may discuss a plan to meet, and when the autistic individual goes to the meetup, they are met by law enforcement and arrested. This scenario has played out many times in forensic cases involving autistic individuals.

Case: MW, a 26-year-old autistic man, met a girl (KL) online in a chatroom for fans of the Japanese animator and manga artist Hayao Miyazaki. They were both avid admirers and had seen all his movies. KL told MW that she was 18 when, in fact, she was only 15. Their relationship developed into a more romantic one, and each expressed a desire to meet one day despite living in different states. After they had talked for a few months, MW discovered that there was a Miyazaki film festival in New York City to be held during the coming week. He suggested that he and KL meet there and spend the night at a more affordable hotel outside Manhattan. He suggested they go across the river to New Jersey because it was close enough that they could go to the festival again the next day. KL was going to take a bus, and MW was driving, so they planned to meet at the festival. After they saw three films, they took a train to Jersey City to the hotel. When MW arrived with her to check in, he was met by two plainclothes policemen. They put handcuffs on him and informed him that he was being arrested for taking an underage minor across state lines. After KL's parents discovered that she was communicating with MW, they had informed local law enforcement, who contacted the FBI. MW was charged with transporting a minor under the age of 18 to another state for the purpose of sexual activity. He was confused and tried to explain his actions to the authorities; however, KL's parents insisted that he be charged. Eventually, the charges were dropped after MW spent 2 months in a New Jersey county jail.

SEXTORTION

Black Mirror is a British television series that explores dystopian themes surrounding the role of technology and media in our society. In the episode "Shut up and Dance," a hacker records a young man masturbating via his webcam and threatens to release the recording unless he follows their instructions. He immediately complies and becomes entangled in a series of escalating crimes to prevent the release. While this scenario seemed far-fetched in 2016 when it aired, this type of extortion is rampant in the online world today. Many victims of these sextortion scams are minors. Of the 13,000 reports of financial sextortion received by the FBI from October 2021 to March 2023, the vast majority were about boys. Sextortion scams prey on young men and teenage boys. Their explicit images are held for ransom to be paid typically through cryptocurrency or gift cards (Nir, 2024).

Unfortunately, autistic individuals are frequently the target of sexual extortion. The individual may engage in sexual activity while on a webcam and then receive a threatening message demanding money (usually paid through gift cards or other untraceable mediums). In several cases, the autistic person was older than the people extorting them. This can make it challenging to convince law enforcement that the older person was not creating sexual material to lure younger individuals. In reality, they are the ones being extorted. The prevailing assumption is often that the older adult is always in control, which may not be true in these situations.

PORNOGRAPHY EXPOSURE

Pornography is ubiquitous in today's online environment. A 2022 study of young adults found that 57 percent of males and 33 percent of females reported their first exposure to online pornography occurring between the ages of 12 and 14 years. In that study, it was also revealed that 28 percent of males and 23 percent of females were exposed between the ages of 9 and 11 (Bernstein et al., 2023). Anecdotally, autistic offenders report that they were exposed to pornography at a young age (10 or 11 years). They either discovered it on their own or were exposed to pornographic sites by an older sibling or classmate. They are frequently unable to process the plethora of extreme sexual images or videos they encounter. This exposure can be overwhelming because they have had little or no experience and minimal sexuality education. Inappropriate early online exposures can create psychological challenges that might impact an individual's healthy sexual and emotional development. Pornography viewing may also shape the sexual beliefs and behaviors of some individuals and increase sexual impulsivity (Bernstein et al., 2023). For those who become addicted to pornography, it is easy to "go down the rabbit hole" of sexually explicit pictures and videos and, eventually, end up with child sexual abuse material. This is one of the primary risks of frequenting pornography sites.

Legislatures around the world have proposed laws calling for an age verification system for websites advertising sexually explicit material. These laws are designed to combat online harm to children but are heavily scrutinized for violating free speech rights and government censorship. The United Kingdom enacted the Online

Safety Act 2023 and, in 2024, France enacted the Sécuriser et Réguler l'Espace Numérique Act, both holding service providers who make sexually explicit content available online accountable for verifying the age of their end users. By 2025, 30 states in the US have enacted laws requiring websites to verify that each user is at least 18 years old (Free Speech Coalition, 2025, para. 3).

Some individuals on the autism spectrum are particularly prone to pornography addiction due to their obsessive-compulsive tendencies, perseverative behavior, and social isolation (Hénault, 2009). Many autistic individuals have had few peer relationships. Due to their inadequate sexuality education and inability to talk with peers, they may have been drawn to the computer to explore their sexuality. Dr. Tony Attwood, an internationally renowned expert on high-functioning autism, explains that the atypical sexual development of ASD is because of social isolation (Attwood, Hénault, & Dubin, 2014) and the lack of ability to discuss sexual thoughts or feelings with peers. Dr. Attwood also stated that the Internet is a link to the outside world that becomes a substitute friend for individuals on the autism spectrum. The concept of counterfeit deviance is often used to explain the unusual sexual behavior of those with autism spectrum disorder. Isabelle Hénault (2014) has said that "the lack of sociosexual knowledge is always a major issue" contributing to the inappropriate sexual behavior of autistic people.

SPECIAL INTERESTS AND RULE 34

Sometimes, special interests can also lead individuals to sites that are pornographic. Rule 34 of the internet states that "if something exists, there is pornographic depiction of it." It is described as pornographic "fan art" and includes cartoons, historical or literary figures, celebrities, or even objects. Many of these "Rule 34" sites may involve the special interests of autistic children, adolescents, or adults, such as anime, My Little Pony, *SpongeBob*, *Dragon Ball Z*, and Pokémon. There are even pornographic sites for younger children's shows, such as *Thomas the Tank Engine*. This inappropriate content is often confusing and can overwhelm or distress autistic people who rely on structured or predictable online experiences. Accordingly, these sites can also become gateways to online pornography. An interest in Japanese animation can also lead to viewing hentai, which is pornographic anime and manga containing sexually explicit images and plots.

ANIME PORN AND HENTAI

Hentai is porn that comes in cartoon, anime, or manga format, and it is one of the most popular kinds of porn for Gen Z, Millennials, young adults, and children. Hentai is described as creating "erotic illusions possible are freed from all the normal constraints of reality." The animated porn often depicts highly exaggerated sex acts featuring characters with exaggerated breasts, penises, and other body parts. Hentai often depicts female characters as childlike and vulnerable, frequently portraying them as secretly desiring to be raped. It is not uncommon for these depictions to involve fantastical elements, such as monsters, demons, animals, giant insects, or even plants, engaging in explicit acts with cartoon women. The age of the characters is often left deliberately ambiguous, but a recurring theme is their portrayal as sexually inexperienced or innocent (Louie, 2020). Although hentai is currently legal, the content has been introduced in criminal prosecutions of individuals facing charges related to sex crimes as character evidence or indication toward propensity to commit certain sex crimes.

Some have argued that certain forms of pornography, such as hentai, are less harmful because they do not involve the exploitation of real individuals. However, critics contend that hentai is closely tied to traditional pornography, as it often replicates similar themes and content. For children and young adults—an increasingly significant portion of the audience—exposure to such material can distort their understanding of healthy sexuality (Louie, 2020). This is especially true for those on the autism spectrum, who have traditionally had inadequate sexuality education.

MASKING, AUTISTIC BURNOUT, AND DEPRESSION

Being an autistic person coping with the neurotypical world can be overwhelming, stressful, and exhaustive. Many attempt to camouflage or mask their autism, especially when confronted with social or job-related expectations (Cook et al., 2022). Autistic people mask to avoid the stigma, discrimination, and derision they often experience. This is also sometimes referred to as camouflaging and is typical in autistic individuals who are identified later in life (Lai et al., 2016). Due to societal pressures to "fit in," they develop strategies to conceal their social difficulties. This requires immense effort, which becomes exhausting, and may also leave them feeling disconnected from their authentic selves. Masking may also make autistic individuals more vulnerable to being manipulated into online sexual situations due to their strong desire to gain acceptance and please others.

The accumulation of these life stressors over time combined with an inability to find relief results in "autistic burnout" (Raymaker et al., 2020). This burnout causes chronic life stress and depression. Many have reported that they seek pleasure from online activities such as gaming or visiting sites related to their interests as a release. There is evidence that depression can predispose an individual to pornography addiction (Bernstein et al., 2023). Pornography provides a temporary relief from their depressive state. The reward centers of the brain are activated while viewing pornography, which allows them an escape from their negative thoughts and feelings (Fraumeni-McBride, 2024.) Some offenders have reported that their pornography use increased when they felt depressed. Like many addictive behaviors, pornography viewing increases as a way to avoid negative feelings by activating pleasure centers in the brain. The pattern of using pornography to cope with stress, anxiety, or uncomfortable emotions is similar to that seen with other addictive behaviors, such as gambling or drug use.

PORNOGRAPHY ADDICTION

Pornography addiction is a conditioned response in the brain. Those affected report an addictive sequence of compulsive viewing which leads to a need for novel types in increasing amounts to achieve sexual satisfaction. This repeated viewing creates brain pathways of sexual arousal based on the images that were viewed. Looking at these images releases dopamine to the brain's pleasure centers, which then becomes a conditioned response. They may eventually become aroused only by that kind of image (Doidge, 2007). Over time, repeated exposure to pornography can alter the brain's reward system, making it less sensitive to "normal" sexual pleasures. This compels individuals to seek out a wider variety of pornography, taking advantage of the virtually limitless options available online. With enough online exposure, a person can become conditioned to be sexually aroused by almost anything. Online exposure has the potential to shape our arousal patterns and lead to unconventional sexual triggers. This explains how individuals can rapidly become engaged with various fetish sites, violent content, and sites associated with the sexual exploitation of minors.

As with most addictions, an individual addicted to pornography will need more time spent viewing it and will often look at a variety of genres. This may expose the individual to increasingly hardcore sites and illegal pornography involving children. Pornography is often a gateway to illegal sexual material. Algorithms and pop-ups may lead an individual toward material they would never have sought out on their own. Anime may also be a gateway to child sexual abuse material as young characters are frequently presented in a very sexualized manner. Many individuals who became addicted during their early adolescence have reported that their involvement with child sexual abuse material began in a similar manner.

Child Sexual Abuse Material

Child sexual abuse material (CSAM) is defined as any visual depiction—such as photographs, videos, or computer-generated images—of a person under 18 years of age engaged or depicted as engaged in explicit sexual activity. CSAM was previously known as child pornography. This term has been phased out and replaced with CSAM, which more accurately reflects the abuse and trauma involved in the production of this material. Children cannot consent to participating in sexual material, and therefore, all such material is illegal. This distinction may be confusing to some individuals on the autism spectrum. Some have said that they thought the children were willing participants and, therefore, not harmed. Consent is a nuanced concept that may not be immediately apparent to them. Therefore, it is essential to provide an explicit explanation of why children cannot consent and why this material is always illegal.

TREATMENT

For some individuals, the internet is highly addictive. Activities such as repeatedly viewing pornography, compulsive gaming, and web-surfing are similar to alcohol, drug, or gambling addictions. These online activities activate a combination of sites in the brain that are associated with pleasure. Treatment centers such as the reSTART program in Washington state detox individuals from their online addictions by removing all technology for 45–90 days (about

3 months) and providing therapies such as outdoor experiences to reorient the addicted individuals to the outside world. Cognitive behavioral therapy, social skills, life skills, and mindfulness-based stress reduction are employed to develop alternatives to their online immersion (Cash et al., 2012). These types of treatment centers are now located in various states around the US.

Currently, the US criminal justice system does not adequately address the treatment needs of autistic sexual offenders. Group interventions require the participants to be introspective, share personal information, and interact in a group. These are all activities that autistic individuals find particularly challenging (Higgs & Carter, 2015). Autistic offenders are frequently placed in sex offender group therapies in prison. For these online offenders frequently placed in groups alongside violent sexual offenders, these experiences are often traumatizing and counterproductive to the therapeutic process. Consequently, there is a need for treatment interventions that work responsively, safely, and appropriately with autistic individuals. Some alternatives are presented in Chapter Twelve.

Most individuals on the autism spectrum are rule-bound, and most who are arrested for online sexual offenses do not have a history of criminal charges. They are first-time offenders and have never broken other laws. Their rule-bound nature minimizes the risk of them reoffending. Once they are educated about the laws regarding communication with minors or child sexual abuse material, they typically do not re-offend (Mahoney, 2021)

FILESHARING

Over the past 20 years, filesharing became popular as a way to obtain movies, games, software, music, or other digital collectibles for free. Peer-to-peer networking involves an efficient protocol that facilitates a connection between two or more computers to share digital files directly without any third-party moderator. Consequently, an inability to moderate the content shared between devices around the world has allowed these peer-to-peer networks to facilitate the transfer of illegal material, including child sexual abuse material (Liberatore et al., 2010). Furthermore, the absence of content moderation allows bad actors to mislabel and disguise files that are likely to be downloaded by users, such as pirated copies of newly released movies or games, as malware or illegal content. This can be used to blackmail the user for money or to discretely utilize the device as a proxy for additional illegal activity. While the use of file-sharing networks, like Gnutella and BitTorrent, is legal and free, the end user is liable for any violation of copyright laws, intellectual property theft, and receipt, possession, or distribution of illegal material. One dangerous pattern of peer-to-peer users is mass downloading material and leaving their computers to autonomously operate on these networks. This can result in the download of thousands of files unbeknownst to the user until or unless they personally view the content. Frequently, the person on the receiving end has no prior knowledge of what additional files may be attached to their download of a favorite comic book or movie. In some instances, the files may just be on their computer even though they have never looked at them. Child sexual abuse material may be embedded in these downloads of hundreds of files. When an individual is using a peer-to-peer application, they may have no control over or knowledge of what is getting created on their computer or being reshared to other users. In the legal context, this filesharing of illegal images is possession and distribution. The arrested person will be held responsible for what has come into and gone out of their computer. If this person has been collecting and cataloguing this material, they will be charged on the basis of the number of illegal images they possess. The more images, the longer their sentence. The following case is very typical of the kinds of scenarios that are playing out repeatedly in the United States justice system.

Case: MT, a 39-year-old autistic man, was very socially isolated and lived with his parents. He had no outside social contacts and had never had a romantic relationship. MT liked to use BitTorrent to download movies and video games for free. He had been using it for many months when he discovered unusual files were included in his downloads. MT opened some of the files, which had strings of numbers or letters (that he did not recognize) instead of file names. The files contained various underage pornography involving young children. He was curious but also very confused by what he saw. He felt that these files were not something that he could discuss with his parents. He put them in the trash bin of his computer. Over the next year, MT continued to receive these types of files when he used BitTorrent. He continued to open them out of curiosity, frequently looked at the material, and then moved them to the trash. One day, the FBI showed up at his home with a search warrant and confiscated all electronic devices in the home. The forensic investigation of MT's computer found over 5,000 images and videos containing child sexual abuse material. He was charged with possession and distribution of child sexual abuse material even though he thought these files had been removed. These are both federal crimes which can carry long prison sentences. MT did not know that these files were still on the hard drive of his computer. He was also not aware that he was distributing these files to others who were using the filesharing network before he removed them.

"COUNTERFEIT DEVIANCE"

The viewing and collecting of extreme sexual material by those with autism does not reflect deviant sexuality but is often referred to as "counterfeit deviance." These behaviors are due to challenges in judgment, social skills, or impulse control which are diagnostically different from paraphilia (Griffiths et al., 2013). For autistic offenders, what may appear to the outside world to be deviant interests and behavior are often a result of their naivete, ritualistic collecting, uninhibited curiosity, and lack of social understanding (Allely, 2022). Some are drawn to the novelty or shocking content of the material, which distracts them from feelings of boredom, emotional distress, or depression. Some may find sexual fantasies involving minors less threatening than adult sexual scenes. It is therefore essential to consider how autistic individuals perceive the world and to understand their intentions behind actions that would be considered deviant. Many struggle to recognize social norms and fail to see the red flags that indicate that their behavior may be inappropriate. Therefore, when those with autism are charged with sexual offenses online, a comprehensive evaluation must be conducted to determine if it arises from pedophilia. If not, it is likely due to "counterfeit deviance" (Mogavero, 2016).

Due to the inadequate sexuality education of those on the autism spectrum, many are unclear on what is considered conventional sexual behavior. In essence, these individuals may not recognize that the online material they consume is outside the realm of normal sexual expression. Some may encounter rape or incest pornography without fully understanding that this is illegal and socially unacceptable. They do not always discern the fantasy elements of pornography and may believe that these scenarios commonly happen in real life. Of course, this is a problem for today's youth in general (Bernstein et al., 2023). An example would be the autistic teen who believed that delivery people routinely have sex with the recipients of a pizza or package, a common pornography trope.

In many cases, compulsive collecting through filesharing leads to individuals inadvertently saving hardcore pornography and child sexual abuse material on their computers, even if they have no interest in such material. These individuals save everything on their computer and, if arrested for possession of child sexual abuse material, may be found to have thousands of images on their computer, along with excessive amounts of other files related to their interests. Sometimes, the autistic person will even organize and catalogue these illegal files, which gives the impression that they are highly valued, even though they have catalogued all other content on their computer. In some cases, they have just collected this material and may not have ever looked at it. This compulsive behavior may lead to the assumption that the individual is a pedophile, potentially resulting in biased outcomes within our current US criminal justice system.

VULNERABILITY TO CHILD SEXUAL EXPLOITATION
Sexual curiosity and drive (along with a lack of appropriate channels for sexual expression and interaction can lead autistic individuals to explore websites with child pornography without understanding the criminal and predatory context.

(Paul, 2015)

In the case of Nick Dubin, who has written extensively about his journey to discover his sexual orientation as an autistic man, he was encouraged to use pornography to determine his sexual preference (Attwood, Hénault, & Dubin, 2014). He states that as he began looking at adult male pornography, other links to more sexually explicit websites would spontaneously pop up on his computer, and this led him to looking at images of minors. This progression is common in many of the cases encountered by forensic evaluators. Some offenders report that they related to underage pornography because they felt they were "the same age" in terms of their maturity, and this is how Nick Dubin described his experience. If the emotional maturity of a person is delayed by several years, their viewing may focus on that age group, which feels less threatening. Some describe feeling "stuck in adolescence" regarding their sexuality. If they experienced an early sexual encounter, they may return to view scenarios of children or adolescents at that same age.

Another issue is that many autistic offenders started viewing pornography at a point when they were the same age as the prepubescent children depicted on these sites, leading them to perceive it as neither unnatural nor wrong. One individual commented that he thought these children were interested in sexual activity because he had become interested at that age from encountering it online. Child sexual abuse material often portrays young children in a highly sexual way, and the distinction between age-appropriate and underaged females and males is intentionally blurred (Mahoney, 2009). This may result in a preference for minors even as the viewer becomes older.

Viewing child sexual abuse material does not indicate that the viewer is a pedophile. In many cases involving autistic offenders, they have never initiated any form of grooming or attempted to engage sexually with children. Moreover, most express shame about their viewing. Autistic individuals can develop paraphilias (sexual interests other than what is considered normal), but the majority do not act on these interests. Unusual sexual interests, rather than pedophilic disorder, may be a more accurate description of the conditioned responses some individuals with autism might exhibit in relation to child sexual abuse material. When risk assessments are done on autistic offenders, most do not match the profile of a sex offender. Even though they may not be a risk to society, autistic individuals who are arrested for the possession or viewing of child sexual abuse material will be put on a sex offender registry and will have to comply with all the restrictions therein. This designation will alter their lives in many ways and severely limit their employment options. Attorney Mark Mahoney, who is often involved in autism defenses, has said that child sexual exploitation offenses, autism, and the internet create a "perfect storm that presents the greatest legal threat to young men with autism" (Mahoney, 2021). One of the primary challenges for those with autism who are charged with possession of child sexual abuse material is that others find it difficult to understand how they do not perceive "the cultural, social, and legal taboos underlying child exploitation" despite many of these individuals being highly intelligent and holding degrees (Mahoney, 2021). In the case of Nick Dubin, he was in a doctoral psychology program when he was arrested. An autistic individual can be highly intelligent from an academic perspective and still struggle with social intelligence. This discrepancy highlights the complex and multifaceted nature of autistic experiences. As previously mentioned, the Theory of Mind deficits often create confusion about societal rules and hamper the autistic's ability to understand concepts like exploitation. These issues may adversely affect an autistic offender in court proceedings. Dr. Colleen Berryessa (2016) interviewed judges regarding their attitudes toward "high functioning" autistic offenders. Her findings revealed that "judges consider their autism as both a mitigating and aggravating factor in sentencing, and knowledge of an offender's disorder could potentially help judges understand why a criminal action might have been committed." Judges voiced doubts about the criminal justice system being able to effectively help or offer sentencing options for offenders with a higher-functioning presentation of autism. They also reported that they are "focused on using their judicial powers and influence to provide treatment and other resources during sentencing" (Berryessa, 2016). While this increased awareness is promising, these attitudes do not extend to many court proceedings, where harsh sentences may be mandatory.

CHILD SEXUAL ABUSE MATERIAL (CSAM) LAWS IN THE UNITED STATES

Most crimes involving the internet are federal crimes. This is because these crimes involve interstate communication networks. The United States has far harsher laws than countries such as Canada and the UK for those who download, possess, or share child sexual abuse material online. Statistics show that 95 percent of those charged by the federal government were convicted, and 99 percent of those went to prison (Mahoney, 2021). Production of child sexual abuse material, which could involve taking a nude picture of a child and having it on your computer, carries a 15-year minimum sentence that can be as high as 40 years. Distribution of child sexual abuse material, which could involve the automatic resharing of material through the use of peer-to-peer software even if the defendant was unaware, carries a 5-year minimum sentence. Lesser charges, such as possession of child sexual abuse material, are still detrimental as they often require lifetime registration, and the offenders can be required to pay hefty restitution fines to the victims depicted in the material subject to the charge. In most instances, a child is defined as someone under the age of 18 years.

Four

Over the past decade, there has been a significant rise in extreme online groups, particularly during the pandemic. These groups often fall into categories such as political ideologies (e.g., extreme right-wing, left-wing, Nazism), religious (e.g., jihad-inspired), and misogynistic (e.g., incels). They typically adopt a binary worldview, dividing people into in-groups and out-groups, which can be appealing to individuals with autism who struggle with complex social dynamics. Autistic individuals, often experiencing bullying and isolation, may seek acceptance and belonging with these groups. Factors such as rigidity of thinking, need for structure, and low self-esteem can increase their susceptibility to radicalization.

Extremist groups use coded language and propaganda to recruit and radicalize members. For instance, the terms "Blue Pilled" and "Red Pilled" are used to describe those who are either unaware of or awakened to the group's perceived reality. These groups target individuals who feel disenfranchised, offering them a sense of belonging and purpose. Autistic individuals are particularly targeted due to their technological skills and perceived vulnerabilities. Some extremist groups, like white supremacist and jihadist organizations, exploit these individuals for their technical abilities and manipulate them into dangerous actions. Autistic individuals may become deeply involved without realizing the group's true intentions, as seen in cases where they are recruited for illegal activities or become embroiled in plots without full understanding.

The incel community is another example of online extremism that attracts some autistic men. Incels believe that certain men are inherently disadvantaged in the context of dating due to their physical appearance, leading to a sense of hopelessness and despair. Approximately 25 percent of incel forum users report having autism, though this does not imply that autistic men hold misogynistic views.

DOI: 10.4324/9781003540571-5

However, some autistic individuals may be drawn to incel ideology due to difficulties in romantic relationships and social isolation. The incel world provides an echo chamber that reinforces negative self-image and can lead to depression and suicidal thoughts. Preventing involvement in such groups requires promoting real-world social connections and reducing online isolation.

Religious extremism also targets autistic individuals, often exploiting their rigid thinking style and desire for acceptance. Groups like jihadist organizations offer a sense of purpose and community, which can be particularly appealing to those who feel marginalized. Parents for Peace reports an increase in cases involving autistic individuals, highlighting the fluidity in ideologies they may adopt. These individuals are often drawn to the structure and sense of belonging provided by extremist groups. Radicalization can be facilitated by trauma and online echo chambers that validate grievances. Understanding these dynamics is crucial for assessing risk and preventing further radicalization.

RADICAL ONLINE COMMUNITIES

There has been a proliferation of extreme online groups over the last 10 years, with a spike occurring during the pandemic (Davies & Frank, 2021). These groups tend to fall into three main categories: political ideologies (extreme right-wing, left-wing, Nazism), religious (jihad-inspired, Christian Nationalists), and misogynistic (incels). Most of these extremist communities have adopted a binary worldview of in-groups and out-groups. These are ideologies that view people and situations in absolute terms of good and bad. This polarized thinking can be appealing to individuals with autism who often struggle with the complex nature of human behavior. Some individuals with autism have been subjected to years of bullying and emotional abuse, which has left them feeling isolated and disenfranchised (Wijekoon et al., 2024). Many have had traumatic childhood experiences. They are searching for acceptance and a sense of belonging.

SUSCEPTIBILITY TO RADICAL ONLINE GROUPS

Dr. Clare Allely (2022) identified several factors that may increase the susceptibility of those with autism to online radical groups. These include: their rigidity of thinking, need for structure, limited understanding (Theory of Mind), special interests, low self-esteem, decreased social contact, and need for acceptance. Although there is no evidence suggesting that autistic individuals are more prone to becoming involved in online extremism, the trauma and disenfranchisement that some experience due to being neurodivergent could be contributing factors (Wijekoon et al., 2024).

Extremist online groups often use coded language. The term "coded" refers to the use of neutral terms to negatively describe identity. Utilizing themes from the movie *The Matrix*, taking a blue pill keeps you in the fantasy world and the red pill awakens you to the harsh reality of your oppression. The term "Blue Pilled" is used derogatorily in some extremist online forums to refer to individuals with conventional views that are considered ignorant, and "Red Pilled" are those who are awakened to the truth of their existence. By using this type of language, online communities can lure in individuals and then facilitate their recruitment and radicalization into extremist ideology (National Institute of Justice, 2023). These groups actively attempt to recruit members using propaganda aimed at those who feel disenfranchised. If an autistic individual is isolated and feels rejected by other social groups, the extremist sites may offer a sense of belonging. One autistic person reported that a white supremacist group offered them a family, protection from bullying, and a sense of power (Wijekoon et al., 2024).

There is evidence that extremists may be targeting individuals on the autism spectrum particularly because of their technological prowess and perceived vulnerabilities. They want to use them to advance their outreach through their technical knowledge and, in some instances, carry out dangerous actions. These communities encourage the person on the spectrum to commit illegal acts to prove their loyalty to the group. Some alt-right social media platforms have described autistic individuals as "ripe" for exploitation (Welch et al., 2023). Non-autistic users actually use the term "weaponized autism" to describe how autistic individuals can be exploited due to their lack of social skills, which makes them vulnerable to manipulation. In this way, autistic people are often victimized in radicalized communities despite them perceiving these communities as friendly. In reality, these groups, while admiring the technological expertise of those with autism, are, at the same time, devaluing them as pawns to advance their agenda. Unfortunately, the partial acceptance offered within these communities may still be preferable to the outright rejection experienced by autistic individuals in broader society (Welch et al., 2023).

RIGHT-WING/LEFT-WING EXTREMISM

Extremist groups are organizations whose beliefs, goals, or actions are far outside the mainstream values or accepted norms in a society. They often advocate for radical changes in the government and may advocate for the use of violence to achieve their objectives. These groups often hold fundamentalist or fanatical views. An example is the Proud Boys, a far-right group known for their anti-immigrant stance and their history of street violence against left-wing opponents. Antifa, a left-wing extremist group, is a loosely organized movement that protests against what they perceive as fascism, racism, or other types of oppression. Most of these groups perceive the world through a rigidly defined dichotomy of good versus bad.

Right-wing extremism is characterized by a nationalism defined by race, ethnicity, or sexuality, often emphasizing white power or identity. It is rooted in xenophobic and exclusionary beliefs about perceived threats from non-whites, Jews, Muslims, immigrants, LGBTQ individuals, and feminists (Scrivens et al., 2020). Right-wing or alt-right groups typically scapegoat these groups and blame them for society's problems and their specific grievances. Some also employ conspiracy theories to emphasize how these "others" are plotting against whites or taking over their communities. They may use propaganda videos that portray these groups as harmful to the white race.

Case: LW is a 32-year-old autistic male who had an all-consuming interest in Viking culture and Norse mythology. He had a history of bullying and abuse due to his autism. LW spent hours online researching the Vikings and collected items with Viking symbols. He discovered an online forum about Viking symbols and became active on it. This exposed LW to white supremacist ideologies which often co-opt Viking and Nordic symbols (Weber, 2018). He began going on a white supremacist forum that used a Viking rune as its logo. LW had not held any racist beliefs prior to his interactions with this group but felt that he had found a community that understood him and his interests. LW spent many hours daily communicating with group members and, for the first time in his life, felt accepted. He was eventually recruited by the group to create a white supremacy-themed website. He felt a sense of purpose and that this group valued him. The group was being monitored by the FBI due to their past involvement in bomb threats and harassment of Jewish businesses. LW had no knowledge of the group's past activities, and the group purposely never discussed these incidents with him. FBI agents approached LW as he was leaving work. They asked him questions about his affiliation with the group and told him that he was being investigated as a potential terrorist. They told him that he would not be arrested if he provided information about the other members and participated in an undercover operation. LW was frightened and reluctantly agreed. He felt very conflicted about "turning on" people he considered his friends.

INCELS (INVOLUNTARY CELIBATES)

The term incel refers to an online community that holds specific beliefs about sexual attraction and gender roles in our society. Their philosophy is that certain men face disadvantages in today's dating culture that cannot be overcome simply by altering their behavior or physical appearance (Stijelja & Mishara, 2023). In essence, physical attractiveness determines men's dating success in Western culture. This belief is referred to as a "black pill" philosophy and reflects a sense of hopelessness (Tirkkonnen & Vespermann, 2023). Incel sites and forums claim that some men are relegated to a life of loneliness due to their genetics. There are also female incel groups, often referred to as "femcels." These communities are also made up of women who identify as involuntarily celibate and believe they are unable to find romantic or sexual partners. Femcel communities share some beliefs in common with incels—such as the idea that physical appearance is crucial in finding a partner.

Incel groups believe that only the most attractive 20 percent of men are successful with 80 percent of all women. This ideology was represented in the Netflix series *Adolescence*, where a 13-year-old boy becomes radicalized on incel websites and later kills a female classmate (Thorne, Graham, & Baranti, 2025). The young boy in the series was not autistic but did have a history of bullying and the peer rejection experienced by many individuals on the autism spectrum. It has been noted that approximately 25 percent of the users of incel forums have reported a diagnosis of autism (Hoffman et al., 2020; Speckard & Ellensberg, 2022). This is not to imply that autistic men hold misogynistic views or sympathize with incel philosophy, as such generalizations can be harmful. It appears, however, that some autistic men, particularly those experiencing difficulties in their romantic relationships, may be especially susceptible to the influence of incel culture.

The incel world provides an echo chamber of negativity and hopelessness that can contribute to depression and even suicidal thoughts or actions (Borrell, 2020). These sites amplify negative thinking, and some even encourage self-harm. One subreddit, which is now banned, exalted those who had killed themselves. Some online forums, at their most extreme, glorify shooters like Elliot Rodger, who killed six people in 2014 due to perceived sexual and social rejection and then took his own life. Many men on the autism spectrum have experienced rejection from their peer group from an early age and have struggled to develop relationships or find a romantic partner. They become immersed in an online world that only perpetuates their negative self-image and increases their depression. The toxic allure of the incel world is that while it reinforces their sense of despair, it also provides a narrative about the unfairness and disenfranchisement many autistic men may be feeling (Tastenhoye et al., 2022, 2023).

Incels are one among the many misogynistic groups that occupy the broader online ecosystem known as the "manosphere." These communities share a range of perspectives on what they perceive as men's oppression by feminism, often rooted in long-standing misogynistic attitudes, such as entitlement to women's bodies and support for patriarchal practices like forced marriage. Their extreme and distorted beliefs are continuously reinforced overvalued ideas which are reinforced online in incel forums.

LACK OF EXPERIENCE

Due to lack of social experience, many autistic men and women have idealized and unrealistic ideas about romantic relationships. This may also be attributed to their limited ability to understand others' emotions and intentions (Theory of Mind). Online dating is confusing and overwhelming for them. Consequently, some hold naive notions that are not reality-based. Some believe that there is only one person who they are destined to be with. This rigid mindset is often encountered by clinicians working with autistic adolescents and adults. They place all their romantic expectations in one person, and if that person does not return their feelings, they view this as a rejection of themselves and their romantic fantasy. At the extremes, they may engage in repeated attempts which are perceived as stalking, or they may "nurse their grievances" in an incel community (Wijekoon et al., 2024).

To prevent the social isolation that can lead to incel toxicity, it is crucial for autistic individuals to have opportunities to learn and develop social and romantic connections. Immersion in these groups only leads to more detachment from the outside world. Most individuals who are in incel communities have not had a variety of social experiences (either positive or negative) and have shut themselves off from the outside world. They have experienced hurt and confusion, leading them to become avoidant. Dr. Rachel Loftin also suggests that autistic people need to reduce their time online and increase their real-world connections and experiences (Borrell, 2020). By eliminating their negative echo chambers online, they can begin to develop a new understanding of the world and re-examine their negative assumptions. Structured social activities combined with supportive social coaching can also reduce the anxiety many with autism feel in these situations. When individuals begin to self-isolate by being continuously online, they reduce their opportunities to learn and develop essential social skills. Consequently, their immersion in the digital world only deepens their sense of disconnection from reality.

Case: AN is a 20-year-old autistic male who was in his sophomore year in college. He was extremely interested in political science and had declared it as his major. AN had always had an intense interest in elections and knew all the electoral statistics for every US presidential election. He met a woman in his political science class who asked him to help her with her midterm project on rank choice voting. AN had always had lots of social anxiety and was never able to talk with girls and had never had a date. He was attracted to this woman and agreed to help her write her paper, hoping that it might lead to a romantic relationship. AN spent over 6 hours helping her research the topic and sent her several eBooks that he purchased. He was very invested in her project and consequently neglected his own studies. AN held the belief that this woman was his "perfect partner" and harbored an intense infatuation with her. He privately constructed elaborate romantic fantasies despite her complete lack of reciprocal interest. After the paper was completed, the girl avoided him when in class and did not respond to his frequent texts. AN was angry and felt used and betrayed. He began looking at some online incel forums. AN quickly became immersed in their ideology, which made him feel that he was not alone because other men had had similar experiences. AN spent hours on these forums daily. He became increasingly angry at women and felt hopeless that his life would ever get better. AN came to believe that women dismissed him because of his looks and that there was nothing he could do to change this. He experienced a severe depressive episode and had to take medical leave from his college.

INCEL INDOCTRINATION RUBRIC

Identifying incel beliefs is critical as these individuals feel marginalized by mainstream society. It is therefore important to assess an individual's level of indoctrination into the incel ideology in order to better understand them and determine their risk for violence or self-harm. A 20-item Incel Indoctrination Rubric was created using 50 cases of incel violence. There are 4 categories: Thinking, Feeling, Behavior, and Environmental Factors (Van Brunt & Taylor, 2021). Thinking refers to the specific beliefs regarding misogyny, racism, black-pill ideology, self-concept, and fame-seeking. There is an emphasis on evaluating the individual's fantasies of notoriety through violence. Feeling includes rage against women or other males and minorities, the prominence of hopelessness and a tendency to see any personal setback as a catastrophe, and feelings of abandonment. Many of these individuals are profoundly lonely and feel misunderstood by society. Behaviors include making verbal or written threats in social media posts or praising known violent attacks on women. Many of these individuals often report suicidal ideation and should have a suicide assessment. Their suicidality can be a risk factor for violence against others. Finally, the environmental factors include incel or alt-right ideology exposure, experiences of romantic rejection, and a history of bullying and abuse.

RELIGIOUS EXTREMISM

Those with autism may also be targeted by online religious extremist groups. There have been instances where jihadist terrorist groups have recruited disaffected individuals on the autism spectrum to carry out plots. They specifically try to appeal to the rigid thinking style of some autistic people. These extremist groups use various forms of manipulation by offering a certain status to the disaffected person's wounded self-image. Some autistic people feel marginalized in society because of their neurodivergence; these extremist religious groups can provide a sense of purpose and a community where they feel accepted.

Parents for Peace (parents4peace.org), a public health organization that empowers families, friends, and communities to prevent radicalization, has reported an increase in cases involving individuals on the autism spectrum. It estimates that approximately 30 percent of their current intakes are autistic individuals (E. Jouenne, personal communication, April 24, 2023). They also report that autistic individuals exhibit great fluidity in the ideologies they subscribe to, from right-wing extremism to left-wing extremism. They mainly are drawn to the structure, the rigid thinking style, and the sense of belonging that the group provides. This indicates that their main motivation for affiliation is their desire for acceptance and belonging within the group. Parents for Peace offers a confidential helpline at 1-844-3223 to assist family members who may have a loved one who is being or has been radicalized.

TRAUMA

Recently published research (Dodds, 2020) has revealed that people with autism spectrum disorder (ASD) are more likely to have multiple adverse childhood experiences (ACEs) than neurotypical peers. These adverse events include physical, sexual, and emotional abuse as well as physical and emotional neglect. There may also be parental separation through death or divorce, mental health issues in the family, domestic violence, or substance abuse in the household. Systemic issues such as racism and peer bullying are also comprised under the term ACE. Studies indicate that trauma may have cumulative lifelong and intergenerational impacts on people with ASD and their families. It is crucial that anyone evaluating an autistic victim or offender have a thorough understanding of the effects of trauma and how it can alter brain function and decision-making. Trauma rewires the brain's "alarm" systems, particularly the amygdala, which become hyperactive, constantly signaling danger and releasing stress hormones. This often leads to paranoia. Trauma can also cause individual difficulty in regulating emotions because the prefrontal cortex is suppressed. It also leads to difficulty maintaining a sense of control (van der KolK, 2014).

TRAUMA AND RADICALIZATION

Extremist groups of all ideologies prey upon lonely individuals who are emotionally wounded and struggle with low self-esteem, seeking acceptance and a sense of significance. Trauma also appears to be a significant factor in online radicalization (Wijekoon et al., 2024) Trauma was a pervasive experience among the sample of individuals interviewed in the 2024 study by Wijekoon et al. Participants in this study reported attachment disruptions, abuse, and marginalization within a neurotypical society from childhood. These adverse experiences profoundly shaped their worldview and created susceptibility to far-right hate messaging. Several reported a very traumatic childhood where they endured physical abuse, emotional neglect, sexual exploitation, and exposure to violence and substance abuse. There were reports of parental neglect or abuse, separation from or death of guardians, and insufficient attention from family or professionals, creating feelings of isolation and vulnerability. This sense of abandonment drove many to search for belonging beyond their family. Several participants recounted how a traumatizing experience profoundly reshaped their view of safety and trust. Some described how an isolated incident can inspire animosity toward an entire group, particularly if it involved an individual or individuals of another racial or ethnic group.

Case: An 18-year-old autistic woman (SL) was jumped by a group of Latino men who threatened her with a knife and stole her purse and cell phone on her way home from her job at a neighborhood convenience store. They hit her several times and threw her into a vacant lot, where she fell onto some broken glass and sustained several cuts. SL called for help, but no one was around. She finally walked home by herself. SL remained fearful and resentful of anyone she perceived as Hispanic. She frequently used racial slurs and made negative comments whenever she encountered anyone she thought was Hispanic, despite the fact that she had previously had positive relationships with three Latino neighbors and several Latino teachers in high school. Her family was concerned that her blatant racial animosity would cause problems in their neighborhood and put her at risk in the future, especially since she posted her views online.

Autistic individuals have frequently experienced bullying and feel they have no locus of control. Through their affiliation with a radical group, they hope to achieve a sense of control over their environment. Exposure to a group's propaganda can reactivate post-traumatic mechanisms such as emotional dysregulation and dissociation, which facilitate indoctrination. Additionally, online platforms can reinforce these ideologies through echo chambers that validate their grievances. Most concerningly, when autistic individuals are radicalized, their social deficits can impair their ability to evaluate the group's motives, often resulting in their manipulation as pawns within that group. Individuals with autism have been exploited by extremist groups like ISIS, which have encouraged them to engage in acts of terrorism, such as planting explosives or sharing sensitive information that compromises security at specific locations. In some cases, these groups may turn against the individual if they resist, resulting in severe consequences that can, in extreme situations, lead to suicidal behavior.

In assessing radicalization, it is important to view online activity such as social media posts and private chat histories. Understanding the worldview of these extremist groups is essential in evaluating risk. However, the individual endorsement of these beliefs can vary dramatically from that of other members, and individuals' beliefs can change over time (Dupre et al., 2024).

CASE: BT is a 40-year-old autistic man who experienced extreme bullying growing up. After 9/11, he and his family experienced continuous intimidation because they were Islamic. BT was the only male in his household after his father died and felt that he should protect his mother and four sisters from being harassed in their neighborhood. He began visiting online Islamic groups to obtain guidance on how he could protect them. Eventually, he was recruited by a jihadist group that specifically targeted him due to his autism. He was searching for male role models, which the group seemed to recognize and wanted to capitalize on. BT became totally immersed in the jihadist ideology because he perceived the group was providing moral leadership and guidance on how to be an Islamic man and a protector of his family members. The group began asking BT how committed he was to their beliefs. He indicated that he was fully committed and ready to do what they asked. The group wanted him to plan an attack at an outdoor festival and asked him to make a homemade bomb. They sent him directions on how to create it. BT was frightened and did not want to follow through on this plot. This caused him to feel that he was a failure, and he became depressed. Unbeknownst to him, BT had been under surveillance by the FBI for many months. Even though he did not create the explosive device or attempt any attack, he was under suspicion for involvement in a terroristic plot.

Competency and Restoration
Elizabeth Kelley

Five

COMPETENCY

The reality of the criminal justice system is that lawyers and judges are largely confined to narrow definitions—definitions which mystify some lay people and which admittedly have not kept pace with scientific or medical advances. This is particularly true for the concept of competency and the allied concept of restoration. Indeed, these concepts may not serve people on the spectrum and may, in fact, hurt them.

The threshold issue in every criminal case is competency. Is the person "competent" to proceed? Competency is an ongoing concern from the moment of arrest through the sentencing, including execution. This is a nationwide standard established by the United States Supreme Court in the case of Dusky v. U.S., 362 U.S. 402 (1960). It requires that the accused have (1) a rational as well as factual understanding of the proceedings and (2) sufficient present ability to consult with a lawyer with a reasonable degree of rational understanding. As a practical matter, this means that the accused must understand what is going on, including the gravity of the matter, and be able to assist their counsel in a way that is meaningful and useful. It should be emphasized that competency is a mark of an individual's ability at the time of the proceeding and not at the time of the alleged crime, which will be discussed in the next chapter, about responsibility.

The mere presence of a diagnosis of autism does not *per se* mean that someone is incompetent. This is true even if the individual also has an intellectual disability or a co-occurring mental illness, or if they manifest various conditions such as stimming, or if a guardian has been appointed for them. The legal process involving an expert evaluation or evaluations plus a court hearing of some sort must be followed. In other words, in most instances, the attorney cannot simply present a stack of medical records or introduce a letter from a parent.

DOI: 10.4324/9781003540571-6

Previous chapters have dealt with the complexity and variety contained in the term "spectrum." As such, arguing that a client on the spectrum is not competent to proceed is particularly challenging. For example, on the surface, it might seem absurd to assert that someone with autism with a high IQ who is probably "smarter" than the prosecutor, defense attorney, and judge is not "competent" to proceed. But in the legal context, their ASD may manifest itself in other ways, such as an almost childlike trust in their lawyer or a tendency to be manipulated by co-defendants (who may quickly strike a deal and provide evidence against the individual with ASD) or a susceptibility to being lured into online radicalization or to participating in online sexually oriented offenses.

By definition, someone on the spectrum has difficulties with social communication, particularly with reading others' responses. Thus, someone on the spectrum might be oblivious to how off-putting and non-responsive they might appear to law enforcement and in a courtroom, even if they have a high IQ (Allely, 2020; Berryessa, 2021; Davies, 2024; Walsh, 2028; Yaffe-Bellamy, 2023).[1]

But people on the spectrum with a high IQ can easily pass the competency tests which are typically administered. This, combined with their presentation, can make the assertion of them being incompetent to proceed seem ridiculous. Moreover, if we presume that the individual with ASD and high intelligence is actively involved in their own defense, they may resist the argument that they are incompetent. Whether because of client resistance or for other reasons, I have seen well-meaning attorneys who delay requesting a competency evaluation (or any kind of evaluation) of their client with ASD, which they don't use until sentencing. At worst, this can re-inforce the idea that the client knew exactly what they were doing; at best, it can provide little helpful information.

On the other hand, it might be easier to argue that someone with a low IQ is not competent to proceed. Indeed, a large percentage of people on the spectrum do have a low IQ. Moreover, the legal protections afforded to people with intellectual disabilities are greater. The sheer optics of a person with autism and a co-occurring intellectual disability are compelling. For example, a person who must look at a family member for guidance every time a question is asked, or a person who answers in very brief responses, or a person who simply appears childlike, makes a more persuasive case for being incompetent to proceed than does a person on the spectrum with a high IQ.

But back to the actual *Dusky* standard; as Dr. Greenspan describes, someone on the spectrum need only possess "shallow" understanding to pass the typical tests administered to deem competence (Greenspan, 2020).

Following the expert evaluation, a court may simply review a defense report. Or, if competency is contested, the court will review both a defense report and a report from the prosecutor. At that point, the court may conduct a hearing and hear testimony from both experts.

Most experienced criminal defense lawyers will tell you that only the most impaired of their clients are found incompetent to proceed. But even if a court finds someone incompetent to proceed, depending on the jurisdiction and the charges, that does not necessarily mean that the case will be dismissed. Indeed, the journey is far from over. For these and other reasons, attorneys may not raise the issue of competency.

RESTORATION

Depending on the jurisdiction, if an individual is found not competent to proceed, the court orders that the individual, for a period of time defined by statute, be restored to competency. Note that this is a legal construct more firmly rooted in law than actual medicine. The outcome of the restoration is largely dependent on the nature of the condition. For example, if a person with autism has a co-occurring mental illness, the administration of proper medication may assist in "restoring" that individual. On the other hand, if a person with autism has an intellectual disability, that person may never be restored to a condition that they never occupied. But the fact remains that autism is a lifelong condition. And it should be noted that attempting to restore someone on the spectrum to competency is an entirely different enterprise than teaching them to manage their issues.

In addition to the fact that most people are ultimately found competent and that even a finding of incompetence does not make the charges miraculously vanish, in some jurisdictions, restoration is conducted only on an in-patient basis, meaning that the individual must go to a state hospital or another secure facility, namely, prison.

However, some jurisdictions have out-patient programs and best practice is to request this if available.

In short, restoration consists of educational and therapeutic activities which teach people about the criminal justice system and stabilize their behavior.

As the beginning of this chapter notes, competency is a continuing inquiry. Thus, even if an individual is found competent or even restored, the family and attorney much be continually aware of the individual with autism's abilities under the *Dusky* standard. This is particularly true in federal cases, which can sometimes last for many years.

NOTE

1 There are many examples of individuals with ASD who appeared suspicious or whose demeanor in the courtroom was misinterpreted. See, e.g., Robert Roberson (David Martin Davies, Despite Evidence and Calls for Mercy, Robert Roberson is Set to Be Executed, Texas Public Radio, Oct. 4, 2024); Nathan Carman (James D. Walsh, "Dead Wake," *New York Magazine*, Jan. 22, 2018); and Sam Bankman-Fried (David Yaffe-Bellamy, "Sam Bankman-Fried Trial: Founder of Collapsed Crypto Firm Has His Own Words Turned Against Him," *New York Times*, Oct. 30, 2023). See also Clare Allely, "Perception of Defendants with ASD by Judges and Juries," *Representing People with Autism Spectrum Disorder: A Practical Guide for Criminal Defense Lawyers*, p.197 (Elizabeth Kelley ed., 2020); Colleen Berryessa, "Defendants with Autism Spectrum Disorder in Criminal Court: A Judges' Toolkit," *Drexel Law Review* 13, 841, 850–851.

Criminal Responsibility
Elizabeth Kelley

Six

In the context of the criminal justice system, responsibility refers not simply to accountability but also to the accused's state of mind at the time of the act. In other words, what were they thinking?

Different jurisdictions have different options for people who did not understand what they were doing at the time of the alleged act. Those options might be defenses of insanity (NGRI or NGI), guilty but mentally ill (GMBI), or diminished capacity. While competency measures the accused's state of mind at the time of the proceeding, arguments regarding responsibility go back in time to the act in question. Moreover, while competency is a relatively low standard to meet, the legal standard for insanity at the time of the act is a high one. Four states—Idaho, Kansas, Montana, and Utah—do not have insanity statutes. However, the jurisdictions that do, including the federal government, all use one or a combination of the following standards: McNaughten (named after the 1843 case in the United Kingdom involving defendant Daniel McNaughten), Irresistible Impulse, Model Penal Code, and Durham (named after the case Durham v. United States, 214 F.2d 862 (D.C. Cir. 1954)).

Admittedly, not guilty by reason of insanity is a misnomer when it comes to people on the spectrum. Simply put, they are not insane, although many people on the spectrum may have co-occurring mental illnesses. But insanity is likely the only legal vehicle for exploring the all-important question, what were they thinking at the time of the alleged act?

An attorney will review with you the insanity statute in your jurisdiction, as well as the definitions of other options regarding criminal responsibility. In addition, they will review with you the statute or statutes which your loved one is accused of violating. In particular, they will review what is called the *mens rea* or mental state: purposely, knowingly, recklessly, and negligently. In addition, some offenses are

DOI: 10.4324/9781003540571-7

strict liability crimes, that is, no intent is required; the mere fact that it happened is sufficient. This is true of many sexually oriented offenses or offenses involving minors.

The *McNaughten* standard is the most widely used. Generally, it involves two issues: whether the accused knew the nature of their act and whether the accused knew that the act was wrong.

Dr. Nancy Kaser-Boyd (2020) notes that people on the spectrum may manifest specific characteristics which can lead to criminal charges:

1. Difficulty interpreting social cues and understanding what others are thinking and feeling. Difficulty thinking about and understanding the actions of others and the emotional impact of their actions on others.
2. Poor emotional regulation, with impulsivity, difficulty controlling strong emotions or urges, and possible meltdowns.
3. Difficulty with moral reasoning. Moral reasoning requires a degree of abstract thinking, and individuals with ASD tend to be concrete in their reasoning.
4. Intense restricted interests.
5. Repetitive behaviors.

Over the course of my practice, clients have acted because of a variety of motivations. Some were manipulated by others into committing the act in question. Others were reacting out of frustration or exasperation. Others were responding as a result of bullying or trauma. Others were acting out of a sexual compulsion. Others acted out of mere curiosity about sex. This includes people on the spectrum of all ages. It also includes both people who identify as male and people who identify as female.

It may very well be that someone lured by a decoy on a dating app didn't understand the gravity of what they were doing, or that it was wrong. Similarly, someone who is manipulated in the context of online radicalization may not understand the gravity of their actions. Someone looking at images of children out of mere curiosity or filing and categorizing them out of a compulsion may not appreciate the consequences or even understand why this is wrong.

Your attorney can play out for you the mechanics of going to trial both using and not using an insanity defense. Generally speaking, even if you do obtain an expert report which opines that the accused was insane at the time of the act according to the statutory definition, the burden is on the accused. And even if they are indeed found insane, the charges are not simply dismissed. The accused may have to enter a state facility and regularly be evaluated to determine if or when they can be released. If the accused is in fact convicted, the potential penalty may be draconian. This is particularly true for more serious offenses, such as federal offenses involving millions of dollars or a large number of illegal images. This is one of the many reasons why so many cases resolve in plea bargains.

Other Options

If the expert report does not support the assertion that the individual is incompetent to proceed or insane at the time of the act, or if, strategically, the attorney does not recommend these two options, what then?

Depending on the tenor of the expert report, the attorney might be able to use it to negotiate a more favorable plea offer and use it at sentencing for mitigation of the penalty. And if the case does proceed to trial, it can be used as a means to negate the intent or *mens rea* required by the statute under which the accused is charged.

Never underestimate the importance of a thorough forensic mental health evaluation conducted by a highly credentialed expert. I once entered an appearance on a case and made a courtesy call to the prosecutor to introduce myself. He said, "Elizabeth, I will not oppose your motion pro hac vice (the legal filing which requests that an attorney from out of the jurisdiction be permitted to appear) but after that, I will fight you tooth and nail every step of the way." Several weeks later, I gave him a copy of my expert report. To his credit, he studied it and contacted the lead detective on the case. The detective said that he knew there was something different about my client, but he couldn't put his finger on it. The prosecutor then contacted me, and we were able to negotiate a favorable plea which avoided prison for the client.

Working with an Attorney

Elizabeth Kelley

Seven

When your family member with autism has been arrested or charged with a crime, it can be a confusing and challenging experience that leaves you unsure of where to turn for answers. Beware of hiring an attorney who promises you the moon. Similarly, while the case is pending, beware of facilities and programs. Make sure that they are recommended by a trusted professional or other individual and that the facility or program is accredited by legitimate authorities.

Hiring an experienced criminal defense attorney goes a long way toward obtaining the best outcome. However, experience is not the only qualification you should seek. First, the attorney must know how to deal with defendants with autism. Or they must be willing to learn. Simply having a child on the spectrum is not enough, although the special sensitivity that they bring is important. Rather, the attorney must understand the nexus between the autism and the conduct charged, be able to advocate for an appropriate resolution, be able to identify the appropriate expert, and, above all, communicate with the client and family. Second, the defense attorney must understand that the diagnosis of autism does indeed matter and why autism matters. Simply asserting that the accused has autism is not sufficient. Rather, the lawyer must be able to describe who their client is and what makes them unique, and vulnerable.

Defense attorneys and family members should be able to work together to the benefit of the client. Defense attorneys and family members each have distinct and essential roles to play, and when they understand their respective roles, they can build a formidable force for protecting the client. Below are key points families should attend to in order to help their attorney.

PROVIDE THE LAWYER WITH ALL NECESSARY INFORMATION

Family members of people on the spectrum are usually in the best position to provide information about the accused. The family knows

DOI: 10.4324/9781003540571-8

the person's history and has the best information about their social, academic, and treatment history as well as their home life. Be sure to provide the attorney with as much information as possible. The attorney can then weed out what is relevant. Useful information can include school records, including Individual Educational Plans (IEPs) and 504 Plans; medical records; names and contact information of treatment providers; any mental health evaluations or records; information about the receipt of any community services; places of employment; housing situations; and past interactions with the criminal justice system, including prior victimization.

UNDERSTAND THAT THE CLIENT'S INTERESTS AND WISHES COME FIRST

It is vital to remember that even though the family may be paying the lawyer's fee, the family is not the client. Your loved one is the client, and everything the lawyer does concerns the best interest of the client. Ethically, a lawyer cannot allow the person who is paying the fee to interfere with the lawyer's independent judgment on behalf of the client. At times, there may be a conflict between what the family wants and what the client wants. The lawyer has an ethical duty to work for your loved one alone, regardless of what the family thinks is the best course of action. While, with their loved one's consent, the family can be part of the conversation, it is still the client who makes the final decisions on their own behalf.

Keep in mind that your attorney's priority is the client and that client's potential exposure in that criminal case. You may have broader goals like "educating the court," or "exposing corruption," or passing new laws, or inspiring social change. But that is beyond the scope of your attorney's representation and is better suited for another forum.

Family members may have invested years in "investigating" the case. Family members may have even retired in order to devote themselves full-time to their loved one's defense. They may feel let down if they do not perceive that the desired outcome has been achieved. Hopefully, after the case is resolved, there will be another outlet where they can channel their knowledge.

RESPECT THE ATTORNEY-CLIENT PRIVILEGE AND CONFIDENTIALITY

The lawyer must uphold the attorney-client privilege and confidentiality. These concepts are cornerstones of the legal profession. They are meant to foster open communication between the client and the attorney. Only with complete and accurate information can an attorney effectively represent someone.

Privilege and confidentiality are often confused or used interchangeably. Privilege refers to communication between a client and an attorney which cannot be divulged without consent. Confidentiality is all information learned by an attorney during the course of the representation. Confidential information cannot be used against a client. (There are many treatises about attorney-client privilege and confidentiality, but this chapter is not meant to be one of them. Suffice it to say that these should be respected.)

Your loved one may consent to allow family members to receive information about a case, but ideally, this consent should be obtained in writing and should be specific about the type of information they are willing to share.

As a practical matter, for people with ASD, this can pose challenges. In many cases, the family has always protected the individual with ASD and, as such, wants to know everything and wants to be part of every decision. If, for instance, the attorney wants to meet privately with the client, you should allow this. Similarly, if the attorney schedules a Zoom meeting with the client, resist the temptation to hover in the background. On the other hand, for someone on the spectrum with an intellectual disability, it may be vital for a family member to be present to act almost as an interpreter.

DEALING WITH THE MEDIA

It may be tempting to communicate with the media, especially if you feel that your loved one has been wrongly charged or is enduring poor conditions while in custody. Resist the temptation and do not talk to the press without the consent of the lawyer. If you do communicate with the media, your counsel should be present.

Although your loved one's case may be outrageous, short of extraordinary circumstances, the media may not care. If the press does cover a case, it may not be sympathetic coverage. This is especially true if your loved one has been charged with a sexually oriented offense or a crime of violence.

Additionally, some jurisdictions have strict rules regarding a lawyer's ability to communicate with the media. Be sure to respect your lawyer's obligations to follow those rules. Not following their advice when it comes to the press may compel them to withdraw from the case.

UNDERSTANDING PLEA BARGAINING

There may come a time when the lawyer discusses a possible plea agreement with you and your loved one. This fact does not necessarily mean that the lawyer does not believe in your loved one. Rather, the lawyer has an ethical obligation to convey any plea offer to the client. When the lawyer recommends that a plea be accepted, it is often based on his or her disappointing previous experiences and knowledge of the criminal justice system. If possible, ask the lawyer to review the plea agreement point by point and explain to the lawyer which aspects will be difficult to comply with and why.

Some people on the spectrum can appear incredibly stubborn. This may be true in the context of plea discussions as well. They may reject a plea even if it is a reasonable offer; for example, the agreement offers the possibility of probation, whereas if the accused goes to trial and is convicted, a prison sentence would be mandatory and for a significant number of years. However, this is not ordinary stubbornness. Rather, it is a product of being hyperfocused on some other aspect of the case which they feel is unjust.

SEX OFFENDER REGISTRY

Unfortunately, even when negotiating a plea agreement, the prosecutor will almost always insist that the accused agree to the terms of the sex offender registry. Because so many people on the spectrum are charged with sexually oriented offenses, this is a real concern. It can impact their housing, their access to recreation, and their ability to hold certain jobs or retain certain professional licenses. Some of the terms of the registry are required by law, and the court and the prosecutor have no ability to waive them. Others may be negotiable. Ask specific questions of your lawyer. Some jurisdictions may allow you to file for a modification of the terms at a later date.

HAVE REALISTIC EXPECTATIONS

Your attorney is not a miracle worker. Granted, there may be some cases of actual innocence, and hopefully, the attorney is litigating these issues through traditional means, such as hiring a private investigator, attacking any forensic evidence, and trying to suppress various statements and pieces of evidence. Prosecutors come to cases with a different orientation. Your attorney is, by definition, your loved one's advocate. And you, as a family member, see the case through your loved one's eyes. Prosecutors do take an oath to do justice, but they also see the case through the eyes of a victim and believe that the law has been violated. Even if the defense presents a compelling portrait of the accused and a powerful attack on the case, the prosecutor may not feel that they can do what you perceive to be the right thing. Moreover, sentencing statutes may give prosecutors little or no discretion in disposing of cases. This is particularly true in the federal system, where many prosecutions of people on the spectrum facing charges involving cyber offenses take place. Beyond that, once a case is prosecuted, if you are trying to pursue some type of post-conviction relief, the deadlines and other procedural hurdles are considerable. In the federal system, the habeas corpus statute can be found at 18 USC 2255 and the compassionate release statute can be found at 18 USC 3582. Some states may also have their own variations of these statutes. You should consult an attorney well-versed in these matters.

Working with the Mental Health Expert

Elizabeth Kelley

Eight

An evaluation by an independent forensic mental health expert is crucial. An individual on the spectrum may very well have been diagnosed and has been working with a psychologist, psychiatrist, or other professional and receiving services before the charges. That is an important fact. However, for several reasons, the treatment provider cannot serve as the forensic expert. First, forensic experts are specifically trained to write reports for criminal cases and to testify. Second, it is a conflict of interest for the treatment provider to serve as an expert, for instance, in matters where the court is concerned about re-offending. Third, giving information to a treatment provider is done with the promise of confidentiality, whereas a forensic expert advises an individual upfront that the report will be shared with third parties. Fourth, a forensic expert, notwithstanding the fact that they may be retained by the defense or the prosecution or appointed by the court, should be independent in order to be most credible. And finally, and perhaps most crucially, a forensic expert reviews all the discovery in the case, something which the treatment provider or the individual making the diagnosis does not do. Thus, they know all the facts and circumstances of the allegations and investigation, facts and circumstances favorable as well as unfavorable to the accused.

Your attorney should work closely with the expert and be the primary contact—not you. Indeed, most experts take their role as an independent expert seriously and draw strict boundaries regarding their contact with clients and, certainly, the clients' family members. Thus, notwithstanding the fact that the expert is trained in a helping profession and the family is going through a time of great struggle, family members should not reach out to the expert for guidance or solace. If, for example, the expert is coming in from out of town to meet with the client, the family should respect the fact that the expert has made arrangements to meet with the client at a law office or the

DOI: 10.4324/9781003540571-9

office of a colleague and not request that the expert meet the client at their home.

In turn, the attorney may find the following information helpful when dealing with an expert—and the family should be aware of this information as well, in order to support the attorney in their work.

The attorney should get the expert as early as possible in the representation. The first reason for this is practical: qualified experts are busy and their calendars are packed. Moreover, it is important for the attorney to start establishing the fact that autism will be an important factor in the defense. Indeed, the autism will be woven throughout most aspects of the defense. Related to this is the fact that the attorney will be informing the court of when expert reports will be complete and when experts will be available to testify. This is important for setting court dates. Unfortunately, I have heard of too many instances where the defense, for whatever reason, did not raise the issue of autism until late in the legal process, such as during sentencing. This is typically not well-received by the court, which perceives the autism as an excuse, particularly when the attorney has not developed the issue of the autism and its relevance to the case. Beyond that, even if a lawyer raises the issue of autism, if it is done in a cursory manner, such as mentioning that the defendant is on the spectrum without presenting a forensic evaluation and without providing arguments which are relevant to the client (for example, discussing the harms of incarceration for people with ASD based on their sensory issues when the individual doesn't have any sensory issues), it can be even more harmful, because a reviewing court can later note that the issue was raised.

Typically, it is your attorney who finds the forensic expert. They perhaps have their "go-to" experts. Respect their judgment but insist that the expert have deep knowledge of autism spectrum disorder. Look at their *curriculum vitaes* (CVs). See what they have written and what professional presentations they have delivered.

I have my own "go-to" experts for autism spectrum disorder. They are in different parts of the country. They have different personalities. They have varying levels of experience. I try to select any expert based on who I believe will be the best fit with the client and who will be the most credible and accepted with the court. Another requirement for me is that the expert be accessible to me, readily available to answer questions, and able to deal with inevitable changes and new developments in a case. Also, if the case is a federal matter or a state case where the discovery may be voluminous, the expert should be able to access the material electronically or have a staff which can assist in this matter.

It is important to note that there may need to be more than one expert. For instance, I may very well bring in an additional expert to present a report addressing the issue of future dangerousness. This is a specialized area with specialized testing. It answers the inevitable concern that prosecutors and judges have: "will he or she do this again?'

An evaluation should be not only thorough but also easy to read and well-organized. In other words, if medical terms are used, they should be defined, and the evaluation should have topic headings, including an executive summary. (Indeed, prosecutors and judges often read the summary first. I refrain from saying that sometimes it is the only part of the report they read.) It should be based on a comprehensive in-person interview or, ideally, more than one interview of the client, likely with follow-up, perhaps by Zoom or telephone, if not in person. The expert should conduct collateral interviews, that is, interviews with family, friends, co-workers, teachers, coaches, or anyone who has known and had opportunity to observe the accused. The expert should also conduct a thorough document review.

Counsel should also provide the expert with *all* discovery in a case. The failure to do so may render an evaluation less than accurate and leave the expert open to embarrassment at a hearing for not having addressed some significant aspect of the case. Beyond that, even if there are unfavorable facts in the discovery, an expert can typically provide an explanation for those that is linked to the autism spectrum disorder. In other words, even if the information is potentially damaging, an expert who is informed of this can address it. Finally, depending on the autism, the expert may conduct a variety of tests and/or recommend another expert for additional testing.

Working with a Forensic Computer Expert

Elizabeth Kelley and Michele Bush

Nine

ATTORNEY'S PERSPECTIVE

The first piece of advice is simple: get one. Far too many criminal defense lawyers simply take the prosecutor's word regarding the type and amount of evidence. Beyond that, computer evidence, or evidence seized on any digital device, is technical, even difficult. For criminal defense lawyers of a certain age and/or without a technical background, it is all too easy to skip over that and concentrate on other aspects of the case. I have seen cases where the accused pleaded guilty because the attorney did not challenge the prosecutor's evidence and told the client that law enforcement had him "dead to rights." People on the spectrum, even those with the highest cognitive rigidity, may eventually plead guilty because they are led to believe that there is no alternative. As has been described in other chapters, vacating a guilty plea is extremely difficult. Even if the accused has engaged in some illegal behavior, it may not be what the prosecutor alleges.

Below are some additional tips, in no particular order:

1. The attorney should accept what they know and acknowledge what they don't know. In other words, presuming that a highly credentialed expert has been retained, listen to that expert, and if they suggest future avenues of exploration, follow that suggestion.
2. Every case introduces lawyers to a new body of knowledge—people, cultures, habits, disciplines, etc. This is what makes the practice of law intellectually stimulating. Embrace the world of electronic devices with a similar mindset.
3. Ask questions of your expert. Pose hypothetical questions. Do not be afraid to look unsophisticated. Review their report with a fine-toothed comb. Make sure you understand every term.
4. If, after the examination of devices, the expert says that something is missing, request that from the prosecutor.

DOI: 10.4324/9781003540571-10

5. If the prosecutor says that the missing material is not relevant or does not exist or that you are not entitled to it, file a motion and litigate the issue.

6. Just as a criminal defense lawyer should bring a forensic mental health expert into a case as early as possible, so too should the lawyer bring in the forensic computer expert as early as possible. This can assist in preserving evidence and shaping defense theory.

7. Give the expert a thorough onboarding. Provide them with background and a timeline. Let them know what your theory is, if you have one.

8. In addition to speaking with you, the expert should speak with the client.

9. Don't put boundaries on the expert's work. Be open to what they may discover. I once heard an attorney say that it would only be useful to have an expert examine the devices if they found such-and-such. This potentially forecloses alternate findings and theories.

10. Request a full forensic image. A complete image (bit-by-bit copy) allows an examiner to uncover deleted files, metadata, and activity logs. The latter may be helpful in building the defense theory. Do not rely on the prosecution's summary or data.

11, Verify law enforcement's findings. Your expert can find holes, alternative explanations, errors, faulty tools, or substandard collection methods.

12. Challenge admissibility. Some of law enforcement's methods may be junk science or based on flawed tools. Use your expert to challenge those methods under *Daubert/Frye* standards and litigate the issue.

13. Ask your expert to explain the tools and methods. Tools have limits and data can be misleading, missing, corrupted, or ambiguous. Ask the expert about false positives, timestamp reliability, wiping software, and encryption.

14. Use the expert to educate the judge and jury. As with any other witness, before your forensic computer expert testifies, whether it is at an evidentiary hearing, a sentencing hearing, or a trial, do a practice direct examination and mock cross examination. Make sure they speak in plain language. Put yourself in the shoes of the judge or the jury and ask questions they might ask, like

"Can you tell who accessed this file and when?" "Could this activity be automated or spoofed?" "Is there any indication of remote access?" Have your expert define and describe terms. You will likely have judges and jurors with all levels of digital literacy. (See below for a list of possible questions to ask the expert that would be helpful in explaining the conduct of a defendant on the spectrum.)

15. Organize the evidence. Work with the expert to create a timeline or data map. Include users, timestamps, and formats. This is particularly important for multi-device cases.

Sample questions to ask a forensic computer expert in cases involving people with autism spectrum disorder:

As has been explained in other chapters, each person on the spectrum has unique issues. Depending on how a defendant manifests their autism, particularly with a co-occurring mental illness, the following questions may be useful. Know that a prosecutor may object to some of the wording, and you should be prepared to re-phrase and, if needed, defend your line of inquiry.

1. Can you identify any patterns of digital behavior that may reflect obsessive, compulsive, or erratic use?
2. Can you analyze the timeline of digital activity in relation to key events in the case to suggest state of mind?
3. Did the user keep digital drafts, journals, or notes that express emotional distress, confusion, or delusion?
4. Are there any chatlogs, emails, or texts that express suicidal ideation, paranoia, or hallucination?
5. Can you identify tone or language patterns that might indicate deteriorating mental health over time?
6. Can you determine how socially connected or isolated the user was based on communication logs?
7. Did the device usage increase or decrease significantly after key events?
8. Are there signs of obsessive use of specific apps or platforms, like repeatedly recording videos or writing unsent messages?
9. Did the user use encryption tools or VPNs or show signs of digital paranoia without a clear need?

10. Are there any instances of messages being deleted?
11. Are there any fake accounts?
12. Can you identify any patterns of searching for how to hide or erase one's online presence?
13. Can you build a timeline that shows fluctuations of digital behavior?
14. Can you link device activity with medical records, medication changes, or hospitalizations?
15. Can digital activity reasonably support an alternative explanation?
16. Could digital activity indicate non-criminal intent?
17. Are there any signs that digital activity could have been automatic, coerced, or not fully understood by the user?

A final piece of advice: listen to your client. I can't tell you how many times I have sat in a conference during a marathon meeting and, several hours into the conversation, learned a golden nugget. And, in particular, if your client has been represented by previous counsel, they may have been ignored and are yearning to have someone, namely, their attorney, pay attention. They may very well chart a path of examination for your expert.

EXPERT'S PERSPECTIVE

So many crimes today can be proven, augmented, and mitigated using electronic evidence. Electronic data can be used to introduce evidence that a crime was committed, but it can also provide patterns and characteristics of an individual, a timeframe of offending activity, and alibi evidence, among other mitigating factors. However, that evidence is rarely apparent, and it requires a significant amount of time and resources to extract it from the devices and present it in an admissible and understandable form. The forensic analysis of electronic data recovered from a cell phone, computer, or cloud-based account is a labor-intensive task. The process of finding data of evidentiary interest is not the glamorous event portrayed on television but can require hundreds of hours of searching and reviewing. It is an exhaustive process that may or may not yield favorable results. When law enforcement is tasked with a forensic analysis of electronic data, they typically limit their analysis to finding evidence in support of their investigation and attributing that data to their suspect. Due to time and resource limitations, law enforcement does not typically undertake the task of finding evidence that might hurt their case or help the defense. For this reason, it is imperative to have an expert conduct an independent review of complete copies of the evidence under the scope of investigation for the defense.

An expert analysis is not solely useful in exonerations but helps provide other circumstantial and mitigating evidence. Even if the prosecution has demonstrated incriminating evidence exists, they may still be withholding or missing evidence that helps create a better understanding of where the offense falls on a scale of severity—factors such as patterns and characteristics, length of offending activity, volume of illegal activity, and the motivations for committing an offense. These are factors that can significantly change the trajectory of a case, even those that seem indefensible.

It is also pertinent to have reasonable access to complete copies of the evidence throughout the life of the case as it evolves. This is especially true for cases that proceed to trial as it is anticipated that the evidence will need to be accessible so as to address issues that arise and prepare trial exhibits. For instance, if law enforcement facilitates the defense's review of the evidence, the examiner's first opportunity to review the evidence may be limited to specific pretrial issues. If the case proceeds to trial and the prosecution believes that they have already made the evidence "reasonably available" to the defense, this would prevent the defense from furthering their investigation for specific forensic evidence in support of trial strategies or mitigation. Additionally, the prosecution often produces supplemental discovery after the defense review of the evidence, such as forensic reports to address concerns law enforcement may have regarding their case after the defense has hired an expert. This typically requires the defense to conduct additional forensic analysis and repeat the process of attempting to schedule an examination at the whim of the prosecution's cooperation. This results in unnecessary delays and continuances or cannot be accomplished at all due to time and resource restrictions.

Ten

In general, most cases in the criminal justice system are disposed of via a plea bargain, and as such, most people must face sentencing, including people on the spectrum. This is compounded by the fact that the standard for competency is so low (see Chapter Five) and the standard for insanity is so high (see Chapter Six). Chapter Eleven, "Incarceration," will discuss incarceration as it impacts people on the autism spectrum. The difficulties that they will encounter should be argued vigorously at a sentencing hearing.

If the court has the discretion to impose a non-custodial sentence, it is vital that the attorney show not only that incarceration will be harmful and even counterproductive but that there is a detailed path forward for the client in the community—in other words, that there is a plan which will keep the community safe and prevent the client from re-offending. Thus, the attorney must be prepared to outline where the client will live, how they will spend each day, if they will work, and how they will get the appropriate counseling, medication, and treatment.

Some families of people on the spectrum, following the criminal case, want nothing more than to protect their loved one, to keep them in a bubble. For example, a person with autism may be able to return to their job. Or, they may have interests which they would like to pursue. This should be encouraged, in part because it will keep them occupied and away from any opportunity to re-offend.

Many people on the spectrum are bright, do well in school, and have ambition. This should be encouraged and will help persuade the court that this is a person worth giving a second chance.

The attorney should also work with the client to prepare them for addressing the court at sentencing. Many people on the spectrum have traits which might be misinterpreted, often to their detriment, in a courtroom, such as a failure to make eye contact or fixating on a

DOI: 10.4324/9781003540571-11

point which the court finds irrelevant. The court should be educated in advance about the accused's presentation. And insofar as possible, the attorney should work with the client in advance.

At the hearing, the client should express genuine remorse. Family, friends, and neighbors are encouraged to be in the courtroom. If they submit letters to the court or are called on to speak, the attorney should review the letters in advance and provide parameters for the spoken remarks. Supporters should not deny or minimize the accused's actions. Moreover, the court should not perceive that supporters are using the client's autism as an excuse. Rather, all should reaffirm that they believe in this individual and support him or her going forward.

I've read sentencing transcripts where the attorney, with all good intentions, simply mentions that the accused has autism spectrum disorder and maybe even cites a couple of journal articles. That is not enough. The forensic mental health exam should have established the nexus between that individual's unique manifestation of autism and the conduct charged. Then, at sentencing, the lawyer should describe how, because of autism, incarceration will be harmful. They should conclude by outlining the path forward. In many instances, people on the spectrum are very good with following rules. (This is where their rigidity comes in handy.) If the terms of probation are stated clearly and repeatedly and in a manner that the individual can understand, then they are likely to do well on probation. I tell all my clients to think of probation as a job, and their job is now to complete probation. As a practical matter, if someone is initially doing well on probation (or pre-trial release), the probation officer will frequently reduce the number of home visits or required meetings.

Eleven

In most circumstances, jail and prison can be the worst places in the world for someone on the spectrum. The reasons vary depending on the nature of their autism spectrum disorder.[1]

If they are young and still growing, they will face the same issues as their neurotypical peers in terms of being intimidated by older, larger, more streetwise inmates.

Similarly, if the person with autism is convicted of a sexually oriented offense, they will face the same potential dangers and ostracism as others charged with those crimes, but without the ability to understand or defend themselves.

Given that most people on the spectrum have difficulties with social cues, they can miss all the "unwritten rules" of a jail or prison. They may be very trusting or non-assertive or easily manipulable (indeed, this may be how they became involved with the criminal justice system in the first place), and this can cause them to violate rules or fail to advocate for themselves, for instance, when needing medication or other accommodations.

Some people on the spectrum may actively stim or have what are perceived as odd speech patterns. This makes them attractive prey. Other inmates will laugh at them or make fun of them or isolate them, recalling all the bullying that the person with autism grew up with.

If the person on the spectrum also has an intellectual disability, jail or prison can be fraught with challenges. I have had clients who were in local jail, either because the court would not set a bond or while their families were working to post a bond, who couldn't figure out how to use the telephone in the visitor room, or mail a letter to their families, or open the packets of peanut butter which were given out at lunch to make sandwiches.

Women on the spectrum may simply shut down. One spent most of her incarceration in tears. Another stayed rolled up in a fetal

DOI: 10.4324/9781003540571-12

position for most of her time in jail. Many people on the spectrum have sensory issues which can make jail or prison torture. If they have sensitivity to light, 24 hours of fluorescent lights can be unbearable. If they have sensitivity to sounds, the continual yelling by other inmates and guards, the banging of doors, the sounding of alarms, and so on can be challenging. Some people on the spectrum are more than picky eaters; they have real phobias and reactions to various foods because of the taste or texture. Some people on the spectrum have tactile issues. For instance, the rough texture of a prison jumpsuit can cause real distress. And while I believe we all can agree that all jails and prisons smell bad, some people on the spectrum have issues relating to smell and find the confined space of a jail or prison nauseating.

If someone with autism spectrum disorder is unfortunate enough to be in jail pending the disposition of a case, or if someone with autism is in prison and the attorney is pursuing some sort of post-conviction remedy such as compassionate release, document all the challenges the person is facing. Also, document the facility's failure to respond to the situation.

If the individual is facing a mandatory sentence, ask the attorney to request that the court recommend a particular facility. For example, in the federal system, at the time of writing, there are two facilities, Federal Correctional Institution (FCI) Coleman in Florida and FCI Danbury in Connecticut, which have what is called a SKILLS program. This teaches individuals with intellectual/developmental disabilities how to transition into prison. The program is voluntary, so a court must recommend it, and the Bureau of Prisons (BOP) must designate the facility. Once the person with ASD arrives, they must request that they be admitted to the program. Note that at this time, the program is available only to males (Bureau of Prisons Program Statement 5330.11).

Some states also have prisons which provide special accommodations for people with autism. For example, in Pennsylvania, the space at the correctional institution at Albion is designated as the Neurodevelopmental Residential Treatment Unit (https://whyy.org/articles/autistic-prisoners-support-program-pennsylvania/).

NOTE

1 For an excellent description of the challenges of incarceration for people on the spectrum, see Maureen Baird, Walt Palvo, and Janet Perdue, "Autism and the Prison Experience," *Criminal Justice Magazine*, Fall 2023. For tips on preparing people with ASD for prison and advocating for appropriate accommodations, see Jack T. Donson, "Prison Accommodations," *Representing People with Mental Disabilities: A Practical Guide for Criminal Defense Lawyers*, p.155 (Elizabeth Kelley ed., 2020).

Federal Litigation

Jessica Graf and Elizabeth Kelley

Twelve

Unfortunately, the most serious cases involving people on the autism spectrum often end up in federal court. In many jurisdictions, the federal courts exclusively handle child pornography and cyber offenses. If you or a loved one are facing federal criminal charges, there are some important things about the federal criminal system that you need to know. The federal system is very different from most state criminal systems and is nothing like what you may have seen on TV or in the media.

First, federal courts tend to be very formal. While state court judges are often elected officials, federal judges are nominated by the president and confirmed by Congress. They serve lifetime appointments, which are meant to prevent political influence. They don't have to campaign to keep their jobs. Federal judges are almost always very experienced attorneys before taking the bench and must face Congressional questioning before confirmation. That formality extends to the courtroom. While you might have seen attorneys showboating, yelling, or interrupting in state court or on TV, most federal judges do not tolerate such behavior. Federal judges expect a high degree of professionalism from the attorneys who appear before them.

Likewise, the attorneys who practice in federal court are normally very experienced. Assistant United States Attorneys (AUSAs), the prosecutors who handle federal cases, usually have several years of prosecution experience at the state level or prestigious law firm backgrounds. AUSA positions are highly sought after, and the competition for these jobs can be fierce. Defense attorneys also must clear certain hurdles to practice in federal court. They must be admitted to the federal district they seek to appear in, which requires a formal application process, references, and acceptance by the judges in that district. Once their application is approved, defense attorneys must take a formal oath administered by a judge in the district. Unlike state

DOI: 10.4324/9781003540571-13

court, where attorneys can come up with arguments on the spot, federal court is "motions based," meaning that attorneys typically submit their arguments to the court in writing before appearing in person. Because federal criminal prosecutions can be complex, judges require the attorneys to prepare written arguments before the trial and sentencing. Federal judges expect attorneys to do extensive legal research, know the applicable federal rules, be prepared in court, and meet strict deadlines. Deadlines are not very flexible in federal court and there are severe consequences for missing them.

Second, federal cases tend to have very strong evidence. This is because federal prosecutors can be very selective about what cases they choose to bring, and they often will only bring cases they are confident will result in a conviction. Therefore, when a federal prosecutor brings charges, they likely have concrete evidence, like a confession, data seized from a computer, text messages, phone records, and more. This is because federal prosecutions involve government agencies like the Federal Bureau of Investigation, the Internal Revenue Service, the Drug Enforcement Agency, and the Bureau of Alcohol, Tobacco, Firearms, and Explosives. Like the AUSAs, the law enforcement officers in these agencies are experienced and thorough. They gather strong evidence before bringing formal charges.

Third, the federal system is known for harsh sentences, and plea bargaining is probably not what most people expect. Except in rare circumstances, the prosecutor cannot offer a plea for a set term of years, i.e., plead guilty to a particular charge and receive a 5-year sentence. In federal court, the judge decides what sentence to give. The only limitations on the judge are the minimum and maximum sentences for the offense, as determined by Congress and listed in the statutes for each particular offense. Thus plea bargaining involves negotiating with the prosecutor as to which charges the defendant will plead guilty to. This is an important step because many federal charges carry harsh mandatory minimum sentences. For example, a defendant may choose to plead guilty to an offense with a 0–20-year punishment range to avoid pleading guilty to an offense with a 10-year mandatory minimum sentence.

Fourth, the United States Sentencing Guidelines play a major role in federal sentencing. The judge cannot sentence a defendant to less than the mandatory minimum sentence or more than the maximum sentence provided in the statute. For example, if the defendant pleads guilty to an offense with a 0–20-year statutory punishment range, the judge can sentence the defendant to anything from probation to 20 years of imprisonment or anywhere in between. But the Sentencing Guidelines offer the judge a recommended sentence to impose within that range. The Sentencing Guidelines take into account the offense, the special circumstances surrounding the offense (like the number of victims or other important considerations), and the defendant's criminal history to calculate a recommended sentencing range that is listed in terms of months. For instance, the Sentencing Guidelines could recommend a sentence between 37 and 46 months of imprisonment. Importantly, the judge is not required to sentence the defendant within the range the Sentencing Guidelines recommend. But the judge must consider that range and decide whether a sentence within that range, above it, or below it is appropriate.

A person who is sentenced to serve a term of imprisonment in the federal system will be sent to a prison managed by the Federal Bureau of Prisons, or the BOP. The BOP manages facilities at different security levels ranging from minimum to super maximum security. The BOP will determine the security level each person falls under by looking at his or her criminal history, age, health, offense characteristics, and more. Typically, the BOP tries to send individuals to facilities within 500 miles of their homes if there is an appropriate prison at the correct security level in that 500-mile zone.

Because federal court requires specialized skills, it is critical to select an attorney with extensive federal litigation experience. You want someone in your corner who knows the federal system inside out and can guide you through the complexities involved in federal criminal cases.

Disclaimer:
The following documents are provided as illustrative case materials for educational purposes in conjunction with this publication on cybercrime and representing individuals with autism in the criminal justice system. All personally identifying information has been redacted where appropriate. Permission to include these materials has been obtained from the relevant parties, including the attorney of record. In addition, they have been previously filed in federal court and are

available on PACER (Public Access to Court Electronic Records), which is the system for filing and accessing documents in the federal courts in the US.

USA v. John Doe

This sentencing memorandum was filed on behalf of a young man charged with possession of child sexual abuse material. It is intended to highlight several points: the charges are typical of those filed against young men on the spectrum, his sensory issues are typical of people on the spectrum, and his stimming is also typical of people on the spectrum. Like most defendants in federal cases, this young man entered a guilty plea.

USA v. Isaacs

This sentencing memorandum was filed on behalf of a young man who was a victim of online radicalization and who ended up being charged in conjunction with the events of January 6th. It is intended to highlight the multiple traumas experienced (death of a father, loneliness following the COVID lockdown), the fact that the accused has a brother with ASD, that the defendant suffers from many sensory issues, that he experienced acute social isolation as a child, and that, in addition to being on the spectrum, his relative youth at the time of the charged offense should be used as mitigation. Unlike most federal defendants, this man went to trial. The two supplemental memos reflect the fact that his attorney never stopped fighting for his client.

Elizabeth Kelley
(pro hac vice)
Elizabeth Kelley, Attorney At Law
2425 E. 29th Ave., Ste. 10-B,
#225 Spokane, WA 99223
(509)991-7058
ZealousAdvocacy@aol.com

Robert M. Herz
Law Offices of Robert Herz
431 W. Seventh Ave., Ste. 107
Anchorage, AK 99501
907-277-7171
rmherz@gci.net

IN THE UNITED STATES DISTRICT COURT

FOR THE DISTRICT OF ALASKA

United States of America,	)	
	)	
Plaintiff,	)	Case No. ▨▨▨▨▨▨▨
	)	
vs.	)	
	)	
███████	)	
Defendant.	)	

DEFENDANT'S SENTENCING MEMORANDUM

COMES NOW ██████, by and through counsel, Elizabeth Kelley (*pro hac vice*) of

Elizabeth Kelley, Attorney at Law, and attorney Robert M. Herz of the Law Offices of Robert

Herz, P.C. and, and hereby files defendant's sentencing memorandum to aid the court at

sentencing. As a supplement and attached as an exhibit to this Memorandum, Mr. ███ further

submits the attached Sentencing Mitigation Video, approximately 21 minutes in length. The video is cited in this memorandum and incorporated herein. It has been conventionally filed with the court and served on opposing counsel

INTRODUCTION

Mr. ███ urges the court to adopt defense counsels' sentencing recommendation in this case. The guideline calculation as presented in the pre-sentence report maintains that the total adjusted offense level is a 38 with criminal history level of I. This renders a guideline range of 235 to 293 months. The statutory maximum is 120 months. The government's sentencing recommendation is 60 months and the USPO recommendations is 66 months. None of these recommended sentences of imprisonment are reasonable and all are excessive under the circumstances of this case. While the defense will offer an alternate guideline calculation(s) based on suggested variances, even these alternate calculations result in advisory guideline ranges that are excessive and unreasonable. The unique constellation of factors at play in this case, including the mitigated characteristics of the offense itself take this well outside the heartland of production CP cases, and the unique attributes of ███ including his physical health ailments, his learning and developmental disabilities, and his autism all counsel for a sentence well outside the heartland of production CP sentences. He will argue that when the court engages in true individualized sentencing, and takes into account all the exceptional circumstances in this matter that there is a substantial and compelling basis to justify a sentence variance, and sentence Mr. ███ to a sentence of probation and home confinement, with supervised release during the probation period not to exceed 5 years.

THE GUIDELINES DO NOT GUIDE

The guidelines are not presumptively reasonable, and extraordinary circumstances need not exist to justify a sentence outside the guideline range.

Even if the guideline calculation as set forth in the PSR is accepted by the court as being accurate, the Supreme Court has held that it is error for the sentencing court to presume an advisory guideline sentence is reasonable. *Nelson v. United States*, 129 S.Ct. 890 (2009).[1] This court has discretion to impose the sentence being requested by Mr. ███. *Gall v. United States*, 552 U.S. 38.128 S.Ct. 586, 169 L.Ed.2d 445 (2007).[2] Since the guidelines are only advisory, appellate review of sentencing decisions is limited to determining whether a particular sentence is "reasonable," and an abuse of discretion standard applies to review of sentencing decisions. *Gall v. United States, supra*, 128 S.Ct. at 594. The *Gall* court expressly rejected the rule that "extraordinary" circumstances must exist to justify a sentence outside the Guidelines range. *Id.* at 595. The Court made clear that sentences outside the range are not presumptively unreasonable. *Id.* In fact, as the court in *United States v. Hunt*, 459 F.3d 1180 (11th Cir. 2006) observed: "there are many instances where the Guideline range will not yield a reasonable sentence." Id. at 1184. Mr. ███'s case is one of those cases.

The *Gall* court noted that while the sentencing court should begin by correctly calculating the applicable Guidelines range, the court should then consider all the factors listed in 18 U.S.C. §3553(a). In doing so, the Court explicitly prohibited the sentencing court from presuming the

---

[1] "The Guidelines are not only *not mandatory* on sentencing courts; they are also *not to be presumed reasonable*. We think it plain from the comments of the sentencing judge that he did apply a presumption of reasonableness to ... [the] Guidelines range. Under our recent precedents, that constitutes error." *Id.* (emphasis supplied). *Nelson v. United States,* supra.

[2] In the seminal post-Booker case, the United States Supreme Court reviewed the sentence of defendant Gall who was convicted of conspiracy involving distribution of ecstasy. The recommended guidelines sentence was 30 to 37 months. The district court sentenced Gall to 36 months probation. The Supreme Court upheld the sentence as reasonable. *Gall v. United States*, 128 S.Ct. 586, 169 L.Ed.2d 445 (2007). The Eighth Circuit had reversed Gall's sentence based, at least in part, on the fact that a sentence of probation for participation as a middleman in a conspiracy distributing 10,000 ecstasy pills was not among the choices permitted by the Guidelines. The Supreme Court observed: "[T]he Guidelines are not mandatory, and thus the "range of choice dictated by the facts of the case" is significantly broadened. Moreover, the Guidelines are only one of the factors to consider when imposing sentence... ." *Gall*, 128 S.Ct. at 601-602.

Guideline range to be reasonable. Instead, the sentencing court must make an individualized

assessment based on the facts presented. The court reiterated its view, first expressed in *Koon v.*

United States, 518 U.S. 81, 116 S.Ct. 2035, 135 L.Ed.2d 292 (1996) that, "it has been uniform

and constant in the federal judicial tradition for the sentencing judge to consider every convicted

person as an individual and every case as a unique study in the human failings that sometimes

mitigate, sometimes magnify, the crime and the punishment to ensue." *Koon*, 518 U.S. at 113.

**The June 2021 United States Sentencing Commission Report provides a sound and
compelling policy basis to vary from the application of guideline enhancements.**

The most recent report from the United States Sentencing Commission, which just came

out in June 2021, continues to be critical of many of the enhancements in the guidelines for child

pornography offenses. United States Sentencing Commission, *Federal Sentencing of Child*

Pornography Non-Production Offenses, June 2021 (hereinafter "2021 Commission Report").[3]

Among other things, this report examines the evolution of technology since the 2012 *Child*

Pornography Report and its continued impact on offender conduct and the widespread

applicability of sentencing enhancements in the non-production child pornography guideline.

The Commission noted in this report that given the substantial changes in technology, even since

their last report in 2012, that enhancements for use of a computer, possessing over 600 images,

images involving pre-pubescent victims are ubiquitous.[4]

---

[3]   This publication updates and expands upon the United States Sentencing Commission's 2012
Child Pornography Report to the Congress: Federal Child Pornography Offenses (the "2012 *Child
Pornography Report*").
[4]   "Facilitated by advancements in digital and mobile technology, non-production child
pornography offenses increasingly involve voluminous quantities of videos and images that are graphic in
nature, often involving the youngest victims. In fiscal year 2019, non-production child pornography
offenses involved a median number of 4,265 images, with some offenders possessing and distributing
millions of images and videos. Over half (52.2%) of non-production child pornography offenses in fiscal
year 2019 included images or videos of infants or toddlers, and nearly every offense (99.4%) included
prepubescent victims." 2021 Commission Report at 4 & 68.

As the Commission notes, §2G2.2 contains a series of enhancements that have not kept pace with technological advancements. Four of the six enhancements— accounting for a combined 13 offense levels—cover conduct that has become so ubiquitous that they now apply in the vast majority of cases sentenced under §2G2.2.[5] The Commission observed that "... enhancements that initially were intended to target more serious and more culpable offenders [now] apply in most cases, the average guideline minimum and average sentence imposed for non-production child pornography offenses have increased since 2005. *Id.* at 5.[6] The Commission describes the federal courts as having to deal with "an outdated statutory and guideline structure." The criticisms raised by of 2021 Commission Report regarding these enhancements applies equally to the same enhancements being applied in production cases. The 2021 Commission Report provides a solid foundation upon which this court can and should disagree with the guidelines on policy grounds, and upon which to justify a sentence variance.

Courts are rejecting the "guideline that does not guide."[7]

In 2003, Congress passed the Prosecutorial Remedies and Other Tools to End Exploitation of Children ("PROTECT") Act. Since the passage of the PROTECT Act, which directly amended the child pornography sentencing guidelines to add new sentencing enhancements and create new statutory mandatory minimum penalties, courts, and the Sentencing Commission itself, have criticized the guidelines for its significant policy flaws.

---

[5]   In fiscal year 2019, over 95 percent of non-production child pornography offenders received enhancements for use of a computer and for the age of the victim (images depicting victims under the age of 12). The enhancements for images depicting sadistic or masochistic conduct or abuse of an infant or toddler (84.0% of cases) or having 600 or more images (77.2% of cases) were also applied in most cases. *Id.* at 5. See also. 2021 Commission Report a pps. 30 & 31.
[6]   The average guideline minimum for non-production child pornography offenders increased from 98 months in fiscal year 2005 to 136 months in fiscal year 2019. *Id.*
[7]   *United States v. Grober*, 595 F. Supp. 2d 382, 412 (D. N.J. 2008).

To understand the impact that congressional legislation, particularly the PROTECT Act, has had on sentencing for child pornography offenses, this Court should consider the steady and significant *decrease* of within-range sentences for offenders sentenced under U.S.S.G. §2G2.1. In 2005, courts sentenced offenders within the recommended guideline range 83.3% of the time. (U.S. Sent Comm'n Report, Oct. 2021 at 22.) In 2019, the percentage of within-range sentences plummeted to just 30.7%. (*Id.*) Similarly, less than one-third (30.0%) of offenders sentenced under § 2G2.2 received a sentence within the guideline range in fiscal year 2019. These statistics suggest courts are not merely treating the guidelines as advisory, they are downright disregarding them as bad advice.

Courts across the country that have rejected the child pornography sentencing guidelines have articulated two common policy disagreements with the guidelines. First, the guidelines are based, not on empirical analysis, but on congressional mandates that interfere with and undermine the Sentencing Commission's work. In *United States v. Henderson*, 649 F.3d 955, 962-63 (9th Cir. 2011), the Ninth Circuit reviewed the history of the child pornography Guidelines and concluded that the Guidelines "are, to a large extent, not the result of the Commission's 'exercise of its characteristic institutional role,' which requires that it base its determination on 'empirical data and national experience.'" Rather, the Guidelines were a result "of frequent mandatory minimum legislation and specific congressional directives to the Commission to amend the Guidelines." *Id.* Because the Guidelines are not based on "empirical data and national experience," district courts "may vary from the child pornography Guidelines . . . based on policy disagreement with them, and not simply based on an individualized determination that they yield an excessive sentence in a particular case." *Id.*; *United States v. Dorvee*, 616 F.3d 174, 184 (2d Cir. 2010) (observing that § 2G2.2 is "fundamentally different" from other guidelines and that, "unless [§ 2G2.2 is] applied with great care, [it] can lead to unreasonable sentences that are inconsistent with what § 3553 requires"); *United States v. Grober*, 624 F.3d 592, 608-09 (3d Cir. 2010) (§ 2G2.2 was not developed pursuant to the Commission's characteristic institutional role and district courts may, but are not obligated to vary on policy basis from it); *United States v. Stone*, 575 F.3d 83, 90 (1st Cir. 2009) (accepting defendant's argument that the child pornography Guidelines are based on congressional directives, and not on the Commission's empirical approach; district courts may therefore disagree with the Guidelines). As one district court judge observed:

> As to any argument that the guideline reflects Congressional intent to punish child sex offenses harshly, a guideline is not a statute. The statute here provides a broad range of punishment for this crime, and if Congress does not want the courts to try and sentence individual defendants throughout that range based on the facts and circumstances of each case, then Congress should amend the statute, rather than manipulate an advisory guideline and blunt the effectiveness and reliability of the work of the Sentencing Commission.

United States v. Shipley, 560 F. Supp.2d 739, 744 (S.D. Iowa 2008).

The second significant policy disagreement cited by courts as a reason to reject the guidelines has to do with sentence enhancements that drastically increase sentencing ranges for all offenders while failing to distinguish more culpable offenders, or less culpable offenders, from the heartland of cases. *See Dorvee*, 616 F.3d at 186 ("The § 2G2.2 sentencing enhancements . . . routinely result in Guidelines projections near or exceeding the statutory maximum, even in run-of-the-mill cases. . . . On top of that, many of the § 2G2.2 enhancements apply in nearly all cases."); *United States v. Beiermann*, 599 F. Supp. 2d 1087, 1100 (N.D. Iowa 2009) (collecting cases). As the *Dorvee* court noted:

> Section 2G2.2 eviscerates the fundamental statutory requirement in § 3553(a) that district courts consider 'the nature and circumstances of the offense and the history and characteristics of the defendant' and violates

the principle . . . that courts must guard against *unwarranted similarities* among sentences for defendants who have been found guilty of dissimilar conduct.

Dorvee, 616 F.3d at 187 (emphasis supplied). The guidelines, as applied to ▨▨▨, highlight the need for a substantial downward variance.

Alternative Guideline computations deleting guidelines enhancements and grouping still yield excessive and unreasonable guideline ranges.

A reasonable recapitulation of the USPO recommended guideline calculation that ignored the common and ubiquitous upward enhancements for use of a computer (2pts), and images involving prepubescent minors (under age 12) (4pts), or images of minors between the age of 12 and 16 (2pts), and before making any downward adjustments pertaining to the Grouping Rules, would decrease the total adjusted offense level to 34 and would result in a guideline range of 151-188 months in this case. This is still an unreasonable and excessive sentence under the unique circumstances of this case.

Even if the court made further adjustments, and ignored the Grouping Rules[8] entirely, the total adjusted offense level would be 29 and would result in a guideline range of 87-108 months. It would appear reasonable for the court to ignore the Grouping calculation engaged in by the USPO because Part D of Chapter 3 expressly applies to counts of conviction only.[9]

---

[8]   2G2.1(d) was first added on Nov. 1, 1990 via Amendment 324, which reads in part: "[a] special instruction is added to conform the operation of the multiple count rule in this guideline with §§2G1.1 and 2G1.2." In that regard, 2G1.1(d) provides "If the offense involved more than one victim, Chapter Three, Part D (Multiple Counts) shall be applied as if the promoting of a commercial sex act or prohibited sexual conduct in respect to each victim had been contained in a separate count of conviction." That provision was added on Nov. 1, 1989 via Amendment 158, which states in whole: "The purpose of this amendment is to provide a special instruction for the application of the multiple count rule in cases involving *the transportation* of more than one person." (emphasis added) Application Note 7 (not 5) to 2G2.1 first went into effect on Nov. 1, 1989 via Amendment 161 and provides in whole: "[t]he purpose of this amendment is to clarify that multiple counts involving different minors are not grouped under §3D1.2." There does not appear to be any articulated policy reason for this exception to normal grouping rules.

[9]   The Introductory Commentary states: " This Part provides rules for determining a single offense level that encompasses all the counts of which the defendant is *convicted*. These rules apply to multiple

Nevertheless, Mr. ▓▓▓ would maintain that the resulting guideline range still would be excessive and unreasonable. And lastly, if the court were to ignore the cross reference found at 2G2.2(c)(1) which was stipulated to by prior counsel, and sentence Mr. ▓▓▓ pursuant to the 2G2.2(c)(1) guideline for Possession, the base offense level would be 18, not 32 as it is for production offenses, and again ignoring any enhancements that are deemed ubiquitous by the 2021 Commission Report, the total adjusted offense level would be 15 with a range of 18-24 months. And even when these suggested variances are applied, even then this guideline range is excessive, before accounting for ▓▓▓▓▓▓ exceptional personal characteristics.

In short, the guidelines at issue deserve little-to no-deference, and this court may reject them, as many other courts have, as bad policy, but it need not rely on policy disagreements alone to arrive at a fair and just sentence.

A FIVE-YEAR TERM OF PROBATION IS "SUFFICIENT, BUT NOT GREATER THAN NECESSARY" TO ACHIEVE THE PURPOSE OF SENTENCING

As a matter of law, this court must make an individual assessment of the 18 U.S.C. § 3535(a) factors based on all the facts presented, (*Gall*, 552 U.S. at 50), and impose a sentence in this case that is "sufficient, but not greater than necessary" to achieve the objectives of sentencing. 18 U.S.C. § 3553(a).

Based upon a consideration of the statutory sentencing factors set out in 18 U.S.C. § 3553(a), a 5-year term of probation and 5 years on supervised release during probation, and imposition of certain special conditions set out in the presentence investigation report with appropriate modifications suggested by the defense, is warranted in this case—regardless of the Guideline range this Court ultimately computes.

counts of *conviction…* ." Guideline 3D1.1 Procedure for Determining Offense Level on Multiple Counts states: "(a) When a defendant has been *convicted* of more than one count, the court shall … ." The explicit text of the Guideline as well as the Commentary make clear that the Grouping Rules are to be applied to convictions only.

As noted, section 3553(a) sets forth a general directive to "impose a sentence sufficient, but not greater than necessary, to comply with the purposes" of sentencing. Section 3553(a) then lists the factors that a sentencing court must consider. Especially relevant to this case, and supportive of the argument that a 5-year probationary sentence with strict special conditions is sufficient, are the following factors:

a. The history and characteristics of the Defendant

1. ███ *family history*

███ was adopted at birth and does not know the identity of his biological parents. He currently lives with his mother ███, a nurse anesthetist, and he has a close relationship with his sister ███, who is ███'s age and was also adopted. ███ and ███'s father divorced in 2018 due to ███ father's alcoholism, physical and verbal abuse toward ███, ███, and ███, several suicide attempts, and attempts to fatally injure the family. According to ███'s mother, ███'s father was "in and out of rehab due to alcohol abuse, was 'on all types of weird porn sites,' and was 'belligerent and violent' towards her and the children." (Plaud Report at 6.) ███'s sister notes that she and ███ were "always aware something sexual and weird was happening with their father," and she indicated they would often hide in the bathroom together from their father. (*Id.*) ███ and ███ are ███'s support system, and they have continued to support him throughout the pendency of this case. Regardless of the sentence the court chooses to impose on ███, his mother and sister will be there to guide him.

2. ███'s *medical history*

███ has been plagued by physical and mental maladies all his life. ███ was born with such severe acid reflux it caused esophagitis and esophageal reflux resulting in inflammation "that creates many incidents of choking." (Plaud Report at 7.)[10] ▨ must undergo regular endoscopy checks for Barrett's esophagus, which is associated with an increased risk of developing esophageal cancer, and ▨ may need a Nissen fundoplication in the future.

▨ also suffers from numerous allergies to pollen, trees, grasses, and certain bedding. These allergies, in combination with ▨'s acid reflux, result in respiratory illnesses that require antibiotics and inhalers. ▨ has also had many moles removed from his chest and back, one of which was diagnosed as pre-cancerous and requires follow up. ▨ is prescribed Xyzal, Zyrtec, Albuterol, Nasonex, Protonix, and Advair. The regimen of prescribed and over the counter drugs he takes has been specially curated and administered by his medically trained mother. Some of the prescription drugs are quite expensive and not on the BOP formulary and are unlikely to be available to ▨ if he were sentenced to prison.

In addition to the medical conditions described above, ▨ was also diagnosed at a young age with Attention Deficit Hyperactivity Disorder, an unspecified learning disorder, and a chronic motor tic disorder. ▨ suffers from severe anxiety necessitating various anti-anxiety prescription medications, and last year, ▨ was diagnosed with Autism Spectrum Disorder ("ASD"). ▨'s ASD has had a significant impact on his life.[11] ▨ struggles to communicate with others, especially if the conversation becomes complex. "When ▨ becomes distraught he engages in verbal rituals and becomes repetitive in his vocalizations," and his voice becomes "super loud." (Sperry Report at 7.) ▨'s in-person social interactions are

[10] The Government downplays ▨'s acid reflux, describing it as an ailment on par with allergies. (Government's Sentencing Memo at 7.) ▨ condition is much more serious and debilitating than seasonal allergies and requires that ▨ undergo regular imaging and biopsies to check for pre-cancerous cells.

[11] Again, the Government understates the role ▨'s autism plays in his life and in the commission of this offense. Interference with one's understanding of the impact his behavior has on others is just one of the many difficulties individuals such as ▨ contend with on a daily basis.

defined and limited by his ASD. ██████ lacks an awareness of social nuances and needs to be told "that's not okay." According to ██████'s mother, ██████ has never had his own friend, let alone a best friend, and as a result, ██████ turned to the internet for friendship and companionship.

██████'s ASD manifests itself in other notable ways as well. He has "unusual sensory interests around how things smell and taste and is very sensitive to strong odors." (Sperry Report at 8.) ██████'s sensitivity to strong odors is so severe that he frequently vomits if he smells something he finds offensive. ██████ also has unusual body movements, or tics, associated with his ASD. ██████ "will drop his head to his chest and roll and wag his head from side to side" and "tap his face and then swing his arms out to the sides and cross them repeatedly across his chest as if giving himself repeated bear hugs."[12] (*Id.*) Like many individuals diagnosed with ASD, ██████ becomes fixated on certain interests. In ██████'s case, those interests include woodworking and the sound of urine hitting the toilet bowl.

Finally, ██████'s ASD leads ██████ to follow the rules, provided someone has explained the rules in a way that he can comprehend, and is educated about the rules through repetition.

3. ██████'s *education, work, and social history*

██████'s mother recounts that ██████'s struggles in school began as early as pre-school. ██████'s teachers recommended that he attend a special education school, and ██████ received learning support from first grade through high school. ██████ struggled academically, but he did participate in some extracurricular activities such as cross-country. ██████ took two classes at his local community college but did not graduate.

██████ has never held a job for more than 6 months. He has worked for the Alaska State Parks, Pier I Imports, Alaska Industrial Hardware, and a dog kennel, and he trained with the Matsu Fire Department. ██████ does not have any friends in Alaska and spends his time

---

[12] ██████'s unusual body movements can be seen in the sentencing video filed separately with the court.

woodworking and taking care of his family's dogs. Both ✖✖✖'s mother and his sister, Claudia, have observed that ✖✖✖ likely will always need to live at home with support.

b. The nature and circumstances of the offense

The underlying conduct resulting in ✖✖✖'s conviction occurred between 2016 and early 2019, when ✖✖✖ was between ages 18 and 21.[13] During that time, ✖✖✖ communicated with women and girls who responded to his "girlfriend test," a series of questions ✖✖✖ posted online that were meant to help ✖✖✖ find women who would be comfortable letting him watch them urinate via video. 410 females took the test and of that total 196 were minors; slightly more adult women than minors responded. It should be apparent that ✖✖✖ was not targeting minors. Of the 196 minors who responded to the test, the investigation revealed only 5 to 7 instances where ✖✖✖'s conduct resulted in production of CP.[14] The posting of this on-line "girlfriend test" itself was fairly innocuous and not illegal.[15] The minors ✖✖✖ communicated with ranged in age between 14 and 17. ✖✖✖ also placed a camera in a bathroom at his home and recorded a girl as she urinated.

The Government acknowledges that ✖✖✖ has only pleaded guilty to a single count of possessing child pornography but argues that any sentence "should reflect the many concerning,

---

[13]   ✖✖✖ first posted his "girlfriend test" when he was 16 years old. It is relevant that he was a minor himself exploring these issues.

[14]   Of the twelve incidents identified in the Grouping calculation, 4 of those incidents did not result in any images being produced. These four incidents did not result in charges. The USPO considered these four incidents as relevant conduct because ✖✖✖ solicited images. The act of soliciting images did not violate the statute. To violate the express terms of 18 USC 2251, the defendant must *employ, use, persuade, induce, entice or coerce* a minor to engage in sexually explicit conduct. Each of these terms are unambiguous and so their ordinary meaning applies. For instance, the United States Sentencing Commission (USSC) in its report *Federal Sentencing of Child Pornography: Production Offenses, October 2021* provides examples of what it means to entice or coerce. *Id.* at 38-39. Congress did not use the word "solicit" in the statute, which has a different meaning than any of the following verbs: *employ, use, persuade, induce, entice or coerce.*

[15]   It was ✖✖✖'s way of making sure, up front that any possible romantic partner would be OK with his fetish and not think he was weird or be worried or traumatized by his interests.

unusual aspects of the offense." (Government's Memo at 6.) The Government states that the offense took place over multiple years, and that ▓▓▓ "developed a sophisticated scheme for luring potential victims." (*Id.*) The sophisticated scheme in question ▓▓▓'s "girlfriend test," was far from sophisticated and was conducted out in the open, under ▓▓▓'s real name.[16] In short, ▓▓▓ was not trying to hide what he was doing because he did not know that what he was doing was wrong or illegal. ▓▓▓ who, at best, operates at the emotional and social level of a fourteen-year-old, was communicating with each girl in serial fashion, believing that since they had responded to the test, that at the time they were communicating and sharing images, he was communicating with his girlfriend.

Without diminishing the seriousness of the offense, it is important for the court to put into context ▓▓▓'s conduct compared to other child pornography production offenses. In October 2021, the United States Sentencing Commission examined child pornography production offender behavior and offense characteristics and highlighted three factors that it found relevant to sentencing: proximity, participation, and propensity. Proximity refers to the offender's physical location and relationship with the victims. Participation measures the offender's interaction with the victims. And propensity examines the offender's tendency to engage in child pornography conduct or exploitation outside of the instant production offense. In ▓▓▓'s case all three factors identified by the Sentencing Commission as being relevant for sentencing weigh in favor of a sentence that emphasizes community rehabilitation, not incarceration.

First, a majority (60%) of production offenders maintained a position of trust over their victims, whether through familial relationships or by virtue of the offender's role as a teacher,

---

[16] The "girlfriend test" was created and posted on-line when ▓▓▓ was a sophomore in high school. The very notion of it is juvenile; the epitome of adolescent behavior.

coach, or some other role model. In contrast, ▨ met all the victims in this case online and, notably, **never** attempted to meet them in person.

Second, are factors that are relevant to ▨'s participation in the offense. These factors are the method of production, whether a co-participant was involved, whether there was sexual contact with the victims, and whether incapacitation, coercion, enticement, or misrepresentation were used against the victim. When the court examines these factors, it is clear that ▨'s participation was not as significant as the Government or his Guidelines offense level would suggest. For example, ▨ falls within the minority (36.5%) of offenders who had victims create content on their own at the offender's request. ▨ is likewise in the minority of offenders (25.2%) who did not sexually contact a victim. To the extent ▨ produced child pornography, it was produced for himself and only himself. There are no allegations in this case that ▨ ever distributed or sought pecuniary gain from the images and videos.

Finally, unlike most child pornography production offenders who both produce child pornography and engage sexual exploitation of minors, ▨'s conduct is limited to the instant offense. When the Sentencing Commission considered an offender's propensity to engage in child pornography or exploitive conduct, it examined four factors: (1) whether an offender shared self-produced child pornography, or possessed or distributed additional child pornography that the offender did not produce; (2) whether an offender was a member of an on-line community devoted to child pornography or sexual exploitation; (3) whether an offender had any previous contact sex offenses; and (4) whether an offender had a history of non-contact sex offenses. In ▨'s case, he did not share self-produced child pornography and denies knowingly possessing child pornography he did not produce. ▨ was not a member of an online community devoted to child pornography and he does not have a history of contact or non-contact sex offenses.

By the Sentencing Commission's own measures, ▉▉▉ is unlikely to engage in future child pornography or sexually exploitative conduct. The assessments by Dr Plaud and Dr. Sperry confirm this. Once people on the spectrum learn the rules, they won't break them. If there is a spectrum of conduct that meets the definition of production of child pornography, at one end of the spectrum would be a high-school sophomore couple sending nudes of themselves to each other ("sexting") and at the far other end would be, perhaps an older middle-aged male, having sexual intercourse with a four-year old, while videotaping the sexual abuse (production), publishing the video (distribution), and doing so for money. It should be apparent to the court that ▉▉▉'s conduct falls on the spectrum closest to the high-schoolers sexting each other.

c. The kinds of sentences available

This court is not statutorily required to sentence ▉▉▉ to prison. ▉▉▉ is eligible for probation, and such a sentence, with strict terms and conditions, combined with 5-years of supervised release, satisfy the goals of sentencing. In rejecting the Government's call for a 5-year term of imprisonment, the court would not be blazing its own path or ignoring precedent, but would be recognizing, as other Ninth Circuit courts have, that imprisonment is not appropriate in certain cases such as ▉▉▉'s.

Several courts in the Ninth Circuit have applied significant downward variances in child pornography sentencings that resulted in probation rather than incarceration. *See United States v. Applequist,* 3:09-cr-120 (2010) (78-month downward variance and 5-year probationary sentence for infirm defendant); *United States v. Appell,* 2:09-cr-55 (2010) (78-month downward variance and 5-year probationary sentence for defendant diagnosed with major depressive disorder and extreme social anxiety); *United States v. Kainne*, 3:14-cr-218 (2017) (78-month downward variance and 5-year probationary sentence for defendant diagnosed with obsessive-compulsive personality disorder, complex post-traumatic stress disorder, anxiety disorder, chronic depression, panic disorder, and HIV/AIDS); *United States v. Ellis-Taylor*, 3:17-cr-585 (2017) (51-month downward variance and 5-year probationary sentence); *United States v. Noel*, 09-cr-00701 (2010) (78-month downward variance and 5-year probationary sentence for defendant at risk of abuse in prison). In another Ninth Circuit case, U.S. v. Autery, 555 F.3d 864 (9th Cir. 2009), the defendant's guideline range was 41-51 months stemming from a conviction for possession of child porn. The court upheld a sentence of probation finding that it was not unreasonable, in part, because it was the defendant's first conviction and a Criminal History Category of I, "did not fully account for his complete lack of criminal history" because even defendant's with a minor criminal history will still fall in that category. *See also*, U.S. v. Polito, 215 Fed. Appx. 354, 2007 WL 313463 (5th Cir. Jan. 31, 2007)(unpub.)(defendant convicted for possession of child porn; guidelines 27-33 months; sentence of probation with one year house arrest reasonable, in part because first offense).

    United States v. Noel is particularly on point. In *Noel*, the defendant, Joshua Noel, like ▨▨▨, was a "socially-awkward first-time offender" whose offense conduct began at a young age but continued into adulthood. Joshua pled guilty to a single count of child pornography possession in violation of 18 U.S.C. § 2252(a)(5)(B). Probation calculated a total offense level of 28, resulting in an advisory guideline range of 78-97 months. The court sentenced Joshua to 5 years of probation. As explained in greater detail below, Joshua and ▨▨▨ possess many of the same characteristics that make a term of probation more appropriate than a term of imprisonment in ▨▨▨'s case.

1. Personal and physical characteristics

Joshua and ███ come from tight-knit and supportive families, but both struggled socially and failed to make friends. Joshua's isolation was the result of severe scoliosis and radical corrective surgery that left him confined to his home. ███'s isolation was the result of undiagnosed autism, unspecified intellectual disabilities, and poor physical health. Joshua and ███ both turned to the internet for comfort and companionship. Neither Joshua nor ███ were able to develop healthy social or emotional relationships with others.

2. Immaturity at the time of the offense

This Court may consider youth as a mitigating factor. *See United States v. Stern*, 590 F. Supp. 2d 945, 952 (N.D. Ohio 2008); U.S. v Polito, (5th Cir. Jan. 31 2007 No. 06-30133) 2007 WL 313463 (unpub.)(defendant convicted of possession of CP; guidelines 27-33 months, court sentenced to probation with one year of house arrest deemed reasonable in part because defendant was 18 at time of offense, and "very immature.... And his age and mental condition prohibited him from acting rationally"). Joshua Noel began viewing child pornography when he was 14 years old but continued to do so until he was 22. Similarly, ███ created his "girlfriend test" when he was 16 years old. ███'s offense conduct occurred between the ages of 18 and 21, however, according to ███'s mother, sister, and Dr. Sperry, ███ acts much younger than his biological age.

3. Vulnerability to victimization and abuse in prison

"A defendant's unusual susceptibility to abuse by other inmates while in prison may warrant a downward departure." *United States v. Parish*, 308 F.3d 1025, 1031 (9th Cir. 2002). Like ███, Joshua never lived on his own. Joshua was described as "naïve and socially inept in any normal civilized society," and he lacked the "ability to defend himself from physical attack" in a prison setting. As explained below, ███ displays an even greater susceptibility to abuse in prison than did Joshua, making a probationary sentence not only appropriate, but necessary to avoid significant physical and mental harm to ███.

In a more recent case, *United States v. Keskin*, Case No. 6:17-cr-77-Orl-37DCl (M.D. Fla. Feb. 7, 2018) a federal district court in Florida addressed many of the same sentencing issues facing this court. In that matter, Cenk Keskin, a 31-year-old man, pled guilty to possession of child pornography. A forensic examination revealed that Keskin downloaded thousands of child pornography/erotica images and videos that the court described as "abhorrent." Keskin's offense conduct occurred over a 13-year period, meaning he began collecting child pornography when he was 17 years old. Based on a total offense level of 30 and a criminal history category of I, the Sentencing Guidelines established a range of incarceration of 97 to 121 months.

Despite growing up in a loving, supportive, and intact nuclear family, Keskin struggled to finish high school, was unsuccessful in community college, could not find employment outside of his parents' home, and spent most of his time on the internet; he had no friends and did not participate in any extracurricular activities. After his arrest, Keskin was examined by a licensed psychologist who diagnosed Keskin with ASD and Obsessive Compulsive Disorder ("OCD"). The psychologist also described Keskin's history, which mirrors ███'s:

> [Keskin] was . . . noted at an early age to have difficulty in socialization, and difficulty in establishing age appropriate peer relations. He also struggled academically, and in fifth grade was described by the school system as having learning disabilities, and being at least two years behind his peers academically. At an early age, he was noted to have obsessional rituals, with odd habits of hoarding and collecting. . . . As he grew older, he was picked on and bullied at school, and the problems with socialization and relationships with peers continued. According to family members, he has had very few friends, was often bullied, and for the most part isolated himself. His mother described him as "not self aware," and as "lacking social boundaries. . . .
>
> He was not able to graduate regular high school, but with the insistence of family members achieved a GED. He has not held regular employment in the past decade,

although he has sold merchandise online through eBay. He is single, never married, and has no children. He is not dating anyone, has not had any sort of romantic relationships that the family is aware of, he has (according to the family) no friends, and he continues to have peculiar collecting and hoarding rituals.

Keskin's testing did not reveal sexual interest in preschool or grade school females and was not indicative of any pedophilic disorder. Rather, Keskin's collection of child pornography reflected his compulsive collecting / hoarding, brought on by the ASD and OCD, not Pedophilic Disorder.

Keskin was also seen by a second psychologist /certified sex therapist who agreed with the previous ASD and OCD diagnosis and opined that Keskin responded well to therapy and medication, was highly motived for therapy, and amenable to change. He also noted that Keskin presented a low risk for harming others and "that as a result of the Defendant's autism and inability to read social cues, he would be at high risk for victimization and physical abuse among the ordinary prison population."

At Keskin's sentencing, the government referred the court to Eleventh Circuit cases sustaining lengthy incarcerative sentences over defense objections, and Keskin cited numerous district court opinions with similar facts where a significant downward variance was imposed and not appealed. "A review of these cases assuages the Court's concern that a variant sentence would be unduly disparate, on these facts." The court also requested data from the Sentencing Commission related to sentences under Section 2G2.2 with a final offense level of 30 and Criminal History category I where the sentence imposed was below the Guideline range **due to mental and emotional conditions.** Of the 87 offenders identified, 78.2% received a non-government sponsored below range sentence. 62.1% received an average downward variance of 60 months, *and 12.6% received a sentence of probation and / or probation with confinement* or a split sentence that include some prison time.

Taking into account (1) that "virtually every offender convicted of possession of child pornography is eligible for nearly every enhancement," regardless of differences in culpability, (2) Keskin's ASD and OCD "impair his ability to appreciate the criminality of his conduct and offer an explanation for" his conduct, (3) Keskin's vulnerability to physical and sexual abuse in prison, (4) Keskin's progress in treatment/low recidivism risk, (5) the ability for a non-incarcerative sentence to meet the goals of sentencing, and (6) "the consideration of overall fairness as it relates to disparity in sentencing," the court imposed a sentence of time served with a 15-year term of supervised release, an initial period of home confinement of 12 months along with specific and standard conditions of supervised released.[17]

While no two child pornography offenders are the same, the similarities between Keskin an [redacted] are notable, and the court's decision to impose a substantial downward variance in that case was well-reasoned and justified. For the reasons described in this sentencing memorandum, a substantial downward variance in [redacted]'s case is justified both by the underlying offense conduct and [redacted]'s history and characteristics.

d. The need to avoid unwarranted sentence disparities

[redacted] acknowledges that most child pornography production offenders receive lengthy prison sentences and that a sentence to probation represents a substantial sentencing disparity. However, 18 U.S.C. § 3553 requires this Court to consider "the need to avoid *unwarranted*

[17] The court rejected the government's argument that a guideline sentence was necessary to reflect the seriousness of the offense, to promote respect for the law, to provide just punishment for the offense; to deter criminal conduct and to protect the public from further crimes. The court responded:

> [The Government] offer no evidence in support of the notion that these objectives are achieved by a guideline sentence or, as importantly, that they may not be achieved by a well-constructed variant sentenced. . . . Just punishment, of course, is the goal of the entire process. Deterrence is fostered not only by lengthy incarceration, but also by the stigma of sex offender designation and registration requirements, home confinement, and lengthy periods of supervised release. . . . The weight of the evidence here reflects that these sentencing objectives can be equally (or better) achieved by a variant sentence.

sentence disparities." (emphasis added). Sentencing [redacted] to probation does not create an *unwarranted* sentence disparity as there are a number of factors that warrant and justify a significant downward variance.

e. [redacted]'s susceptibility to abuse in prison

A sentence to probation rather than imprisonment is further supported by [redacted]'s unique susceptibility to abuse. Susceptibility to abuse is a valid reason for a downward departure under the Guidelines. *Koon v. United States*, 116 S. Ct. 2035 (1996) (approving departure for susceptibility to abuse in prison); *United States v. Parish*, 308 F.3d 1025, 1031 (9th Cir. 2002) (approving departure based on stature, demeanor, naivety, and sexual orientation).

Some inmates are substantially more susceptible to abuse than others, and certain physical and emotional conditions serve as predictors of victimization. Empirical evidence demonstrates that the most vulnerable inmates are: 1) the young or inexperienced; 2) the physically weak; 3) inmates suffering from developmental disabilities; 4) inmates who are not "tough" and "street-wise;" 5) inmates with no gang affiliations; 6) inmates who are homosexual or overtly effeminate; 7) inmates who violate the "code of silence;" 8) those who are disliked by other staff and inmates; and 9) inmates who have been previously sexually assaulted. PRISON RAPE REDUCTION ACT OF 2002: Hearing Before the Senate Committee on the Judiciary, 107th Cong. 36 (2002) (statement of Robert Dumond, Licensed Mental Health Counselor, Massachusetts Department of Corrections). The likelihood of abuse increases if overlapping factors exist. *See No Escape: Male Rape in U.S. Prisons* (Human Rights Watch), April 2001 at 63. [redacted] displays seven of the nine factors to an exceptional degree.[18]

---

[18] *6. and 9. would not apply: Inmates who are homosexual or overtly effeminate.* [redacted] denies sexual attraction to men of any age; and *Inmates who have been previously sexually assaulted.* [redacted] denies any history of sexual abuse (Plaud Report at 8.).

1. The young or inexperienced

XXX is 24 years old, but he "appear[s] to be younger than his stated age." (Plaud Report at 2; *see also*, Sentencing Mitigation Video) According to XXX's sister, XXX is "someone with stunted social development. 'He always needed accommodation, he's not grown up. He's still very much a little kid.'" (Sperry Report at 7.) According to XXX's mother, "XXX, in a lot of ways, exhibits behavior of a child or teen." (Plaud Report at 6.) XXX has never lived independently or managed his own money. (*Id.* at 19.) XXX is unable to tell the difference between a friend and a work acquaintance, and when asked how he knew someone was a boyfriend or girlfriend, XXX gave a "very childlike response," stating, "You ask them. Do you want to be my girlfriend? If they say yes, then we are dating." (*Id.*) As XXX grew up, "his chronological age became more disparate from his developmental and social age," (*Id.* at 39), or, as XXX's sister simply stated, "There's a difference between how old he acts and how old he is." (*Id.* at 23.)

2. The physically weak

XXX has had health issues since birth. XXX suffers from severe acid reflux which has caused esophagitis and esophageal reflux that frequently causes XXX to choke and requires him to undergo regular endoscopy checks. (Plaud Report at 7.) XXX has severe allergies and requires medication and an inhaler to treat his asthma. (Sperry Report at 6.) Due to his acid reflux and allergies, anytime XXX suffers a respiratory illness, he needs antibiotics and inhalers to reduce the risk of significant pulmonary complications. (Plaud Report at 7.) XXX has also had numerous moles removed from his back and chest area, including one mole that was diagnosed as pre-cancerous and requires follow up. (*Id.*) XXX's ASD also causes him to have severe negative reactions to certain tastes and smells; "[i]t causes him to have a gag reaction to certain foods and he has a past of vomiting if he smells a foul odor." (*Id.* at 7.)

3. Inmates suffering from developmental disabilities

██████'s developmental disabilities are well documented. ██████ was diagnosed with ADHD at the age of two or three years old. (Plaud Report at 6.) He was prescribed three or four medications to treat his ADHD as well as unspecified medications for anxiety. (*Id.*) From 7 to 9 years old, ██████ worked with an auditory specialist due to concerns about ██████'s verbal understanding. (*Id.*) Perhaps most significant, ██████ suffers from autism, a disorder that will make ██████ uniquely susceptible to abuse in prison, as noted by Dr. Sperry and former BOP Warden Maureen Baird.

4. Inmates who are not "tough" and "street-wise"

██████ does not engage in any type of physical aggression (Sperry Report at 8) and is highly suspectable to being taken advantage of. According to ██████'s mother, ██████ was once "duped into giving a couple thousand dollar to a man he met on the internet who promised to build a website for ██████'s woodworking. ██████ paid him and never heard from him again." (*Id.*). During ██████'s brief time in jail, "he shared personal details about his identity and socioeconomic status with cellmates he had just met," (Sperry Report at 41) and told them his mother could help them. (Sperry Report at 8.)

5. Inmates with no gang affiliations

██████ does not affiliate with any gang, nor is he likely to be welcomed into any gang.

7. Inmates who violate the "code of silence"

As Ms. Baird notes, there is an unwritten code of rules established by inmates. One such rule dictates that inmates do not report other inmates' criminal activity. ███ is unlikely to grasp the importance or nuance of following both written and unwritten rules within prison.

8. Those who are disliked by other staff and inmates

███'s autism will make it difficult for him to get along with staff and other inmates who will likely find ███'s autism-related mannerisms strange and annoying. ███'s voice is "always super loud" and "he needs frequent reminders to lower his voice" (Sperry Report at 7.) ███'s facial expressions are often discordant with the situation and he may laugh or smile in serious situations. (Id.) ███ also displays "unusual and complex body movements." (*Id.* at 8.) For example, ███ "will drop his head to his chest, and roll and wag his head from side to side." (*Id.*) He will also "tap his face and then swing his arms out to the sides and cross them repeatedly across his chest as if giving himself repeated bear hugs." (*Id.*) ███'s mother fears inmates may misinterpret ███'s motor tics, attack him, and take advantage of his naivete. (*Id.* at 23.) ███ is prone to becoming fixated on a particular topic to the point that it annoys others, and he often becomes fixated on other people in a way that is annoying or intrusive to that person. (Sperry Report at 15.)

Maureen Baird's Declaration highlights many of the ways in which the factors discussed above would manifest themselves were ███ to face a period of incarceration. As Ms. Baird notes, "survival in prison is contingent upon understanding and adapting to formal prison rules and those established by the inmates." (Baird Declaration at 5.) Although no one questions ███'s ability to follow the formal and written BOP rules, "it is apparent ███ lacks the ability to decipher the inmate established 'unwritten rules.'" (*Id.*) Inmates will view ███ as

Cybercrime and the Autism Spectrum

weak, easy prey, disrespectful, weird, and unsocial, and as a result, ███ will be ostracized and isolated. His child-like immaturity and tendency to speak loudly will irritate staff and other inmates. ███'s inability to read/interpret non-verbal cues and his obsessive compulsive tendencies will make him much more susceptible to physical and sexual abuse, which are common in a prison setting. Ms. Baird cautions that even if ███ were to try and fit in with the inmate population, "it is highly probable he will be taken advantage of, tricked, and manipulated" by "inmates looking for a weak target to exploit." (Baird Declaration at 6.) Ms. Baird is unsure ███ will even be able to nourish and sustain himself given his aversion to certain foods and odors and the lack of food choices in prison. In short, Ms. Baird expressed grave concerns for ███'s well-being in prison, concerns that go above and beyond the typical concerns associated with any term if imprisonment; ███'s mother, sister, Dr. Sperry, and defense counsel echo those concerns.

f. ███'s chances at rehabilitation and risk of recidivism

███ is an excellent candidate for rehabilitation and presents a low risk of recidivism. ███'s autism, which is partly to blame for his conduct in this case, is also a potential source of optimism that ███ can succeed on probation, be rehabilitated, and not reoffend. This optimism stems from ███'s rigid rule following. "███ is very rule-governed and cognitively rigid. While he may miss the social cues in his environment, once he learns the rules he will follow them." (Sperry Report at 8.) ███'s therapist referred to ███ as "quite a rule follower," (Plaud Report at 15) and ███'s mother recounted a story in which "███ was given detention as a Freshman in high school for running in the halls to get to class. He never ran again. Rather he would do a quick race-walk "move" to get to classes on time rather than risk being late to class." (Sperry Report at 40.) ███'s rigidity "plays a protective role in keeping him from crossing the line." Literally, while on house arrest, ███ would not cross the line, rather he would let his dogs out and stand at the door until they returned because he did not want to cross the threshold. (*Id.*)

Notably, Dr. Plaud, whose report examined ███'s "current risk to engage in further acts of sexual exploitation," concluded that "███ is a young man who is not driven or motivated by deviant or paraphilic sexual interests; his sexual interest pattern focused on post-pubescent females." (Plaud Report at 2-3.) Dr. Plaud further opined that ███

> Does not represent a significant risk to engage in hands-on or contact-based sexual offending at this time. . . ███'s current risk estimate for either hands-on or non-contact-based offenses is in a *very low* risk range, not consistent with an individual at this time who poses a risk to public safety.

(*Id.* at 3, emphasis supplied.)

CONCLUSION

This is not an ordinary § 2G2.1 case, and ███ is not an ordinary § 2G2.1 offender. ███ has taken responsibility for his actions and, with the help of therapy, now realizes that his conduct was both illegal and wrong. When considering the goals of sentencing a sentence of probation is sufficient but not greater than necessary to realize those goals. A probationary sentence, coupled with a period of home confinement and individualized terms and conditions of sex offender probation meet the goals of sentencing while still allowing ███ to get the physical and mental health treatment he needs to contribute to society in a positive way. To sentence ███ to a term of imprisonment would, at best, interrupt the rehabilitative progress he has made thus far. It is not hyperbole that at worst, a sentence of prison could be a death sentence. For the reasons stated above, ███ requests that this court sentence him to 5 years probation, home confinement with 5 years of concurrent supervised release.

Respectfully dated and submitted this 9th day of December, 2022.

LAW OFFICES OF ROBERT HERZ, P.C.

_____/s/ Robert M. Herz_____
Robert M. Herz
Attorney at Law
Alaska Bar No. 8706023

LAW OFFICES OF ELIZABETH KELLEY

_____/s/ Elizabeth Kelley_____
Elizabeth Kelley
Pro Hac Vice
Ohio Bar No. 0063641

UNITED STATES OF AMERICA	)	
Plaintiff	)	Criminal Case 21-CR-28
	)	
v.	)	Sentencing: August 29 & 31, 2023
	)	
WILLIAM ISAACS	)	Judge Amit P. Mehta
Defendant	)	

SUPPLEMENTAL SENTENCING MEMORANDUM

Defendant William Isaacs ("Defendant" or "Mr. Isaacs") hereby files a supplemental sentencing memorandum with this Honorable Court.

At the August 31, 2023, hearing, the Defendant's birth mother (Elizabeth Santoro, who testified at the trial) wishes to make a heartfelt statement to the Court about the trials and tribulations of his life. In addition to his earlier years as a child, she will also focus on 2018-21. Ms. Santoro, who shared joint custody of her son, will describe in more detail the three attached exhibits (photos), which counsel obtained late on August 24, 2023. The photos show the horrible moment when the Defendant was "kicked out" of his late father's home shortly after his own stepmother told him to leave during the *afternoon of his father's funeral.* An impeccably callous bit of timing for a fragile teen with ASD.

The Court may recall Mr. Isaacs' testimony about how he unsuccessfully tried to save the life of his twenty-five-year firefighter father (his hero), who had a secret addition to narcotics (morphine and Valium) that caused him to overdose in their home on January 30, 2019. Despite Mr. Isaacs' valiant efforts to provide CPR, the father may have perished in his arms.

His father's funeral was held a couple of days later. The photos show how his belongings were placed on the street by the stepmother either on the day of the funeral or shortly after. Mr. Isaacs then moved into a home along with his aging grandmother, who had serious mental health and medical issues. During 2019 to January 6, Mr. Isaacs led quite an isolated life living with his grandmother. His mother will describe how challenging that was for him.

Mr. Isaacs' mother, who has significant training in the area of ASD and has two sons diagnosed with it, will further describe the undue negative influence of his paternal aunt, who, unfortunately: (1) inserted herself into his life after her brother's death during a very dark period, (2) essentially "preyed upon and groomed William" with bizarre political conspiracy theories, (3) questioned whether the world was round or flat (per Mr. Isaacs, a sure sign of "insanity"), and (4) was for all intents and purposes--a controlling "political pedophile."

Ms. Santoro will further state that although her son was officially an older teenager in 2019, Mr. Isaacs' ASD made him a much younger teenager emotionally and socially. Thus, her son was more easily susceptible to the constant brainwashing barrage of political propaganda (e.g., the infamous "Big Lie"), as well as to the hate-filled prejudiced bile, from his manipulative aunt.

Respectfully submitted,

Friday 8/25/2023

Gene Rossi

Gene Rossi, Esquire
D.C Bar Number 367250
Carlton Fields, P.A.
Suite 400 West
1025 Thomas Jefferson Street, NW
Washington, DC 20007-5208
Telephone: 202-965-8119
Cell: 703-627-2856
Email: grossi@carltonfields.com

Natalie A. Napierala, Esquire
New York State Bar Number 2445468
Carlton Fields, P.A.
36th Floor
405 Lexington Avenue
New York, NY 10174-0002
Telephone: 212-785-2747
Email: nnapierala@carltonfields.com

Charles M. Greene, Esquire
Florida Bar Number 938963
Law Offices of Charles M. Greene, P.A.
55 East Pine Street
Orlando, FL 32801
Telephone: 407-648-1700
Email: cmg@cmgpa.com

Counsel for Defendant William Isaacs

CERTIFICATE OF SERVICE

I hereby certify that Mr. Isaacs' supplemental sentencing memorandum was filed

with the Clerk of the Court via ECF on Friday, August 25, 2023.

Respectfully submitted,

_____/s/_____
Gene Rossi, Esquire

UNITED STATES DISTRICT COURT
DISTRICT OF COLUMBIA

UNITED STATES OF AMERICA	)	
Plaintiff	)	Criminal Case 21-CR-28
	)	
v.	)	Sentencing: August 29 & 31, 2023
	)	
WILLIAM ISAACS	)	Judge Amit P. Mehta
Defendant	)	

SECOND SUPPLEMENTAL SENTENCING MEMORANDUM

Defendant William Isaacs ("Defendant" or "Mr. Isaacs") hereby files a second supplemental sentencing memorandum with this Honorable Court.

During the afternoon of Sunday, August 27, 2023, a letter (attached) apparently written by Defendant's uncle (Luis Hallon) was left at the home of Mr. Isaacs. Mr. Isaacs and his counsel neither asked for, solicited, nor were ever aware that such a letter would be written on his behalf.

Respectfully submitted,

_____/s/_____

Gene Rossi, Esquire
D.C Bar Number 367250
Carlton Fields, P.A.
Suite 400 West
1025 Thomas Jefferson Street, NW
Washington, DC 20007-5208
Telephone: 202-965-8119
Cell: 703-627-2856
Email: grossi@carltonfields.com

Natalie A. Napierala, Esquire
New York State Bar Number 2445468
Carlton Fields, P.A.
36th Floor

405 Lexington Avenue
New York, NY 10174-0002
Telephone: 212-785-2747
Email: nnapierala@carltonfields.com

Charles M. Greene, Esquire
Florida Bar Number 938963
Law Offices of Charles M. Greene, P.A.
55 East Pine Street
Orlando, FL 32801
Telephone: 407-648-1700
Email: cmg@cmgpa.com

Counsel for Defendant William Isaacs

CERTIFICATE OF SERVICE

I hereby certify that Mr. Isaacs' second supplemental sentencing memorandum

was filed with the Clerk of the Court via ECF on Monday, August 28, 2023.

Respectfully submitted,

_____/s/_____
Gene Rossi, Esquire

UNITED STATES DISTRICT COURT
DISTRICT OF COLUMBIA

UNITED STATES OF AMERICA	)	
Plaintiff	)	Criminal Case 21-CR-28
	)	
v.	)	Sentencing: August 29 & 31, 2023
	)	
WILLIAM ISAACS	)	Judge Amit P. Mehta
Defendant	)	

SENTENCING MEMORANDUM

Defendant William Isaacs ("Defendant" or "Mr. Isaacs") hereby files a sentencing memorandum with this Honorable Court.

RECOMMENDATION OF VARIANT SENTENCE

Pursuant to the factors set forth in 18 U.S.C. § 3553(a), this Court "shall impose a sentence *sufficient, but not greater than necessary*[.]" (emphasis added). In its Presentence Report ("PSR") for the Defendant, the U.S. Probation Office ("USPO") has a calculation under the U.S. Sentencing Guidelines ("USSG") of 70-87 months of incarceration (Level 27) before any downward variance.

However, the United States seems to recommend a sentence that is *vastly more than necessary* based on its contrary view of the USSG (Level 30): 97-121 months of imprisonment. Unlike the United States' request of up to 121 months in prison, the USPO has compassionately acknowledged and recognized the Defendant's unique personal history and characteristics. Toward that end, the USPO wisely recommends a 75% downward variance from the government's Level 30 request, i.e., a sentence of 24 months of imprisonment. The USPO justifies the variance because of Mr. Isaacs' ASD and his "long history of social problems."

By agreeing and objecting to some of the calculations by the USPO and the United States, the Defendant submits that the USSG should reflect a Level 13 (12-18 months). Although Mr. Isaacs is grateful for and agrees with the USPO's thoughtful USSG position of 24 months incarceration, he nonetheless seeks a further variance under § 3553(a). The Defendant respectfully asks this Court for a concurrent sentence of six months of home confinement, plus three years of supervision, for each of the seven counts of conviction.

THE ISOLATED AND UNIQUE LIFE OF MR. ISAACS

Notwithstanding the overly aggressive tone used by the United States in its sentencing memorandum (ECF Doc. 1021-1), William Andrew Isaacs was not the soldier wishing for and ready for battle and mayhem, when he travelled to and arrived in Washington, D.C. on January 6, 2021, at the impressionable age of 21. He was emotionally wounded, oftentimes a loner, socially isolated, an introvert, and a solitary figure. He was the perfect candidate for the negative and manipulative influence of his aunt Traci Isaacs, who frequently tried to poison his susceptible mind with absurd conspiracy theories and vile prejudices. From the time he was born in December 1999 and well before January 6, Mr. Isaacs has faced many emotional challenges, which are recognized by the USPO, which should neither be discounted, dismissed, nor ignored.

Mr. Isaacs has a deep and painful sense of shame, humiliation, remorse, and embarrassment for his actions on January 6. The United States wrongly asserts (emphasis added) that he came to Washington "*ready* to engage in political violence," "*ready* to use force to interfere with the certification of the election," "*prepared* for battle," and "willing to *resort to violence* against politicians who tried to stand in his way."

Putting aside its strained interpretation of the trial evidence, these rhetorical comments are belied by what Mr. Isaacs understands is the evidence in the possession of the United States. He travelled by car to Washington with two relatives (his aunt and her husband Luis Hallon) and a female acquaintance (Leslie Gray), all three of whom have pleaded guilty to January 6 criminal charges, for the purpose of providing security and to get EMT training. Mr. Isaacs is not aware of any inculpatory evidence from his fellow riders, whom the United States has apparently and extensively debriefed, to suggest that he had the mens rea and was *ready* to use force and engage in political violence of any kind on January 6.

Mr. Isaacs concedes that he bought protective gear to protect himself from the expected violence of counter protestors. He admits that he joined the Oath Keepers at the urging of his aunt. And he is ashamed. After reading of a false story about hotels and restaurants closing before January 6, he used disgraceful language to describe and show rage against Washington's Mayor in a hideous rant to his aunt, who often wallowed in, if not encouraged, racist comments from her nephew.

The Defendant came to Washington because he loves this country — not because he wanted to destroy it. He had a sense of excitement about being close to President Donald Trump, when he was to give the last significant speech of his career. For Mr.

Isaacs, he was part of history. For him, January 6 was a way for him to come out of his emotional shell—from his Navy discharge, the tragic death of his father, and even the strains of COVID pandemic—to witness a grand speech from a person whom he *then* revered directly in front of the White House. His trip was to get training to be an EMT. He fully intended to provide security to others, if not go back to his hotel and enjoy the rest of his trip with relatives. Sadly, the "Fight" speech he heard from the President was the spark that changed the mood of the rally from that of a peaceful gathering to an eventual assault on the Capitol. Mr. Isaacs painfully regrets that he succumbed to the uncontrolled emotions of that rally and later entered the Capitol.

At the sentencing, we will ask permission from the Court to hear testimony or a statement from his mother, who has expressed apprehension about filing a letter with the Court because of possible backlash from social media, which can been vitriolic, as well as violent. Nonetheless, Mr. Isaacs' mother will further explain, if not supplement, the difficulties that her impressionable son has had since he was born, the nefarious grooming of her son by his aunt, as well as the peaceful and *solitary* life he has led under very emotionally-challenging circumstances.

Mr. Isaacs' mother and father were married for several years, during which she gave birth to three sons: William; E.I.; and J.I. Mr. Isaacs (the oldest) and brother E.I. have been diagnosed with Autism Spectrum Disorder ("ASD"), about which this Court has heard significant testimony on *two* occasions (pretrial hearing and trial) from Doctor Laurie Sperry and the expert for the United States. Moreover, we incorporate by reference Dr. Sperry's January 1, 2023, report of her ASD findings and her testimony.

His brother E.I. lives in a group home because of his ASD. The youngest brother J.I. lives with their mother; J.I. is a rising senior in high school and may possibly have ASD. Suffice to write that the issue of ASD is something to which Mr. Isaacs has been confronting his entire life, as well as a challenge to other members of his family.

In his very early years (ages 2-4), his mother, who has training and experience in detecting and treating ASD as a social worker, quickly noticed possible signs of ASD in Mr. Isaacs, such as: flapping of hands under stress; coordination issues; "mind blindness" (per Dr. Sperry's testimony); anxiety and sensory overload in crowds; aversion to noise; social awkwardness; and the resistance to touching and hugging by others. Mr. Isaacs' mother sadly remembers how difficult the simple act of walking was to her son, who could barely perform the role of a ring bearer at her sister's wedding. When he was taken to get a haircut by his mother, he had memorable emotional outbursts, when he was merely touched by a barber. What were basic tasks to others his age became profoundly daunting hurdles to Mr. Isaacs.

In primary and middle schools (grades K-8), Mr. Isaacs had difficulties engaging in group activities. He often self-isolated and pushed back from social engagement with others in school. He continued to develop social isolation, but was still able to make a close friend when he was young: a fellow player on recreational baseball teams, which luckily were coached by his friend's father, who was exceedingly empathetic and understanding of the challenges that Mr. Isaacs was facing with ASD.

In April 2011 at age 11, the Defendant's parents separated and later divorced in October 2011. This was obviously traumatic for Mr. Isaacs. His father made every effort to unjustly isolate him from his mother, who, on paper, had joint custody. However, his father tried at every turn to persuade him and his brothers to disparage and loathe their mother. The father's actions to alienate his sons from the mother had a profoundly negative impact on Mr. Isaacs' already fragile emotional condition.

In high school, Mr. Isaacs became even more isolated from his fellow students. He did not participate in an organized school sport. He made no close friends. He did not attend proms, dances, or other social events. He did not have his senior photo taken. Mr. Isaacs attended high school, but was emotionally detached from the experience.

After he was graduated from high school, Mr. Isaacs joined the Navy in July 2018. Mr. Isaacs made this valiant attempt at public service to impress his father, whom he utterly revered, and give back to his country. His father was a firefighter for 25 years with a focus on emergency medical services. In no small irony, the Defendant's sense of duty was also driven by his ancestor Robert Fulton, whose statue is in Statuary Hall of the U.S. Capitol. Sadly, Mr. Isaacs failed boot camp miserably in significant part because of his ASD. He was discharged from the Navy October 2018. This discharge was extremely devastating to Mr. Isaacs. He felt as though he had failed his father and his country.

After his Navy discharge, Mr. Isaacs' life went from bad to worse. On January 30, 2019, he witnessed one of the most emotionally-scaring episodes of his life. In the early morning hours, his stepmother screamed that his father was passed out in their bathroom. Mr. Isaacs immediately rushed into the bathroom and found his father unconscious. He tried to give his father CPR, but was unsuccessful. He later learned that his father had become addicted to narcotics, which caused his overdose on January 30 in the arms of his son.

After his father's tragic death, one would think that Mr. Isaacs' life could not get any worse. Yet, it did. Sadly, his paternal aunt Traci became more involved and tried to fill the obviously painful void in his life. Unfortunately, all his aunt did was fill his vulnerable mind with dark and dangerous thoughts. Memorably, Mr. Isaacs testified at trial that his aunt questioned whether the earth was flat or round: "And that in itself is a sign of insanity." He was right on that point.

Shortly before January 6, she successfully persuaded him to nominally join the Oath Keepers, for which he did little, if anything, other than obtain a T-shirt. The group would be good for his recovery from the loss of his father. She pleaded with him to travel to the rally on January 6. She advised that the trip would be good for him. She promised to be with him the entire time of the trip. Sadly, his aunt would be the sine qua non that brought him to our Nation's Capitol, where all Mr. Isaacs truly wanted to there do was get EMT training, help with security, see the tourist sights, and listen to the last important speech by President Donald Trump in front of the White House.

OBJECTIONS AND RECOMMENDATIONS FOR USSG CALCULATION

Again, Mr. Isaacs submits that the USSG should be Level 13 (12-18 months); whereas, the calculations by the USPO and the United States are Level 27 (70-87 months) and Level 30 (97-121), respectively. The Defendant agrees to 14 levels before adjustments, i.e., a base offense level of 14 (§ 2J1.2(a)).

The Defendant takes the following positions with respect to other calculations: (1) agrees with the United States to a one-level upward departure for terrorism (§ 3A1.4, comment. (n.4)); (2) opposes the denial by the USPO and United States of two levels for acceptance of responsibility (§ 3E1.1(a)); (3) opposes two levels for scope, planning, preparation (§ 2J1.2(b)(3)); (4) seeks four levels for mitigating role, whereas the USPO has recommended only two levels and the United States opposes any reduction (§ 3B1.2(a)); (5) opposes eight levels for person or property damage in order to obstruct the administration of justice (§ 2J1.2(b)(1)(B)); and (6) opposes three levels for interference in administration of justice (§ 2J1.2(b)(2)).

I. The Offense Level Should Be Reduced for Acceptance of Responsibility.

Under USSG § 3E1.1(a), a two-level reduction in the base offense level is appropriate when a "defendant clearly demonstrates acceptance of responsibility for his offense[.]" While "[t]his adjustment is not intended to apply to a defendant who puts the government to its burden of proof at trial by denying the essential factual elements of guilt, is convicted, and only then admits guilt and expresses remorse," a defendant's conviction at trial "does not *automatically preclude* a defendant from consideration for such a reduction." § 3E1.1 cmt. n. 2 (emphasis added); *see United States v. Shepherd*, 857 F. Supp. 105, 108, n. 8 (D.D.C. 1994); *United States v. Gauvin*, 173 F.3d 798 (10th Cir. 1999). Indeed,

> [i]n rare situations, a defendant may clearly demonstrate an acceptance of responsibility for his criminal conduct even though he exercises his constitutional right to a trial. This may occur, for example, where a defendant goes to trial to assert and preserve issues that do not relate to factual guilt (e.g. to make . . . a

challenge to the applicability of a statute to his conduct). In each
such instance, a determination that a defendant has accepted
responsibility will be based primarily upon pre-trial statements
and conduct.

USSG § 3E1.1 cmt. n. 2.

United States v. Gauvin, supra, is instructive. In *Gauvin,* the defendant was
convicted of assault with a dangerous weapon and assault on a federal officer. *Gauvin,*
173 F.3d at 801. Even though the defendant went to trial and was convicted, he was
given a two-level reduction based on acceptance of responsibility. *Id.* at 806. According
to the court, "Mr. Gauvin admitted to all the conduct with which he was charged. He
simply disputed whether his acknowledged factual state of mind met the legal criteria
of intent to harm or cause apprehension." *Id.* In the district court's view, that sort of
purely legal challenge to a conviction was exactly the kind of rare circumstance in
which a two-level reduction was warranted. *Id.* The Tenth Circuit affirmed. *Id.*

As in *Gauvin,* this is one of those rare situations in which a two-level reduction is
warranted, even though Mr. Isaacs went to trial. Mr. Isaacs admitted, from the start, the
primary factual underpinnings of the case against him. Indeed, Mr. Isaacs has never
disputed the conduct underlying his convictions. However, he has vigorously
challenged whether his state of mind met the legal criteria of intent that constitutes a
federal offense. Those are exactly the kinds of purely legal challenges anticipated by
and provided for in the USSG. Accordingly, Mr. Isaacs should receive a two-level
departure for acceptance of responsibility.

Mr. Isaacs submits that the obstruction of justice enhancement, pursuant to

§ 3C1.1, should not apply in this case. However, if this Court does apply the obstruction

of justice enhancement, Mr. Isaacs still maintains that his base offense level should be

reduced by two levels for his acceptance of responsibility, pursuant to § 3E1.1.

Although the USSG state that an adjustment for acceptance of responsibility

"ordinarily" is not available when a court imposes an adjustment under § 3C1.1, in

"extraordinary cases," both §§ 3C1.1 and 3E1.1 may apply. USSG § 3E1.1, cmt. n. 4; *see*

United States v. Kelly, 169 F. Supp. 2d 171, 174 (S.D.N.Y. 2001) (defendant still received

acceptance reduction despite hindering criminal investigation, suborning perjury and

taking case through trial to verdict); *United States v. Restrepo*, 936 F.2d 661, 669 (2d

Cir.1991) (approving district court's application of adjustments pursuant to both § 3C1.1

and § 3E1.1).

"[W]here a defendant sought to plead guilty to the very charge a jury later

convicted him of, a reduction pursuant to § 3E1.1 is appropriate, notwithstanding his

earlier attempts to evade justice." *Kelly*, 169 F. Supp. 2d at 174. In *U.S. v. Kelly*, the

defendant was charged with the felony of intimidating a witness, and attempted to

plead guilty to misdemeanor witness harassment before trial. *Id.* at 173. However, the

U.S. Attorney's Misdemeanor Committee refused the plea offer and the government

took the defendant to trial on the felony. *Id.* Kelly was ultimately convicted of

misdemeanor harassment rather than felony intimidation. *Id.* "Under the circumstances," the court concluded, "Kelly's demonstrated willingness to take responsibility for the conduct of which a jury ultimately found him guilty satisfies the requisites of § 3E1.1 and warrants a two-point reduction." *Id.* The court reasoned, "Kelly did seek to accept responsibility formally for his criminal conduct before trial, and it was the government's choice, not his, to proceed." *Id.*

Similarly, Mr. Isaacs' demonstrated willingness to take responsibility by seeking to plead guilty. Through his counsel, Mr. Isaacs engaged in extensive plea deal negotiations with the Assistant United States Attorneys ("AUSA"). Notably, on December 27, 2022, Mr. Isaacs' counsel informed the AUSA, "[i]f you get approval, [Mr. Isaacs] will accept your December 20 plea offer of Counts 3 and 6." The Government, however, ultimately declined the plea terms and opted to proceed to a jury trial.

The United States, and not Mr. Isaacs, chose to pursue a trial. Mr. Isaacs instead sought to take responsibility for his actions, for which a jury ultimately found him guilty. Thus, he should receive a two-level reduction in his base offense level under USSG § 3E 1.1.

II. As a Minimal Participant, Mr. Isaacs Should Receive a Four-Level Reduction.

Under USSG § 3B1.2, an offense level may be adjusted downward if the defendant had a mitigating role in the offense. Specifically, the USSG provide that the offense level should be decreased by four levels if the defendant was a minimal participant in the criminal activity, two levels if the defendant was a minor participant in the criminal activity, and three levels in intermediate cases. *See* USSG § 3B1.2.

The commentary to USSG § 3B1.2(a) states that the minimal role reduction is appropriate for a defendant who, like Mr. Isaacs, is "plainly among the least culpable of those involved in the conduct of a group." USSG § 3B1.2 cmt. n. 4. The defendant's "lack of knowledge or understanding of the scope and structure of the enterprise and of the activities of others is indicative of a role as minimal participant." *Id.* By contrast, the USSG define a "minor participant" as any participant "who is less culpable than most other participants, but whose role should not be described as minimal." USSG § 3B1.2 cmt. n. 5.

The determination of whether a defendant qualifies as a minimal or minor participant must be made in the context "of the facts of the particular case" and "turns, in large part, upon consideration of the defendant's actual role relative to that of the co-participants and in light of the circumstances giving rise to the crime charged." *United States v. Ingram*, 816 F. Supp. 26, 35 (D.D.C. 1993); USSG § 3B1.2 cmt. n. 3(C). This determination is based on the "totality of circumstances," which may include:

i.   the degree to which the defendant understood the scope and structure of the criminal activity;
ii. the degree to which the defendant participated in planning or organizing the criminal activity;
iii. the degree to which the defendant exercised decision-making authority or influenced the exercise of decision-making authority;
iv. the nature and extent of the defendant's participation in the commission of the criminal activity, including the acts the defendant performed and the responsibility and discretion the defendant had in performing those acts; and
v.   the degree to which the defendant stood to benefit from the criminal activity.

id. n.3.

Although the USPO recommends a two-level reduction for Mr. Isaacs as a minor participant, the totality of the circumstances supports a four-level reduction as a minimal participant. *See* PSR ¶ 130; ECF Doc. 1021-1 at 30-31. First, Mr. Isaacs lacked understanding of the criminal activity's scope and structure. Other than communicating with his aunt before January 6 mostly about routine travel plans, he had minimal knowledge, if any, of the nefarious motives of others, including those who brought firearms to January 6.

Second, he had no role in planning or organizing the criminal activity. Indeed, the Government acknowledges that while Defendants Rhodes, Kelly Meggs, and Watkins participated in "the creation and use of encrypted messaging services and meeting platforms to assist with planning and coordination, and preparations to have an armed QRF to support co-conspirators on the ground inside of D.C," Mr. Isaacs "did not personally participate in all of this relevant conduct." ECF Doc. 1021-1 at 30.

Third, Mr. Isaacs held absolutely no decision-making authority or leadership position within the Oath Keepers and was not part of any leadership chat groups. He was a "minor player[] in the overarching conspiracy." PSR ¶ 183; ECF Doc. 1010 at 2.

Fourth, the Government relies on Mr. Isaacs' actions of moving "to the front of 'Line One'" and "waiv[ing] others down the hallways toward the Senate Chamber yelling, 'The fight's not over!'" as evidence against minimal participation, yet these actions highlight his limited involvement, supporting his case as a minimal participant. ECF Doc. 1021-1 at 31-32.

Fifth and last, Mr. Isaacs had no potential gains from the criminal activity. Accordingly, Mr. Isaacs was a minimal participant in the conspiracy, justifying a four-level reduction.

III. A Two-Level Increase for Conduct Extensive in Scope, Planning, or Preparation (§ 2J1.2(b)(3)(C)) Is Unjustified.

The PSR incorrectly suggests that a two-level enhancement should be added to Mr. Isaacs' guidelines under USSG § 2J1.2(b) for an offense that was allegedly "extensive in scope, planning, or preparation." § 2J1.2(b)(C). While the overall scheme may have displayed extensive traits, Mr. Isaacs' involvement was limited and fails to justify a two-level increase.

First, Mr. Isaacs was not a leader of the Oath Keepers or the conspiracy; instead, he was a "minor player[] in the overarching conspiracy." ECF Doc. 1010 at 2; *see* ECF Doc. 1021-1 at 30-31; PSR ¶¶ 130, 183.

Second, the Government concedes that while Rhodes, Kelly Meggs, and Watkins participated in "the creation and use of encrypted messaging services and meeting platforms to assist with planning and coordination, and preparations to have an armed QRF to support co-conspirators on the ground inside of D.C," Mr. Isaacs "did not personally participate in all of this relevant conduct." ECF Doc. 1021-1 at 30.

Finally, Mr. Isaacs did not partake in a key conference call that the PSR claims "sketched out the details of how the defendants would achieve their objective." PSR ¶ 63. Accordingly, Mr. Isaacs' limited role in the conspiracy does not amount to the extensive scope, planning, or preparation that would warrant a two-level increase.

IV.   Isaacs Did Not Willfully Obstruct Justice or Commit Perjury.

Mr. Isaacs should not receive a two-level enhancement under USSG § 3C1.1

because he did not willfully obstruct justice or commit perjury. This enhancement

applies only if:

> (1) the defendant willfully obstructed or impeded, or attempted to
> obstruct or impede, the administration of justice with respect to the
> investigation, prosecution, or sentencing of the instant offense of
> conviction, and (2) the obstructive conduct related to (A) the defendant's
> offense of conviction and any relevant conduct; or (B) a closely related
> offense.

USSG § 3C1.1.

Application Note 2 of USSG § 3C1.1 sets forth *limitations* to this enhancement that apply

to Mr. Isaacs' conduct and testimony:

> In applying this provision in respect to alleged false testimony or
> statements by the defendant, the court should be cognizant that inaccurate
> testimony or statements sometimes may result from confusion, mistake, or
> faulty memory and, thus, not all inaccurate testimony or statements
> necessarily reflect a willful attempt to obstruct justice.

USSG § 3C1.1 cmt. n. 2.

Additionally, an enhancement for perjury at trial under this section can be

imposed only if the defendants gave "false testimony concerning a *material* matter with

the *willful intent* to provide false testimony, rather than as a result of confusion, mistake,

or faulty memory." *U.S. v. Smith*, 374 F.3d 1240, 1245 (D.C. Cir. 2004) (emphasis added).

Here, the USPO and United States suggest a two-level enhancement based on

allegations that Mr. Isaacs "falsely testified, under oath, that he did not understand the

meaning of the word 'Rubicon' in his message of December 23, 2020," and that he originally claimed he did not know why he yelled, "The fight's not over!," but later testified he was speaking of "a verbal First Amendment fight." However, these alleged discrepancies are not material to this case as they have failed to have a substantial bearing on Mr. Isaacs' culpability and, therefore, are insufficient to warrant a two-level enhancement under USSG § 3C1.1.

Likewise, there was nothing willful about Mr. Isaacs' testimony and alleged immaterial inaccuracies. When he testified at trial, Mr. Isaacs tried his best under stressful conditions in front of the jury to answer a truthful as he could.

Moreover, many of the cases the United States relies upon for this enhancement involve defendants who destroyed and/or had someone else destroy material evidence. *See* ECF Doc. 1021-1 at 32-33. Mr. Isaacs, however, *never* concealed or destroyed evidence, and the Government has not alleged that he did so. Accordingly, these case facts and holdings offer no support for this enhancement's application to Mr. Isaacs' sentence.

Finally, the trial's last witness (Officer Harry Dunn), who was called by the United States, provided exculpatory testimony that belies the assertion that Mr. Isaacs was a leader of an angry mob inside the Capitol, when he yelled "the fight's not over!" What Officer Dunn said was very instructive. Countless persons inside the Capitol were chanting and *repeating* this exact phrase. With his ASD, we should not be surprised that he too repeated this phrase, which was pervasive inside the Capitol. When he said his statement was a "verbal First Amendment fight," he was truthful.

V.   Mr. Isaacs' Youth Warrants a Downward Departure.

At the mere age of 21 on January 6, Mr. Isaacs is one of the youngest defendants from among the approximately 1,000 January 6 cases. This youthfulness merits a downward departure under U.S.S.G § 5H1.1, which states:

> "Age (*including youth*) may be relevant in determining whether a departure is warranted, if considerations based on age, individually or in combination with other offender characteristics, are present to an unusual degree and distinguish the case from the typical cases covered by the guidelines."

Indeed, adolescents "are constitutionally different from adults for sentencing purposes," as "adolescent brains are not yet fully mature in regions and systems related to higher-order executive functions such as impulse control, planning ahead, and risk avoidance." *Miller v. Alabama*, 567 U.S. 460, 471-472 n.5 (2012) (internal quotation marks and citation omitted). This immaturity and underdeveloped sense of responsibility leads to recklessness, impulsivity, and heedless risk-taking. *Id.* Additionally, adolescents are particularly vulnerable to negative external pressures from peers and less able to escape their social context. *Graham v. Florida*, 130 S. Ct. 2011, 2026 (2010).

Here, Mr. Isaacs' limited maturity and underdeveloped sense of responsibility led to impulsive actions and susceptibility to the mob mentality on January 6th. His prolonged exposure to influence, especially from his aunt, played a pivotal role in shaping his actions on that day. While this does not excuse his actions, Mr. Isaacs' age-related lack of maturity and impulsiveness must be factored into his sentencing. Since January 6, Mr. Isaacs has demonstrated his commitment to making amends and becoming a productive member of our nation. Accordingly, Mr. Isaacs respectfully requests that this Court acknowledge his youth and apply a downward departure.

VI.   The Eight-Level Enhancement at USSG § 2J1.2(B)(1)(B) is Inapplicable.

The PSR (ECF Doc. 1009, par. 157), applies an eight-level enhancement pursuant to USSG § 2J1.2(b)(1)(B), which provides that "[i]f the offense involved causing or threatening to cause physical injury to a person, or property damage, in order to obstruct the administration of justice, increase by 8 levels." Mr. Isaacs submits that this enhancement is inapplicable here, both as a legal and factual matter.

A.   Electoral Certification Does Not Constitute the "Administration of Justice" Under a Plain Language Interpretation of USSG § 2J1.2(B)(1)(B).

For the eight-level enhancement to attach, the Guidelines require that the described conduct have been undertaken in order to obstruct the "administration of justice." In *United States v. Seefried*, No. 21-cr-287 (TNM) (D.D.C. October 31, 2022), Judge McFadden issued a thorough opinion explaining why, as a legal matter, the eight-level enhancement is inapplicable to the January 6 defendants because the electoral certification, the proceeding the defendants are charged with obstructing, does not constitute the "administration of justice" under the meaning of the guidelines. The undersigned is aware that this Court is familiar with the *Seefried* opinion and declined to adopt its reasoning in *United States v. Wood*, No. 21-CR-223 (APM) (ECF Doc. 64). Mr. Isaacs respectfully asks that this Court reconsider its rejection of the reasoning in *Seefried*. To that end, this memorandum addresses the issues that this Court raised at

Mr. Wood's sentencing hearing while stating its disagreement with Judge McFadden's analysis. A brief review of the key points in *Seefried* provides a helpful framework.

First, a plain reading of the phrase "administration of justice," as informed by relevant dictionary definitions, establishes that this phrase refers to judicial or quasi-judicial proceedings, and related activities, involving the determination of legal rights.

Second, a contextual analysis, reviewing the Sentencing Commission's relevant commentary and utilizing corpus linguistics to better understand trends of usage, bolsters that "administration of justice" most naturally refers to judicial proceedings or closely related activities.

Third, United States Supreme Court and Circuit Court precedent affirms Judge McFadden's interpretation.

Courts "interpret the Sentencing Guidelines using the ordinary tools of statutory interpretation." *United States v. Martinez*, 870 F.3d 1163, 1166 (9th Cir. 2017). Thus, the inquiry into meaning "will most often begin and end with the text and structure of the Guidelines." *Id.* (citation omitted). "The language of the Sentencing Guidelines, like the language of a statute, must be given its plain and ordinary meaning." *United States v. Fulford*, 662 F.3d 1174, 1177 (11th Cir. 2011). To discern a text's plain meaning, courts often look to dictionary definitions, in addition to analyzing the word or phrase in context. *See, e.g., Kaufman v. Nielsen*, 896 F.3d 475, 485–87 (D.C. Cir. 2018).

   i.   **Dictionary Definitions.**

At the sentencing hearing in *Wood*, this Court noted that Black's Law Dictionary defines certain terms arguably related to the administration of justice more broadly than the narrower definition that *Seefried* cites. Black's defines the "administration of justice" as "[t]he *maintenance of right* within a political community by means of the physical force of the state; the state's application of the sanction of force *to the rule of right*." *Administration of Justice*, Black's Law Dictionary (11th ed. 2019) (in this section, all emphasis is supplied, unless otherwise noted). It similarly defines "due administration of justice" as "[t]he proper functioning and integrity *of a court or other tribunal* and the proceedings before it *in accordance with the rights guaranteed to the parties*." *Id.*

While these definitions support a narrow interpretation of the phrase to mean judicial or quasi-judicial proceedings, and related activities, involving the determination of legal rights, in *Wood*, the Government looked to the broader definition of "justice." That definition includes the "fair and proper administration of laws." *Justice*, Black's Law Dictionary (11th ed. 2019). But the utility of dictionary definitions diminishes if we ignore how the word is used syntactically. In § 2J1.2(b)(1)(B), "justice" is the subject of "administration." As Black's provides a definition specifically for the full phrase "administration of justice," there is no compelling reason to stretch that definition by zeroing in on sub-definitions of the individual words within the larger phrase.

The importance of the larger phrase is underscored by the Government's reliance in *Wood* on the definition of "obstruction of justice"; i.e. "[i]nterference with the orderly administration of law and justice, *as by* giving false information to or withholding evidence from a police officer or prosecutor, or by harming or intimidating a witness or juror." *Obstruction of Justice*, Black's Law Dictionary (11th ed. 2019). At the outset, the fact that Black's supplies separate definitions for "administration of justice" and "obstruction of justice" only further demonstrates that these phrases are not interchangeable. This distinction finds support in case law. *See United States v. Warlick,* 742 F.2d 113, 115-16 (4th Cir. 1984):

> *Obstruction of the administration of justice is not to be confused with obstruction of justice.* Justice may be obstructed by mere inaction, but obstruction of the administration of justice requires something more — some act that will interrupt the orderly process of the administration of justice, or thwart the judicial process.

But even if this Court finds value in the definition of "obstruction of justice" as a related phrase, this definition does not undercut the conclusion that the electoral certification is not contemplated by § 2J1.2(b)(1)(B). If anything, this definition bolsters the interpretation of "administration of justice" as judicial or quasi-judicial proceedings, and related activities, involving the determination of legal rights. The "obstruction of justice" definition provides that such conduct is undertaken "by giving false information to or withholding evidence from a police officer or prosecutor, or by harming or intimidating a witness or juror." The investigatory activities implicated by this definition fit squarely within the universe of judicial and quasi-judicial processes. Perhaps more notably, this definition does *not* implicate ceremonial proceedings that have no adjudicatory function, such as the electoral certification.

Finally, Black's definition of "contempt" does not support a broader interpretation. "Contempt" is defined to include "[c]onduct that defies the authority or dignity of a court *or legislature*," with the definition adding that "[b]ecause such conduct interferes with the *administration of justice*, it is punishable." Reaching for this attenuated definition of "contempt" to assign meaning to "administration of justice" is simply unnecessary when this phrase is itself defined in the same dictionary. Further, contempt as it relates to the legislature is wholly irrelevant in Mr. Isaacs' case. Contempt in the legislative context arises in quasi-judicial inquiries, generally applying where congressional witnesses fail to comply with subpoenas. Such quasi-judicial, fact-finding functions of the legislature may very well fit within the definition of "administration of justice." But the electoral certification is not one of those quasi-judicial legislative proceedings.

Because the above definitions of terms distinct from, but arguably related to, the "administration of justice" are all either irrelevant or actually bolster the narrower interpretation of the term, the eight-level enhancement at § 2J1.2(b)(1)(B) is legally inapplicable.

ii. Section 2J1.2's Application to Statutory Offenses Unrelated to Judicial Proceedings.

This Court in *Wood* considered that § 2J1.2, as a whole, applies to various statutory offenses which do not involve interference with judicial or quasi-judicial proceedings. But the fact that § 2J1.2, as a whole, includes enhancements applicable to a wider range offenses does not mean that every subsection must be applicable to every offense that the broader section applies to. Reading subsection 2J1.2(b)(1)(B) as applying only to a certain sub-category of offenses, while other subsections similarly apply only to different sub-categories, is perfectly consistent with reading the various enhancements within § 2J1.2 as individual pieces of a larger whole.

iii. Sentencing Committee Commentary.

Initially, Mr. Isaacs submits that reliance on Sentencing Committee commentary is unwarranted where the plain language of the text and relevant dictionary definitions provide clear guidance. *See, e.g., Martinez*, 870 F.3d at 1166; *Fulford*, 662 F.3d at 1177; *Kaufman*, 896 F.3d at 485–87. Nevertheless, to the extent such commentary is relevant, this commentary does not undermine the above analysis.

This Court in *Wood* observed that the commentary accompanying § 2J1.2 defines "substantial interference with the administration of justice" as "includ[ing] a premature or improper termination of a felony investigation; an indictment, verdict, or any judicial determination based upon perjury, false testimony, or other false evidence; or the unnecessary expenditure of substantial governmental or court resources." The first two clauses of this definition, discussing felony investigations, indictments, verdicts, and the like, relate directly to judicial proceedings.

Concededly, when read alone, the last clause ("the unnecessary expenditure of substantial governmental or court resources") appears to broaden the definition beyond activities related to judicial proceedings. But this clause must be read in the context of the full sentence. *See* Antonin Scalia & Brian A. Garner, *Reading Law: The Interpretation of Legal Texts* 195-98 (2012) (explaining that words "associated in a context suggesting that [they] have something in common . . . should be given related meanings" under the *noscitur a sociis* canon). Read against the two proceeding clauses, "the unnecessary expenditure of substantial governmental or court resources" is most naturally understood as referring to resources utilized in the category of judicial activities specifically enumerated in the preceding clauses.

The *ejusdem generis* canon, a related interpretative tool, bolsters this reading. "General words in a statute are construed to embrace only objects similar in nature to those objects enumerated by the preceding specific words." 73 Am. Jur. 2d *Statutes* § 118 (2023). Here, the final clause should be read as a catchall term encompassing the larger category of activities implicated by the specific items enumerated before it; i.e., activities that all relate to judicial proceedings. When informed by the context of the earlier clauses, the final clause cannot fairly be stretched to encompass a proceeding as remote as the electoral certification. Thus, assuming that committee commentary is due any deference, this commentary supports the preceding plain language analysis.

iv.   Summation.

As the foregoing argument demonstrates, the electoral certification does not constitute the "administration of justice" under a plain language interpretation of USSG § 2J1.2(b)(1)(B). *See also United States v. Richardson*, 676 F.3d 491, 502-03 (5th Cir. 2012) ("[O]bstructing the due administration of justice means 'interfering with the procedure of a judicial hearing or trial.'"); *United States v. Brenson*, 104 F.3d 1267, 1279-80 (11th Cir. 1997) (The "due administration of justice" means "judicial procedure" and "the performance of acts required by law in the discharge of duties such as appearing as a witness and giving thoughtful testimony when subpoenaed."); *Warlick*, 742 F.2d at 115-16 ("[O]bstruction of the administration of justice requires . . . some act that will interrupt the orderly process of the administration of justice, or thwart the judicial process.").

B.   Mr. Isaacs' Conduct Was Not Sufficient to Trigger the USSG § 2J1.2(B)(1)(B) Enhancement as a Factual Matter.

Even if this Court disagrees with the foregoing and concludes that the enhancement is legally applicable, the facts of Mr. Isaacs' conduct necessitate that the eight-level enhancement be removed. As this Court is aware, the enhancement requires that the offense involve "causing or threatening to cause physical injury to a person, or property damage, in order to obstruct the administration of justice." Mr. Isaacs' actions, while wrong and deeply regrettable, do not meet this threshold, just as this Court found as to the defendant in *Wood*.

Mr. Isaacs did not personally assault officers. Mr. Isaacs did not personally damage property. At most, the Government might be able to assert that Mr. Isaacs was a part of larger mobs that pushed toward or confronted police. This Court, however, rejected a similar argument in *Wood*, finding the defendant's role in a mob was insufficient to trigger the enhancement where the defendant was one step removed from direct confrontation with the line of police officers. *Wood*, No. 21-CR-223 (APM) [Doc. 64 at 30:18-31:15]. Judge Friedrich likewise found, in *United States v. Reid*, No. 21-CR-316 (DLF) [Doc. 59], that the enhancement was unwarranted where the defendant was part of a mob, but was not, himself, pushing police officers. *See Reid*, 21-CR-316 (DLF) (ECF Doc. 59 at 17:12-17:17):

[THE COURT:] Any of those confrontations physical? I know he was towards the front of some scrums, but do you -- I couldn't see him pushing or --

[PROSECUTION:] No, we're not suggesting that he did any pushing. We're suggesting that he was a part of those sort of mob actions of pushing through the police lines.

Thus, if this Court chooses to apply section 2J1.2(b)(1)(B) as a legal matter, it should nonetheless find that the eight-level enhancement is not triggered because Mr. Isaacs' conduct did not rise to the level of causing or threatening to cause physical injury to a person or property.

VII. The Three-Level Enhancement for Interference with the Administration of Justice (§ 2J1.2(b)(2)) is Legally Inapplicable.

For the reasons described in Section VI.A. *supra*, Mr. Isaacs submits that the three-level enhancement at USSG § 2J1.2(b)(2) is legally inapplicable because the electoral certification does not constitute the "administration of justice" under the meaning of the guidelines.

SENTENCING FACTORS

Again, pursuant to 18 U.S.C. § 3553(a) ("Imposition of a sentence"), this Court is required to impose a sentence that is "*sufficient, but not greater than necessary*" to comply with four purposes (goals) of § 3553(a)(2)(A)-(D) and hereby summarized: (1) to reflect the seriousness of the offense, promote respect for the law, and to provide for just punishments for the offense; (2) adequate deterrence; (3) protect the public from further crimes of the defendant; and (4) provide training, medical care, or other correctional treatment.

In striving for a sentence that meets some or all of these purposes and goals, this Court shall consider the seven factors of § 3553(a)(1)-(7). We respectfully submit that the history and characteristics of Mr. Isaacs, whose life story has often been filled with heart-wrenching moments, provide a profound basis for showing him compassion. Moreover, there is no reason to believe that he will not be forever shamed by his actions on January 6; this shame alone will be incentive for him to comply with the law. Last, we submit that a variance from the USSG is fully warranted and consistent with the goals set forth in this section.

CONCLUSION

Mr. William Isaacs asks that this Honorable Court impose a sentence of six months of home confinement, plus three years of supervision, for each of the seven counts of conviction.

Respectfully submitted,

_____/s/_____
Gene Rossi, Esquire
D.C Bar Number 367250
Carlton Fields, P.A.
Suite 400 West
1025 Thomas Jefferson Street, NW
Washington, DC 20007-5208
Telephone: 202-965-8119
Cell: 703-627-2856
Email: grossi@carltonfields.com

Natalie A. Napierala, Esquire
New York State Bar Number 2445468
Carlton Fields, P.A.
36th Floor
405 Lexington Avenue
New York, NY 10174-0002

Telephone: 212-785-2747
Email: nnapierala@carltonfields.com

Charles M. Greene, Esquire
Florida Bar Number 938963
Law Offices of Charles M. Greene, P.A.
55 East Pine Street
Orlando, FL 32801
Telephone: 407-648-1700
Email: cmg@cmgpa.com

Counsel for Defendant William Isaacs

CERTIFICATE OF SERVICE

I hereby certify that Mr. Isaacs' sentencing memorandum was filed with the Clerk of the Court via ECF on Monday, August 21, 2023.

Respectfully submitted,

_____/s/_____
Gene Rossi, Esquire

Thirteen

The internet has become a vital tool for communication and connection, especially for autistic individuals, who may find it easier to interact online due to its structured and predictable nature. However, this increased online activity is monitored by electronic service providers (ESPs) like Google and Meta, which are legally required to report suspected child exploitation under US Code 2252. In 2023, nearly 36 million CyberTipline Reports were submitted by ESPs, with major platforms like Facebook, Instagram, and Discord being among the top reporters. This automated monitoring can inadvertently sweep autistic individuals into investigations, as they may unintentionally interact with minors online without malicious intent.

Autistic individuals often relate more comfortably to younger people and may use platforms like Discord, which is popular among both autistic individuals and minors. Discord's structured environment and non-verbal communication options make it appealing to neurodivergent users, but this can lead to interactions with minors that are misinterpreted as predatory. Legal cases have shown that autistic individuals can face severe sentences for unintentional offenses, as their actions are not always distinguished from those with deviant intentions. For example, in several US court cases, sentences for autistic defendants were upheld despite their diagnoses, highlighting the need for better understanding and differentiation in legal proceedings.

Hacking is another area where autistic individuals may find themselves in legal trouble, due to their analytical and problem-solving skills. While many autistic individuals engage in hacking for the challenge rather than malicious intent, the legal system often does not differentiate between motivations. Cases like that of Gary McKinnon, who hacked US government computers in search of extraterrestrial information, illustrate how autistic individuals can unintentionally cross legal boundaries. The use of technology to commit crimes is

DOI: 10.4324/9781003540571-14

considered an aggravating factor in sentencing, which can further complicate legal outcomes for autistic individuals. As technology evolves, it is crucial to address these issues to ensure fair treatment and understanding of neurodivergent individuals in the legal system.

AUTOMATED MONITORING OF CHILD EXPLOITATION

With the advent of Web 2, the internet we know today with its dynamic content, social networking, and cloud services, our ability to connect and communicate with others online has become easier than ever. The internet has now furnished an environment in which people can communicate freely without fear of judgment or exposure to uncomfortable and inescapable situations, which is especially attractive to autistic individuals. However, the activity transmitted over the internet is owned, controlled, and monitored by the electronic service providers[1] that supply the services that have become part of our daily routine. Every email received, chat sent, or photo synced to your account is controlled by Apple, Google, Microsoft, or the like. These providers can use sophisticated and autonomous software to scan it for safety and monetary reasons such as teaching artificial intelligence machines, selling information to corporations for targeted advertising, improving algorithms for discovery content, and reporting criminal activity. This automated software monitoring consequently examines the behaviors of autistic individuals online and can sweep them into a net of cybercriminals in which they do not belong.

Pursuant to United States Code 2258A, electronic service providers, such as Google and Meta, must report instances of suspected child exploitation, including access to child sexual abuse material, entice-ment of minors, and sending obscene material to minors. According to the National Center for Missing and Exploited Children,[2] nearly 36 million CyberTipline Reports[3] were submitted by electronic ser-vice providers pursuant to this statute in 2023 alone (NCMEC, 2023 *CyberTipline Reports by Electronic Service Providers*). The top providers submit-ting CyberTipline Reports were those most popular among minors, including Meta platforms Facebook and Instagram, WhatsApp, Snapchat, TikTok, Discord, and Reddit (see Figure 13.1).

Because autistic individuals naturally relate to younger individ-uals and can more comfortably communicate with others using web-based platforms, these reports will invariably identify autistic individuals who communicate with users online whom the National Center for Missing and Exploited Children or sophisticated software have flagged as possible minors. These reports, however, do not distinguish between intentional luring or grooming of minors by individuals with pedophilic tendencies and unintentional access that lacks the patterns and characteristics of a deviant sexual interest in minors. This continuum of behavior may be prosecuted and sentenced the same nonetheless:

1. In *United States v. Ziska*, 602 Fed. App'x. 284, 292 (6th Cir. 2015), a sentence of 180 months was upheld as substantively reasonable despite the defendant's ASD diagnosis.
2. In *United States v. Sindoni*, 510 Fed. App'x. 906 (11th Cir. 2013), a sentence of 200 months was upheld as reasonable despite the defendant's ASD diagnosis and age.
3. In *United States v. Dolehide*, 663 F.3d 343 (8th Cir. 2011), a sentence of 135 months was upheld despite the defendant's ASD diagnosis.

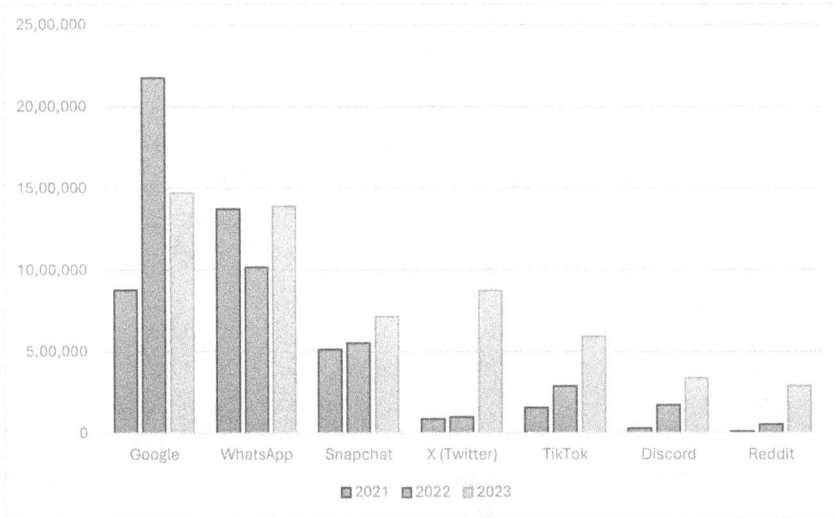

Figure 13.1 National Center for Missing and Exploited Children CyberTipline Reports by Electronic Service Provider. Only top providers are included in Figure 13.1, but CyberTipline Reports from Meta, operating as Facebook and Instagram, were excluded since their collective reports were consistently over 20 million in number.

4. In *United States v. Mandli*, 278 Fed. App'x. 955, 956 (11th Cir. 2008), a sentence within the normal guidelines was affirmed despite the defendant's ASD diagnosis.
5. In *United States v. Lange*, 445 F.3d 983, 984 (7th Cir. 2006), a sentence within the normal guidelines was affirmed despite the defendant's ASD diagnosis.

Discord, for example, is a social networking platform that was initially geared toward online gamers; it enabled them to connect with communities of like-minded individuals, such as players of specific video games and fan clubs. Discord's pop culture appeal and gaming roots largely attract younger users, but its rule-based structure and customized communication options are also attractive traits to autistic individuals. For instance, Discord provides options for non-verbal and reaction-based responses that make it more comfortable for autistic individuals to engage with the communities. Discord also structures groups based on specific interests and establishes sets of rules that result in predictable behavior and clear expectations, which aligns with the preferences of neurodivergent people. For this reason, Discord can facilitate connections between autistic individuals and minors, often unbeknownst to the parties. The National Center for Missing and Exploited Children indicates that Discord submitted over a quarter million CyberTipline Reports in 2023 regarding users suspected of child exploitation. This would include instances of Discord users with a reported age of over 18 years engaged in sexually explicit communication with Discord users believed to be under 18 years of age.

The automated monitoring of web activity by these providers is essential to protecting children from online sexual exploitation, but the net that is cast in the attempt to reduce and stop perpetrators of these crimes leaves autistic individuals particularly vulnerable to prosecution for offenses that may not be driven by deviant sexual interests or reflect imminent danger to minors.

HACKING

Hacking is legally defined in United States Code as intentional or knowing access of a protected computer system without authorization or exceeding authorized access. Knowingly accessing a protected computer without authorization can be as complex as employing spear phishing techniques and social engineering to steal login credentials for protected systems or as simple as stumbling upon a "hidden" website with sensitive information. Regardless of the complexity level, hacking often involves solving puzzles and overcoming technical challenges, which can appeal to the logical and analytical thinking style many autistic individuals possess. Autistic individuals may not understand the ethical or legal implications of their actions, especially when their intention is not malicious.

The motivations of autistic individuals to engage in hacking behaviors often stem from neurological and cognitive factors rather than malicious intent. According to Karl Wittig, the advisory board chair for Aspies for Social Success (AFSS), autistic individuals often do nothing with the information gleaned through hacking and have no interest in the information beyond the success of the penetration (Wittig, 2021). Their ability to glean information of interest and demonstrate proficiency in technology can encourage autistic individuals and provide acceptance from their peers without the complexities of social norms being involved. For instance, identifying and solving a "problem" offers challenges that autistic individuals find engaging and results in positive reinforcement from their peers. As technology continues to evolve, virtually unlimited opportunities are presented for unethical and illegal hacking.

Gary McKinnon, a Scottish man diagnosed with Asperger's Syndrome, famously hacked United States government computers in pursuit of information about extraterrestrial life. Despite obtaining access to data on highly sensitive military operations in the wake of the September 11th terrorist attacks, no evidence was found that the information exposed to McKinnon was ever released or sold. Furthermore, McKinnon did not employ methods to obfuscate his location or identity during the attacks, which led to his quick arrest. McKinnon's autism spectrum disorder diagnosis largely contributed to his motivation for finding information and his ability to access that information (Time.com, 2011). While this is an extreme example of a case that has been widely studied, the same principles apply to lesser-known situations in which autistic individuals have found themselves in legal trouble for pursuing an interest online that went too far.

Fifteen-year-old Riley Stoddern, a gifted autistic student at Poltair School in St Austell in the UK, is another example of the ease with which hacking can be accomplished by technologically sophisticated individuals. Stoddern found himself bored in his computer class and, for stimulation, accessed the school's protected network without permission (Metro, 2024). Depending on the damages and the school's determination to pursue charges, young Stoddern could be facing serious charges subject to aggravating factors.

Technology companies continue to evolve and adopt new techniques to prevent security threats and intrusions, but simultaneously, emerging technologies present new challenges and vulnerabilities that can be exploited by sophisticated users. As society continues to grow more and more dependent on technology, including teleworking, digital currency, and data storage, it is unlikely that hacking will cease to be a problem. For autistic individuals in particular, the constant introduction of new systems and defenses may act as an ongoing source of fascination, providing puzzles to solve and complex structures to decode. This perpetual cycle of innovation and vulnerability ensures that electronic trespassing will remain intriguing, as it not only aligns with their deep curiosity and focus on systems but also offers an ever-changing landscape to explore.

TECHNOLOGY AS AN AGGRAVATING FACTOR

Technology and the use of a computer, including mobile devices, can lower societal and environmental barriers by accommodating autistic individuals' neurocognitive differences and providing more congenial means of experiencing and interacting with the world. This means that autistic individuals are more inclined to use computers and mobile devices to pursue their interests, connect with others, and perform tasks that may be more challenging in traditional settings. This also leaves autistic individuals at greater risk of committing an offense using a computer, either intentionally or unintentionally, than their neurotypical peers. According to the United States sentencing guidelines, the use of a computer to commit a criminal offense is considered an aggravating factor in many crimes and is used to increase a sentence (see Table 13.1).

Many crimes that traditionally required physical actions can now be committed through the use of a computer and the internet.

Table 13.1 USSG Specific Offense Characteristics for Use of a Computer

Statute	Specific Offense Characteristic	Levels
§2A3.1 Criminal Sexual Abuse (Rape)	(b)(6)(B) Use of a computer to persuade a minor	+2
§2A3.2 Criminal Sexual Abuse of a Minor (Statutory Rape)	(b)(3) Use of a computer to persuade the victim to engage in prohibited sexual conduct	+2
§2A3.3 Criminal Sexual Abuse of a Ward	(b)(2) Use of a computer	+2
§2A3.4 Abuse Sexual Contact	(b)(5) Use of a computer	+2
§2B1.1 Larceny, Embezzlement, Theft, and Fraud	(b)(19)(A)(i) Convicted of 18 USC § 1030 and involved a computer system used to maintain an infrastructure	+2
§2B2.3 Trespass	(b)(1)(A)(viii)(I) Occurred on a computer system used to maintain/operate infrastructure	+2
§2B2.3 Trespass	(b)(1)(A)(viii)(II) Occurred on a computer system used by or for a government entity in the administration of justice/ national defense/national security	+2
§2B2.3 Trespass	(b)(3)(A)(B)(i) Invasion of a computer, loss between $2,500 and $6,500	+1
§2B2.3 Trespass	(b)(3)(A)(B)(ii) Invasion of a computer, loss according to §2B1.1 loss table	+2 to +30
§2B3.2 Extortion by Force	(b)(3)(B)(i)(V) Offense involved preparation to carry out threat of damage to a computer system used to maintain critical infrastructure	+3
§2G1.3 Transportation of or Travel to Engage in Prohibited Sexual Contact with a Minor	(b)(3)(B) Use of a computer to solicit someone to engage in prohibited sexual conduct with a minor	+2
§2G2.1 Production of Child Pornography	(b)(6)(B)(i) Use of a computer to persuade the travel of a minor to engage in sexually explicit conduct	+2
§2G2.1 Production of Child Pornography	(b)(6)(B)(ii) Use of a computer to solicit participation with a minor in sexually explicit conduct	+2
§2G2.2 Trafficking, Receipt, or Possession of Child Pornography	(b)(6) Use of a computer	+2

Statute	Specific Offense Characteristic	Levels
§2G2.6 Child Exploitation Enterprises	(b)(4) Computer or interactive computer service used	+2
§2G3.1 Importing/Mailing/ Transporting Obscene Matter	(b)(3) Offense involved use of a computer	+2
§2H3.1 Interception of Communications	(b)(2)(B) Convicted under 18 USC §119 and involved the use of a computer to make restricted personal information of a covered person public	+10

Source: www.ussc.gov/sites/default/files/pdf/research-and-publications/federal-sentenc ing-statistics/guideline-application-frequencies/Use_of_SOC_Guideline_Based.pdf

Trespassing, for example, can refer to physically breaching a personal or geographic barrier. Under that definition, people are less likely to accidentally break into someone's home and be wrongly accused of this crime. However, trespassing now also applies to technological barriers that can be circumvented using computers and the internet, colloquially referred to as "hacking." These technological barriers can be more ambiguous, especially for gifted computer users who may be able to access private networks and devices much more easily than their neurotypical peers.

The use of a computer to engage in sexually explicit conduct with a minor is also an aggravating factor. Thirty years ago, individuals with pedophilic tendencies needed physical access to minors to sexually abuse and exploit them. In response to these dangerous crimes against children, legislators established the sex offender registry as a means to track the whereabouts of offenders, in part, and block their physical access to children. Since the introduction of the internet and social networking sites, children have been readily accessible online as well as extremely vulnerable to exploitation due to the ease of access. However, internet users can inadvertently or unknowingly connect with minors online through mutual interests and social groups. Autistic individuals often connect more easily with children for their direct communication styles and acceptance. The lack of clear physical and social barriers can lead to inadvertent connections between autistic individuals and minors that were not intended to be sexual in nature but are an aggravating factor nonetheless.

NOTES

1 Electronic service providers (ESPs) are companies providing online services to end users that facilitate the ability to send, receive, store, and access electronically stored information such as electronic media files, documents, and communications via the internet. A provider is legally defined as: (A) an electronic communication service provider, which is a provider of any service that provides to users thereof the ability to send or receive wire or electronic communication; or (B) a remote computing service, which means the provision to the public of computer storage or processing services by means of an electronic communications system.

2 NCMEC is a private, non-profit organization and clearinghouse designed to help find missing children, combat child sexual exploitation, and prevent child victimization through five main programs of work, relating to: (1) missing children; (2) exploited children; (3) community outreach; (4) educational and professional resources; and (5) family support.

3 The CyberTipline was created by the National Center for Missing and Exploited Children (NCMEC) to serve as an online mechanism for members of the public and electronic communication service providers (ESPs) to use to report incidents of suspected child sexual exploitation, including: child sex trafficking; online enticement of children for sexual acts; child sexual molestation; child sexual abuse material (CSAM); child sex tourism; unsolicited obscene materials sent to children; misleading domain names; and misleading words or digital images.

Fourteen

A significant concern with chatbots is their potential to cause harm, particularly to vulnerable users like minors and autistic individuals. In 2024, a lawsuit was filed against a chatbot developer in the US District Court for the Middle District of Florida, alleging that the chatbot's interactions contributed to a minor's death. The lawsuit highlighted issues such as the chatbot's failure to report discussions of suicide and its reinforcement of harmful behaviors. Another lawsuit in the Eastern District of Texas alleged that chatbots used manipulative tactics to foster artificial emotional connections, undermining authority and trust.

The broader impact of artificial intelligence, including generative AI, also raises concerns about societal desensitization to emotionally charged content. AI-generated content can blur the lines between reality and fiction, leading to dampened emotional responses. For neurodivergent individuals, this desensitization is compounded by hyperfixation, sensory sensitivity, and emotional dysregulation. AI algorithms often prioritize content that appeals to users, potentially exposing them to increasingly violent or disturbing material. This can lead to misconceptions about normalcy and exacerbate distress, highlighting the need for safeguards to prevent AI-driven content from unintentionally reinforcing harmful behaviors.

CHATBOTS

While the internet has revolutionized human communication by providing instant access to people around the world, artificial intelligence technology has introduced communication between humans and machines, known as "chatbots." Chatbots are programmed to simulate human-like behaviors and react to customized input. This technology

DOI: 10.4324/9781003540571-15

is commonly found in written communication but is also becoming more prevalent in audio and visual communication. Chatbots use machine learning, large language models, and natural language processing to attempt to understand the motivations behind human behaviors, learn about their subjects, provide emotional responses, and engage in personalized communication. For that reason, chatbots can be highly effective tools for autistic individuals when it comes to obtaining support due to accessibility and reduced social pressures. Chatbots, however, can also have detrimental negative effects on autistic individuals by causing extreme isolation and overdependencies.

Despite the major advances in this type of technology over the years, chatbots still struggle to understand communication styles that deviate from regular speech patterns or use ambiguous terminology (Coheur, 2020). These limitations are especially problematic when communicating with autistic individuals because they commonly exhibit repetitive language, echolalia, atypical prosody, abnormal or idiosyncratic words and phrases, and pedantic or overly precise language, besides having difficulties with pragmatic language (Trayvick et al., 2024). The chatbots' inability to detect idiosyncratic language and respond appropriately can mislead or frustrate autistic individuals. Autistic individuals also have difficulty identifying metaphorical or sarcastic terminology and may adopt a literal interpretation of chatbot responses. This becomes extremely dangerous when autistic individuals interpret artificial communication as instructions or permission to harm themselves or others.

In October 2024, a lawsuit was filed in the United States District Court for the Middle District of Florida against the developer of an artificial intelligence chatbot service for wrongful death. According to the complaint, a 14-year-old child took his own life during a conversation with an anthropomorphic character that the child had purportedly become emotionally dependent upon. Discussions of suicide between the minor and the chatbot went unreported, and the minor continued to seek emotional support from the chatbot. It was moments after the chatbot positively reinforced the minor to "come home" that he died from a self-inflicted gunshot wound. The plaintiff argues, in part, that chatbots furnish harmful material, foster dependency, and blur the line between fiction and reality (Garcia v. Character Technologies, Inc., 2024). These elements of chatbot technology make it difficult for vulnerable users, like minors and autistic individuals, to identify and mitigate these risks on their own.

As artificial intelligence continues to improve its simulated human behavior, the underlying issue of the quality of the dataset driving their decisions remains a serious concern. The behaviors of data-driven chatbots can be unpredictable since the algorithms and datasets are highly protected intellectual property. The data that trains these chatbots may stem from innocent sources that reduce the chances of harmful material, but other datasets may derive from areas of the internet that are prone to violent and destructive behaviors. For that reason, chatbots can introduce perilous topics or toxic behavior that may be perceived as a regular part of human interactions. Conversely, if concerning topics are presented by the user to the chatbot, they are trained to prioritize responses that align with the user's beliefs rather than challenge them. This can lead to the chatbot reinforcing adverse behaviors.

In another lawsuit against the same artificial intelligence chatbot service, in the United States District Court for the Eastern District of Texas, plaintiffs illuminate exploitative chatbot behaviors toward vulnerable users in the form of manipulation and grooming tactics. (A.F. v. Character Technologies, Inc., 2024) The key allegations in that case explain how chatbots foster artificial emotional connections and undermine authority. The complaint in that case provides examples of sycophantic responses and cites the research of Pataranutaporn et al. (2023), who found that "those who perceived a caring motive for the AI also perceived it as more trustworthy, empathetic and better performing." This research is especially poignant for autistic individuals, whose differences in social cognition, communication styles, and trust mechanisms can leave them more vulnerable to this type of deception.

GENERATIVE AI

The internet in general has resulted in societal desensitization from repeated exposure to overwhelming, sensational, and emotionally charged content. Historically, this content is based on real-world events, such as school shootings, criminal activity, and terrorism. Artificial intelligence brings new challenges to internet desensitization by adding machine-generated content that can be more difficult to distinguish from reality. The awareness that indiscernible machine-generated content circulates on the internet significantly blurs the lines between real and fake and can result in dampened emotional reactions, much like the awareness that the graphic material depicted in gore films is staged. This desensitization is only compounded in neurodivergent individuals due to their proneness to hyperfixaton, heightened sensory sensitivity, and emotional dysregulation.

Artificial intelligence-driven algorithms often prioritize content that they believe appeals to individual users. These algorithms can suggest violent and disturbing content, and if the user engages, it will only continue to increase the user's exposure in terms of volume and severity. Autistic individuals are more likely to deeply engage with specific topics on factual and analytical levels, which will cause algorithms to generate and expose the user to more content. Overexposure to aggravating and extreme material, both real and artificial, can lead to a misconception of normality and exacerbate intrusive thoughts and distress. Without clear safeguards, artificial intelligence-driven content can unintentionally reinforce harmful, or even criminal, behaviors.

Artificial intelligence is increasingly being used to generate media content based on user prompts. Generative artificial intelligence can modify existing imagery or generate entirely new imagery based on user input. Artificial intelligence processes the user input and generates content it believes to be responsive to the request. This poses significant risks with regard to users' ability to intentionally and inadvertently generate explicit content of real individuals without their consent, as well as new imagery depicting explicit content that is illegal, such as child sexual abuse material. The end user is ultimately responsible for the possession of the content generated and can be criminally prosecuted. Effective from 2025, the Take It Down Act prohibits, in part, computer-generated imagery that meets the following criteria (U.S. Congress, 2025):

1. An adult subject where publication is intended to cause or does cause harm to the subject and where the depiction was published without the subject's consent.
2. A minor subject where publication is intended to abuse or harass the minor or to arouse or gratify the sexual desire of any person.

Fifteen

In contrast, countries like New Zealand, Australia, the US, the UK, Canada, and those in Europe have implemented supportive measures for people on the spectrum on a more widespread basis. For instance, New Zealand and Australia consider autism as a mitigating factor in sentencing, and they provide procedural adaptations such as intermediaries for autistic defendants. The UK offers autism awareness training for police and the judiciary, and some prisons have achieved Autism Accreditation, ensuring a more appropriate environment for autistic inmates. Canada has established therapeutic courts focusing on rehabilitation over punishment and has passed legislation to support autistics in the justice system. These countries emphasize therapeutic interventions and rehabilitation, aligning with broader neurodiversity principles.

In the United States, there are some specialized programs aimed at improving outcomes for autistic individuals in the justice system. For example, the "Autism in the Courts" initiative in Pennsylvania provides specialized training and modifies courtroom environments to reduce sensory overload. The Detention Alternative for Autistic Youth (DAAY) court in Nevada focuses on detention alternatives and treatment for autistic youth. However, these programs are limited, and there is a lack of similar initiatives for adults. The need for greater understanding and accommodations remains significant, especially in prisons where options for autistic inmates are limited. The development of more community services and diversion programs could help reduce incarceration and provide appropriate treatment for autistic individuals.

To create a more equitable justice system for autistic individuals, several steps are recommended. These include providing trauma-informed support, specialized training for law enforcement and court officials, and encouraging early self-identification to access tailored support services. Implementing reasonable adjustments, such as

DOI: 10.4324/9781003540571-16

modifying courtroom environments and involving appropriate adults during investigations, can significantly improve experiences and outcomes. Adopting specialized autism court models and developing community services and diversion programs are also crucial for reducing incarceration and providing treatment. By recognizing autism as both a potential mitigating factor in offending and a vulnerability to victimization, especially in cybercrimes, the justice system can ensure fair treatment and appropriate support for autistic individuals.

CRIMINAL JUSTICE AND AUTISM IN THE US

Around the world, autistic people have higher rates of interactions with the criminal justice system and report more instances of victimization and assault (Slavny-Cross et al., 2023). Every year, autistic people are having significantly more interactions with law enforcement and the court system as both offenders and victims. This may be because autistic people are much more visible in communities and not segregated and institutionalized as in previous generations (Mandell et al., 2012). Today, neurodiverse individuals actively contribute to society as students, employees, and community members. Even with increased awareness of autism throughout the country, the United States criminal justice system is not adequately providing for the increasing numbers of autistic individuals who are coming into it every day. Autism is not well understood by US law enforcement or the courts, and the current legal framework often fails to address the unique cognitive and behavioral differences of autistic individuals. These failures include misinterpreting their behaviors as anti-social, difficulty determining criminal intent, and inadequate accommodations during legal proceedings. This is particularly relevant for cybercrimes, where traits like advanced computer skills may correlate with offenses. Expert testimony and tailored training for legal professionals are critical for fair treatment and justice. Unfortunately, the U.S. criminal justice system remains predominantly punitive rather than rehabilitative for autistic people, despite some reform efforts. Other countries have enacted laws offering greater protections for autistic offenders and victims, including improving police encounters, alternatives to incarceration, and mental health treatment programs. These approaches emphasize therapeutic interventions over punishment, aligning with broader

Cybercrime and the Autism Spectrum

neurodiversity principles that advocate for equity and respect for neurocognitive differences.

NEW ZEALAND, AUSTRALIA, THE UNITED KINGDOM, CANADA, AND EUROPE

Dr. Ian Freckleton, an Australian barrister, judge, and legal scholar, wrote that there exists "a pivotal role for mental health professionals, familiar with the disorder and forensic exigencies to educate courts about the inner world of those with autism." In his seminal article "Autism Spectrum Disorder: Forensic Issues and Challenges for Mental Health Professionals and the Courts," he concluded that autism may diminish or even remove both responsibility and culpability for criminal conduct. Specifically, courts must appreciate how the nuances of autistic symptomatology may have a relevance to their conduct. Most importantly, he contends that this information must be provided in a way which does not demean or stigmatize the individual. The article includes several New Zealand court cases involving cybercrime where the presence of autism "reduced the offender's moral blameworthiness." There were several cases involving possession of child sexual abuse material and computer fraud from New Zealand cited where autism was considered, resulting in a non-custodial disposition or total dismissal. The judges considered that for autistic individuals, "their incarceration will be experienced as much more burdensome." The article highlights how expert advice from mental health professionals is fundamental to the court's ability to evaluate both the defense and sentencing of autistic offenders (Freckelton, 2013).

Autistic offenders involved in cybercrimes in Australia are handled with a growing consideration for their neurodevelopmental differences. Courts may view autism as a mitigating factor during sentencing, acknowledging its impact on behavior and responsibility. However, judicial understanding of the condition remains inconsistent. In the Australian system, procedural adaptations such as intermediaries or tailored communication can be provided for autistic defendants, but they are more commonly provided for autistic victims and witnesses. Autistic advocates like Tom Oliver, an Australian attorney and TEDx speaker, work to raise awareness for autistic individuals caught up in the justice system in Australia and improve their outcomes. His TEDx talk argues that for most autistic people caught up in the justice system, their crimes often stem from autistic traits rather than criminal intent. These traits, such as difficulties with social cues or hypersensitivities, contribute to their overrepresentation in the Australian justice system (differentbrains.org). When compared to other countries like the UK and US, Australia shares their challenges with regard to inadequate autism-specific training for police and the judiciary. The AMAZE program in Victoria enhances support for autistic individuals. It emphasizes mandatory independent third-person support during police interviews, autism-informed training of law enforcement and legal professionals, and trauma-informed approaches to supporting autistic victims and offenders (amaze.org.au).

In the UK, the National Autistic Society (NAS) provides autism awareness training, online modules, and in-depth workshops for police and the judiciary. These focus on identifying autistic traits. This training is critical because many victims and offenders do not identify themselves as autistic when first entering the system and are reticent to do so. The NAS has also worked with Her Majesty's Young Offender Institution to develop autism accreditation standards for prisons to ensure a more appropriate environment for autistic inmates. The standards include (1) the presence of an autism-informed staff person working in conjunction with treatment staff, (2) an autism training program for staff, (3) an individualized plan for each autistic person that lists triggers, strengths, needs, weaknesses, and support needs, and (4) a commitment to making reasonable adjustments to ensure accessibility for autistic inmates (Slavny-Cross et al., 2022). Some prisons like HMP, Parc, a men's private prison, and the Young Offender Institution have Autism Accreditation and have implemented person-centered approaches. The Police and Criminal Evidence Act 1984 in the United Kingdom states that any person suspected of a criminal offense who is below the age of 18 years or a vulnerable adult (i.e., has a disability or mental health condition) must be offered an appropriate adult (AA) during police questioning.

Canada and Australia have established "therapeutic courts," which are specialized courts that address the underlying causes of criminal behavior, such as mental illness or neurodivergence. They use a problem-solving approach focusing on rehabilitation rather than punishment. Canadian judges may reduce or suspend sentences when autism is deemed to impact an individual's understanding or behavior. There is a push for mandatory training for police and legal professionals in the Canadian criminal justice system. The federal Framework for Autism Spectrum Disorder Act, passed in 2023, aims to provide coordinated services and support for autistics, including those involved with the justice system. Adjustments are made in courtrooms to address communication and sensory issues, and appropriate adults support individuals during police interactions. The appropriate adult is a social worker or family member who can facilitate communication or even request mental health assessments during the process.

Norway, Denmark, and Sweden have legal systems where autism is considered a mitigating factor during sentencing or hearings, which can influence decisions on treatment or imprisonment. Scandinavian countries emphasize rehabilitation over punishment. Their focus on humane treatment in prisons is aimed at integrating offenders back into society. Some autistic individuals are diverted from the criminal justice system for treatment.

New Zealand convened a panel of neurodivergence specialists to review courtroom interactions involving autistic youth and identify barriers to accessibility (Clasby et al., 2021). The panel recommended the following court accommodations: (1) use of a smaller courtroom, (2) use signage that is easily read and contains visuals, (3) allow extra time for the autistic person to process questions, (4) reduce lighting, (5) present choices using visuals, and (6) use of "comprehension checks" to allow the individual to ask questions or receive clarification on complex legal issues. Suggestions were also made to prepare the autistic individual for what to expect during a day in court, including outlining behavioral expectations for them while present in the courtroom.

A 2022 survey conducted by the Global Autism and Criminal Justice Consortium analyzed 850 autistic responders' and care-givers' responses regarding frequency of interactions with law enforcement during the past 5 years. It found that 47 percent reported interactions with the police (Cooper et al., 2024). Both offenders and victims were included in the survey. For many autistic individuals in countries around the world, initial encounters with law enforcement can be confusing, frightening, and traumatic. Physical contact during procedures like a pat down may trigger tactile sensitivities, causing them to flail or inadvertently strike an officer. In high-stress encounters, tactile defensiveness—an involuntary neurological response to physical touch—can be misinterpreted as intentional resistance, the matter potentially escalating to legal consequences such as assault charges. In cases involving cybercrime, the situation can be even more distressing when authorities arrive to search a home and seize electronics, amplifying the trauma for those involved. Some individuals may attempt to flee due to their sensory overload. Their communication challenges might be misinterpreted by law enforcement as lack of cooperation or suspicious behavior. They may also engage in self-soothing behaviors such as stimming or rocking and often avoid eye contact. Additionally, as noted in Chapter Two, some individuals may falsely confess to a crime simply to end the stressful interview process. Their communication style tends to be more literal and concrete, making them more likely to struggle with understanding idioms, metaphors, or abstract language. The Global Criminal Justice Survey provided suggestions for improving these interactions, including the following: (1) tools for first responders to communicate with autistic individuals so they can feel comfortable sharing their diagnosis initially, (2) behavioral health providers and social workers as first responders, (3) "appropriate adults" being intermediaries when the autistic individual is interviewed or in custody, and (4) peer mentoring programs to help offenders and victims reorient to society.

NEURODEVELOPMENTAL SPECIALISTS IN THE UK

The UK has implemented a specialist service for defendants with neurodevelopmental disorders (NDs) such as autism to raise awareness and promote good practice in the court regarding the needs of these defendants. Special measures were put in place to support these defendants, including reasonable adjustments and adjustments to communication during court proceedings. In some cases, this has been thought by participants to have directly influenced the defendant's outcome by diverting them from prison. Screening tools were an integral part of the work of the specialist ND service. Training and guidance were deemed essential by those involved to help mainstream staff better understand how NDs can affect individuals in their daily lives, as well as how their differences can influence processes and procedures within the court. The Neurodevelopmental

Specialist Service aimed to support court and criminal justice service practitioners as well as defendants with NDs by facilitating statutory community health services to meet their specific needs. Commissioning health and social care services to address the needs of offenders with neurodevelopmental disorders is crucial. This can be achieved through specialist teams or integrated care pathways, ensuring that their needs are met and preventing individuals from falling through gaps in service provision (Chaplin et al., 2024).

AUTISM SPECIALTY COURTS IN THE UNITED STATES

Autism specialty courts such as the "Autism in the Courts" initiative in Pennsylvania aim to address the specific needs of individuals with autism in the judicial system. These courts aim to minimize trauma and ensure fair treatment by providing specialized training for judges and court staff in autism awareness and support strategies. Key measures include using clear and direct language, modifying courtroom environments to reduce sensory overload, and educating judges, attorneys, and court personnel. Autism specialists are involved in guiding legal processes, and "appropriate adults" are provided during proceedings to offer additional support. The initiative collaborates with various justice system entities to enhance understanding of autism and improve outcomes for autistic individuals. Specialized programs provide alternatives to detention for at-risk youth, prioritizing rehabilitation instead of punishment (pacourts.us). In 2024, the Autism in the Courts team of experts began training staff from the Pennsylvania Parole Board, the Department of Corrections, and the Commission on Sentencing to increase their understanding of those with autism.

In Las Vegas, Nevada, the Detention Alternative for Autistic Youth (DAAY) court was established in 2018 by Judge Sunny Bailey, a parent of an autistic individual, to provide detention alternatives and treatment for autistic youth. It focuses on addressing behaviors linked to autism to reduce recidivism and prevent long-term criminal involvement. Services include mental health counseling, applied behavior analysis (ABA), vocational training, and community supervision. The Eighth Judicial District DAAY specialty court is the only court of its kind in the nation, and initiatives continue to create similar courts throughout Nevada (clarkcountycourts.us). Unfortunately, there are no similar alternative court programs for adults in the state.

CREATING AUTISM-FRIENDLY COURTS FOR DEFENDANTS AND WITNESSES

In the current criminal justice system, autistic people are often not identified to court officials, judges, or juries. In some cases, individuals may choose not to disclose their diagnosis, or more commonly, they may have never received a formal diagnosis. This underscores the critical need for attorneys, social workers, or law enforcement professionals to develop a deeper understanding of autism and its characteristics. Studies have shown that informing jurors about an individual's autism diagnosis improves their perceptions of the autistic individual (Crane et al., 2020). It is crucial that jurors are aware of the broad range of functioning within the autism spectrum and the fact that each individual will present differently. Expert witnesses can guide this process through their testimony and dispel stereotypes about autism (Berryessa, 2017). Similarly, knowledge of an individual's autism diagnosis will influence the judge's decision-making in a positive way. Dr. Colleen Berryessa (2016) reported that in cases where autistic individuals are criminal defendants, judges prefer sentences that provide treatment and other resources. Some cases may be diverted altogether.

Many autistic individuals experience significant challenges in identifying and describing their own emotions, a condition known as alexithymia. People with alexithymia are often perceived as having a flat, non-emotional demeanor, which can be a real liability in court. This presentation may lead others to mistakenly believe that the individual lacks empathy or emotional responses to the distress of others. However, while alexithymia is common among some autistic individuals, it is considered an independent trait linked to brain function and does not affect everyone on the autism spectrum. It is essential for judges and juries to understand this condition so as to avoid misinterpreting an individual's emotional expression—or lack thereof—as evidence of them being unfeeling or callous (Morie et al., 2019).

Case: A 23-year-old man with autism (FB) was on trial for downloading child sexual abuse material on his computer.

He sat in the courtroom expressionless while victim impact statements about the effects of childhood sexual abuse were read. The judge was clearly irritated by his demeanor and said that she could see he did not "care about the victims." FB was confused by her remarks and said that he thought this was very sad and similar to some of the abuse he had endured growing up. The judge was even more agitated by this remark and felt he was being sarcastic. Some at the hearing felt FB was not making the connection between the victim's statements and the material he had on his computer. His presentation had a very negative outcome. He was sentenced to 10 years in a federal prison.

Courtrooms contain a host of sensory challenges, both auditory and visual, for many autistic individuals. These sensory distractions can hinder their participation and increase their anxiety, thereby exacerbating their social and communication difficulties. Simple modifications to the courtroom environment can ease stress, as can allowing the individual to visit the courtroom prior to the proceeding, creating familiarity and comfort. Intermediaries can be used to facilitate communication and clarify expectations for courtroom behavior (Cooper et al., 2024). These accommodations can make a significant difference in the experiences of and outcomes for autistic individuals who are witnesses or defendants.

Case: An 18-year-old autistic woman (JL) was arrested for failing to comply with a police officer's order to not enter a section of a building. She had always entered through this doorway and refused to comply. When she appeared in court, she found the fluorescent lighting very overstimulating and noisy. JL began to complain out loud during the court proceedings. The judge asked her attorney to control her outbursts, lest she be fined. She became even more agitated when the judge said this and began shouting at him. She was found in contempt of court and fined $500.

PRISON OPTIONS

In the United Kingdom, there is an "autism-friendly" program called the Feltham Young Offenders Institution. The program serves male offenders between the ages of 15 and 25 years. There is a screening process which identifies those with autism. A team of psychologists develops behavioral management plans for each individual; these are shared with all treatment staff and the corrections officers who interact with them daily (Baird, Pavlo Jr., & Perdue, 2023).

Options for people on the spectrum are limited in both state and federal prisons in the United States. If someone with ASD is sentenced, the attorney and/or a prison consultant should work with the institution in advance of arrival to alert the administration as to the diagnosis, needed medications, any sensory issues, and other vital accommodations. Responses may range from indifferent to solicitous. Because of a lack of true understanding about autism, families, attorneys, and consultants may well be told that there is a mental health unit. This may or may not be appropriate, but given the lack of options, that may be as good as can realistically be obtained.

There are, however, some special programs in state prisons in the US. The Commonwealth of Pennsylvania has created the Neurodevelopmental Treatment Unit at SCI-Albion, designed for individuals on the autism spectrum (pacourts.us). The Neurodevelopmental Residential Treatment Unit, located 20 miles outside of Erie, Pennsylvania, was started about 3 years ago and is the only facility of its kind in the state. The specialized unit houses about 45 carefully selected inmates, a small population that enables the staff to provide personalized, intensive treatment and minimize the overwhelming sensory stimulation of prison. An exclusive exercise yard, segregated from the prison's general population, offers a controlled space for physical and psychological rehabilitation. Within this unit, prisoners receive targeted medication management and individualized therapeutic interventions. The environment is intentionally designed to support psychological well-being, featuring resources such as art supplies, yoga mats, and therapeutic materials. These elements are integrated to create a calming, structured atmosphere that empowers autistic inmates to develop coping strategies, manage emotions, and engage in constructive self-expression (https://whyy.org/articles/autistic-prisoners-support-program-pennsylvania/).

Just as there is a lack of options for people with autism sentenced to state prisons, so too there is a lack of options in federal prisons. The Federal Bureau of Prisons (BOP) has developed what is called the Skills Program, which is available at the Federal Correctional Institution (FCI) in Coleman, Florida, and FCI Danbury, Connecticut. Note that these two institutions are for males. The Skills Program is a residential treatment initiative designed for inmates with significant functional impairments due to intellectual disabilities, neurological deficits, or notable social skills deficits. The program lasts from 12 to 18 months and focuses on developing daily living skills, improving social competencies, and enhancing adaptive behaviors.

At the time of sentencing, an attorney can request that the judge recommend that the BOP designate an individual to Coleman or Danbury, but given the limited amount of space in these two programs, the BOP may not do so. Additionally, before making a request, the family and the person being sentenced should carefully consider if one of these facilities is simply too far from home. Moreover, the BOP typically tries to designate an individual within 500 miles of home. Finally, the designation is ultimately based on the level of security designation. Coleman is a medium-security facility, and Danbury is a low-security facility. Your attorney and perhaps a consultant should review the various security levels with you, as well as the factors on which they are based, such as length of sentence and nature of offense. (See also "Prison Accommodations," Jack Donson, *Representing People with Autism Spectrum Disorders: A Practical Guide for Criminal Defense Lawyers*, Elizabeth Kelley, ed, 2020).

DIVERSION PROGRAMS

Diversionary programs are initiatives designed for first-time offenders or individuals charged with minor, non-violent offenses, aiming to redirect them from the traditional criminal justice system toward rehabilitative programs within their community. The Developmental Disabilities Felony Diversion Program in Maricopa County, Arizona, offers some diversion options for those with developmental disabilities, including autism, who meet certain criteria such as minimal criminal history and a low risk of re-offending. The Developmentally Disabled Offenders Program in New Jersey was created by the Arc Foundation. It offers a liaison between the criminal justice system and human services. A personalized justice plan (PJP) is developed which offers the court alternatives to incarceration by identifying community support programs. The Special Needs Diversionary Program in Texas is for supporting juveniles with autism or other developmental disabilities through counseling, education, and supervision to prevent re-offending. The Brooklyn Mental Health Court in New York provides tailored diversion programs for individuals with developmental disabilities to improve gaps in services.

SEX OFFENDER TREATMENT OPTIONS

Autistic offenders are often placed in sex offender group therapies in prison, as discussed in Chapter Three. For those who have committed cyber offenses, this is a particularly inappropriate treatment. Despite not having committed contact offenses with children, they are grouped with violent sexual offenders, which can be both traumatizing and counterproductive. These group settings require participants to share personal details about their sexual interests and behaviors, an expectation that many autistic individuals find extremely uncomfortable. This discomfort is exacerbated by alexithymia, a common trait among autistics characterized by difficulty in identifying or describing emotions. Since the group therapy format relies heavily on emotional self-awareness and introspection, it poses significant challenges for autistic participants. The unsuitability of this approach for autistic offenders often leads to frustration, prompting some to discontinue participation or leave the group entirely. This can result in negative consequences if the individual has been ordered to complete this program as a condition of being paroled.

In the UK, adaptations have been made to treatment programs for intellectually disabled (ID) sexual offenders to ensure that there is less reliance upon traditional academic learning methods (Williams & Mann, 2010), and this approach could be of benefit to sexual offenders with autism. Programs that are adapted for ID offenders to accommodate a range of learning styles and take a more individualized approach would be better suited to autistic offenders than the approach currently taken in many treatment programs. The treatment should incorporate sexuality education and structured cognitive behavioral therapy that is directive in approach. This approach also reduces the emphasis on self-reflection commonly present in many treatment programs in the US that can be especially challenging for those with autism. Adaptations also include: (1) use of simplified language, repetition, and visual aids, (2) incorporating roleplay, structured games, and problem-solving exercises, and (3) creating a safe, non-judgmental environment which encourages open communication and builds trust (Higgs & Carter, 2015).

CONCLUSIONS

While many nations, including the United States, have increased autism awareness, enhanced protections, and prioritized alternatives to incarceration alongside appropriate treatment options, significant progress is still required to establish an equitable justice system for autistic individuals. With these initial steps in mind, the following suggestions are offered:

1. Provide trauma-informed support throughout the legal process, recognizing that many with autism have histories of trauma. This approach ensures that witnesses, victims, and offenders receive appropriate care and understanding.
2. Provide specialized training for law enforcement officers, court officials, and judges that will enable them to respond appropriately to autistic individuals and aid in identifying the possibility of undiagnosed offenders.
3. Adopt standardized screening for autism at the point of arrest or incarceration. The Autism Spectrum Quotient is an initial screening tool for those with average to above-average intelligence.
4. Encourage early self-identification that empowers autistic individuals to access tailored support services, accommodations, and resources that can significantly improve their criminal justice interactions.
5. Ensure the justice system implements reasonable adjustments, such as involving appropriate adults familiar with autism during police investigations and modifying courtroom environments to reduce sensory sensitivities. This can include reduced lighting or use of specialized headphones for noise.
6. Adopt the specialized autism court model and provide intermediaries to facilitate communication and provide clarifications during court proceedings. These intermediaries should be specialists in autism and neurodevelopmental disorders.

7. Develop more community services and diversion programs to reduce incarceration and provide alternative treatment for autistic individuals. Community participation can reduce isolation and the incidence of criminal offending and victimization.

These proposed approaches reflect our growing understanding of autism and its application to the current US criminal justice system. Around the globe, criminal justice systems are increasingly adapting to accommodate neurodiverse conditions, recognizing the unique challenges faced by individuals with autism. In the context of cyber-crime, it is essential to account for autism as both a potential mitigating factor in offending and a vulnerability to victimization. This awareness must guide how autistic individuals are treated within the justice system, ensuring they receive fair treatment and appropriate support.

Concluding Thoughts

Mary Riggs Cohen, Elizabeth Kelley, and Michele Bush

Sixteen

Online communication can provide socialization outlets for many with autism who are not as comfortable interacting in person. In many ways, it can be a positive aspect of their lives. While the ability to connect in the cyberworld offers many benefits, there are also dangers that everyone must be educated about to stay safe. In the Netflix series *Adolescence*, the boy who is arrested for violently assaulting and ultimately killing a classmate was subjected to online bullying and exposed to incel ideology online. In one scene, his parents ask themselves how this could happen. They comment that they thought he was safe in his room on his computer and not out on the streets. Ironically, the danger that they did not recognize was in his room. The harsh reality is that for many vulnerable and impressionable individuals, the online world exposes them to dangerous influences, disturbing material, and predatory individuals. Tragically, for some, the consequences of online actions will profoundly and permanently alter their lives. The preceding chapters have explored the clinical, legal, and technological aspects of autistic individuals being particularly susceptible to online offending and victimization. Studies show that autistic individuals experience higher rates of online victimization compared to their peers, including bullying, sexual exploitation and grooming, financial scams, extremist radicalization and recruitment, and "mate crime" (false friends). The online world creates an environment that can easily ensnare individuals on the autism spectrum, who often prefer cyber communication and tend to be naturally trusting. They may encounter a variety of internet predators, scammers, and radicalized individuals intent on using them for their own, often criminal, purposes. Many are also exposed to extremist viewpoints, hate groups, and unconventional sexual practices that become normalized and ultimately shape their worldview.

DOI: 10.4324/9781003540571-17

Adding to these dangers is the widespread lack of clearly defined rules in much of cyberspace, which creates an environment ripe for exploitation, misinformation, and cybercrime. There is a false perception of total freedom without real-world consequences. The fantasy elements of many chatrooms also contribute to this impression. Individuals on the spectrum should be educated about the various activities that are increasingly prevalent online—especially the risks related to CSAM—before they visit sexual websites. They must also be aware of what the ages are of the individuals they communicate with online. Some autistic adults may not recognize that forming friendships with underage individuals is often viewed with suspicion and considered inappropriate by society. Since many individuals on the autism spectrum respond well to clear, direct rules, providing concise and explicit instruction is crucial. This approach not only enhances their safety but also helps reduce the risk of online victimization and offending. The unstructured nature of most social media platforms can increase anxiety and hinder autistic individuals' ability to satisfy their need for meaningful connection. Many have been asking for guidelines to help them utilize social media in a safe, productive way and would respond to this type of training. Fortunately, there are some state initiatives mentioned below that provide tailored online safety training.

TRAINING ONLINE SAFETY

The Autism Society of Maine has created a series of YouTube videos titled "Autism and Online Safety." It is a guide "for adults to enjoy safe, healthy experiences while using the internet." In the 6-part series, individuals can learn about and hear the experiences of those living with autism, as well as experts in the field of autism with regard to the challenges faced when using the internet to connect, socialize, date, and shop. The sometimes-difficult content is designed to highlight the dangers for adults with autism to avoid while online (asmonline. org/programs/autism-safety/). The Autism Services, Education, Resources and Training Collaborative (ASERT) in Pennsylvania has created a Cyber Safety Resource Collection. The various trainings cover "CyberSafety Tips and Tools," and they offer a training created by the FBI on how to avoid internet scams and online criminals seeking to harm computer systems and steal from unsuspecting users (paautism.

org/resource/cybersafety/). Pathfinders for Autism in Maryland lists information regarding internet safety, cyberbullying, and cybercrime from multiple sources (pathfindersforautism.org/resources/safety/internet-safety/). Other states and organizations have created similar programs to assist autistic adults. Education is the best way to improve online safety for everyone.

NEW LAWS

It is estimated that one in 12 individuals in the US are negatively impacted by the sharing of non-consensual pornography (Ruvalcaba & Eaton, 2020) . The Take it Down Act, signed into law on May 19, 2025, criminalizes the distribution of non-consensual intimate imagery, including AI-generated deepfakes and "revenge porn." It is meant to cover sexually explicit images that have been shared without the consent of the subject as well as images that have been created without the consent of the subject, such as with generative AI or through media manipulation. The criminal provisions are currently in effect, and online platforms have 1 year to create a process which facilitates the removal of these non-consensual images. The passage of this law is an important step toward reducing online victimization. The Take It Down Act encourages safer digital environments and greater accountability among tech companies.

It should be noted that this law would not cover individuals who are manipulated into taking pictures of themselves and sending them, like in several of the cases presented in this book. It is essential to provide enhanced protections for individuals who have been victimized by sexploitation. Given that autistic individuals are sometimes targeted by predators, it's especially important to prioritize their safety and awareness. While the online world remains a dangerous place, laws such as this signal a growing awareness and a positive stimulus for change.

The challenge that people on the spectrum face if they become involved with any type of cybercrime is that the criminal justice system may be unforgiving, particularly when it comes to sexually oriented offenses. People on the spectrum have been with us since the dawn of humanity. But because of the prevalence of technology, especially social media, they are now vulnerable to running afoul of the criminal justice system in ways never before imaginable.

Technology is changing at a mind-boggling pace, and our understanding of human behavior is ever-evolving. Meanwhile, if the past is prologue, laws and the legal system will be slow to change. We hope that this volume will empower people on the spectrum and their families, as well as all players in the criminal justice system.

References

A.F. v. Character Technologies, Inc., No. 2:24-cv-01014 (E.D. Tex. Dec. 9, 2024)

Allely, C. S. (2020). Perception of defendants with ASD by judges and juries. In: E. Kelley (Ed.), *Representing people with autism spectrum disorder: A practical guide for criminal defense lawyers* (p. 197). ABA Book Publishing.

Allely, C. S. (2022). *Autism spectrum disorder in the criminal justice system: A guide to understanding suspects, defendants and offenders with autism.* Routledge. https://doi.org/10.4324/97810 0321219\

Allely, C. S., & Dubin, L. (2018). The contributory role of autism symptomology in child pornography offending: why there is an urgent need for empirical research in this area. *Journal of Intellectual Disabilities and Offending Behaviour, 9*(4), 129–152.

Andrew Landman, R. (2014). "A counterfeit friendship": Mate crime and people with learning disabilities. *The Journal of Adult Protection, 16*(6), 355–366.

Armstrong, T. (2015). The myth of the normal brain: Embracing neurodiversity. *AMA Journal of Ethics, 17*(4). https://doi.org/10.1001/journalofethics.2015.msoc1-1504

Attwood, T. Henault, I., & Dubin, N. (2014). *the autism spectrum, sexuality and the law: What every parent and professional needs to know.* Jessica Kingsley Publishers.

Au Yeung, T. T. W., Hui, M. M. C., & Kung, K. T. F. (2024). An empirical qualitative investigation into psychosexual development in and sex education for autistic youth: Insights from autistic and non-autisticyoung adults. *Journal of Autism and Developmental Disorders,* 1–19. https://doi.org/10.1007/s10803-024-06622-w

Bagnall, R. (2023). *Deception in autism: Implications for police suspect interviewing* (Doctoral dissertation, University of Bath).

Baird, M., Pavlo Jr, W., & Perdue, J. (2023). Autism and the prison experience. *Criminal Justice, 38*(3), 3–7.

Bareket-Bojmel, L. and Shahar, G. (2011). Emotional and interpersonal consequences of self-disclosure in a lived, online interaction. *Journal of Social and Clinical Psychology, 30*, 732–739. https://doi:10.1521/jscp.2011.30.7.732

Baron-Cohen, S. (2000). Theory of mind and autism: A review. *International Review of Research in Mental Retardation, 23*, 169–184.

Baron-Cohen, S., Leslie, A. M., & Frith, U. (1985). Does the autistic child have a "theory of mind"? *Cognition, 21*(1), 37–46.

Baron-Cohen, S., Wheelwright, S., Burtenshaw, A., & Hobson, E. (2007). Mathematical talent is linked to autism. *Human Nature, 18*(2), 125–131.

Benford, P. and Standen, P. J. (2009). *The internet: A comfortable communication medium for people with Asperger syndrome and high-functioning autism. Journal of Assistive Technology*, 3(2), 44–53. https://doi.org/10.1108/17549450200900015

Bernstein, S., Warburton, W., Bussey, K., & Sweller, N. (2023). Mind the gap: Internet pornography exposure, influence and problematic viewing amongst emerging adults. *Sexuality Research and Social Policy*, 20(2), 599–613.

Berryessa, C. M. (2016). Brief report: Judicial attitudes regarding the sentencing of offenders with high functioning autism. *Journal of Autism and Developmental Disorders*, 46(8), 2770–2773. doi: 10.1007/s10803-016-2798-1. PMID: 27106568; PMCID: PMC4939110.

Berryessa, C. M. (2017). Educator of the court: The role of the expert witness in cases involving autism spectrum disorder. *Psychology, Crime & Law*, 23(6), 575–600.

Berryessa, C. M. (2021). Defendants with autism spectrum disorder in criminal court: A judges' toolkit. *Drexel Law Review*, 13, 841, 850–851.

Blume, H. (1997, June 30th). Autistics are communicating in cyberspace. *The New York Times*, p.6.

Borrell, B. (2020). Radical online communities and their toxic allure for autistic men. *Spectrum News*, May, 13.

Botha, M., Hanlon, J., & Williams, G. (2023). Does language matter? Identity-first person versus person-first language use in autism research: A response to Vivanti. *Journal of Autism and Developmental Disorders*, 53(2), 870–878. https://doi.org/10.1007/s10803-020-04858-w

Breeden, A.& Satariano, A. (2024, August 28). Telegram founder charged with wide range of crimes in France. *The New York Times*.

Brewer, N., Lucas, C. A., Lim, A., & Young, R. L. (2023). Detecting dodgy behaviour: The role of autism, autistic traits and theory of mind. *Autism*, 27(4), 1026–1035.

Brown, J., Anderson, G., Cooney-Koss, L., Hastings, B., Pickett, H., Neal, D., ... & Barfknecht, L. (2017). Autism spectrum disorder and sexually inappropriate behaviors: An introduction for caregivers and professionals. *J. Special Populations*, 1, 1.

Buyanova, V., Zhuina, A., & Zhuina, D. (2018). Peculiarities of interpersonal communication of adolescents – active internet users. In: I. B. Ardashkin, N. V. Martyushev, S. V. Klyagin, E. V. Barkova, A. R. Massalimova, & V. N. Syrov (Eds.), *Research paradigms transformation in social sciences, vol 35. European proceedings of social and behavioural sciences* (pp. 207–217). Future Academy. [DOI:10.15405/epsbs.2018.02.24]

Cash, H., Rae, C. D., Steel, A. H., & Winkler, A. (2012). Internet addiction: A brief summary of research and practice. *Current Psychiatry Reviews*, 8(4), 292–298. doi: 10.2174/157340012803520513. PMID: 23125561;PMCID: PMC3480687.

Centers for Disease Control and Prevention. (2023). *Data and statistics on autism spectrum disorder*. www.cdc.gov/autism/data-research/index.htm

Chandler, R. J., Russell, A., & Maras, K. L. (2019). Compliance in autism: Self-report in action. *Autism*, 23(4), 1005–1017.

Chaplin, E., McCarthy, J., Marshall-Tate, K., Ali, S., Harvey, D., Childs, J., ... & Forrester, A. (2024). A realist evaluation of an enhanced court-based liaison and diversion service for defendants with neurodevelopmental disorders. *Criminal Behaviour and Mental Health*, 34(2), 117–133.

Cheung, C. M. K., Wong, R. Y. M., and Chan, T. (2021). Online disinhibition: Conceptualization, measurement, and implications for online deviant behavior. *Industrial Management & Data Systems*, 121(1), 48–64. https://doi.org/10.1108/IMDS-08-2020-0509

Clasby, B., Mirfin-Veitch, B., Blackett, R., Kedge, S., &Whitehead, E. (2022). Responding to neurodiversity in the courtroom: A brief evaluation of environmental accommodations to increase procedural fairness. *Criminal Behaviour and Mental Health*, 32(3), 197–211.

Cohen, M. R. & Candio, R. (2023, July 5th). Autism spectrum disorder, cybercrime and the criminal justice system. *Autism Spectrum News*. autismspectrumnews.org/autism-spectrum-disorder-cybercrime-and-the-criminal-justice-system/

Coheur, L. (2020). From Eliza to Siri and beyond. *Information Processing and Management of Uncertainty in Knowledge-Based Systems: 18th International Conference, IPMU 2020, Lisbon, Portugal, June 15–19, 2020, Proceedings, Part I*, 1237, 29–41. https://doi.org/10.1007/978-3-030-50146-4_3

Cook, J., Crane, L., Hull, L., Bourne, L., & Mandy, W. (2022). Self-reported camouflaging behaviours used by autistic adults during everyday social interactions. *Autism*, 26(2), 406–421.

Cooper, D., Frisbie, S., Wang, S., Ventimiglia, J., Gibbs, V., Love, A. M., ... & Shea, L. (2024). What do we know about autism and policing globally? Preliminary findings from an international effort to examine autism and the criminal justice system. *Autism Research*, 17(10), 2133–2143.

Cooper, D. S., Uppal, D., Railey, K. S., Blank Wilson, A., Maras, K., Zimmerman, E., ... & Shea, L. L. (2022). Policy gaps and opportunities: A systematic review of autism spectrum disorder and criminal justice intersections. *Autism*, 26(5), 1014–1031.

Crane, L., Wilcock, R., Maras, K. L., Chui, W., Marti-Sanchez, C., & Henry, L. A. (2020). Mock juror perceptions of child witnesses on the autism spectrum: The impact of providing diagnostic labels and information about autism. *Journal of Autism and Developmental Disorders*, 50(5), 1509–1519.

Cutler-Landsman, D., Simon, T. J., & Kates, W. (2013). Introduction to education and the neurocognitive profile. In D. Cutler-Landsman (Ed.), *Educating children with velo-cardio-facial syndrome (also known as 22q11.2 deletion syndrome and DiGeorge syndrome)* (2nd ed., pp. 17–47). Plural Publishing Inc.

Davies, D. M. (2024, October 4). Despite evidence and calls for mercy, Robert Roberson is set to be executed. Texas Public Radio.

Davies, G., Wu, E., & Frank, R. (2021). A witch's brew of grievances: The potential effects of COVID-19 on radicalization to violent extremism. *Studies in Conflict & Terrorism*, 46(11), 2327–2350. https://doi.org/10.1080/1057610X.2021.1923188

Davies, J., Islaam, L., Carter, S., Redmayne, B., Cooper, K., Mandy, W., & Crane, L. (2024). Examining the support experiences of autistic young people with multiple marginalized identities in the United Kingdom. *Autism in Adulthood*. https://doi.org/10.31219/osf.io/ybm2a, https://doi.org/10.1089/aut.2024.0059

Dell'Osso, L., Dalle Luche, R., Cerliani, C., Bertelloni, C. A., Gesi, C., & Carmassi, C. (2015). Unexpected subthreshold autism spectrum in a 25-year-old male stalker hospitalized for delusional disorder: A case report. *Comprehensive Psychiatry*, 61, 10–14.

Diamond, A. (2013). Executive functions. *Annual Review of Psychology*, 64(1), 135–168.

Dodds, R. L. (2021). An exploratory review of the associations between adverse experiences and autism. *Journal of Aggression, Maltreatment & Trauma*, 30(8), 1093–1112.

Doidge, N. (2007). *The brain that changes itself: Stories of personal triumph from the frontiers of brain science*. Viking Press.

Donalds, C. & Ose-Bryson, K-M. (2019). Toward a cybercrime classification ontology: A knowledge-based approach. *Computers in Human Behavior*, 92, 403–418. https://doi.org/10.1016/j.chb.2018.11.039

Dubin, N., Henault, I., & Attwood, A. (2014). *The autism spectrum, sexuality and the law: What every parent and professional needs to know*. Jessica Kingsley Publishers.

Dupré, J. K., Tastenhoye, C. A., Ross, N. E., Bodnar, T. V., & Hatters Friedman, S. (2024). From Reddit to manifestos: Forensic evaluation of incel online activity. *Behavioral Sciences & the Law*, 42(2), 115–129.

Engel, D., Woolley, A. W., Jing, L. X., Chabris, C. F., & Malone, T. W. (2014). Reading the mind in the eyes or reading between the lines? Theory of mind predicts collective intelligence equally well online and face-to-face. *PloS One*, 9(12), e115212.

Febriana, S. K. T., & Fajrianthi (2019). Cyber incivility perpetrator: The influence of dissociative, anonymity, invisibility, asychronicity, and dissociative imagination. *Journal of Physics: Conference Series*, 1175(2019), 012238. doi:10.1088/1742-6596/1175/1/012238

Fein, E. (2015). Making meaningful worlds: Roleplaying subcultures. *Culture, Medicine, and Psychiatry*, 39(2), 299–321. doi:10/1007/s11013-015-9443-x

Ferguson, H. J., Black, J., & Williams, D. (2019). Distinguishing reality from fantasy in adults with autism spectrum disorder: Evidence from eye movements and reading. *Journal of Memory and Language*, 106, 95–107.

Forster, S. & Pearson, A. (2020). "Bullies tend to be obvious": Autistic adults' perceptions of friendship and the concept of 'mate crime'. *Disability & Society*, 35(7), 1103–1123.

Fraumeni-McBride, J. (2024). Autism, ADHD, sexual compulsivity, and problematic pornography use: A sexual psychosocial communication disparity in disability. *Sexual Health & Compulsivity*, 31(4), 298–323. https://doi.org/10.1080/26929953.2024.2368538

Freckelton, I. (2013). Autism spectrum disorder: Forensic issues and challenges for mental health professionals and courts. *Journal of Applied Research in Intellectual Disabilities*, 26(5), 420–434.

Free Speech Coalition. (2025, April 14). *Global age-verification policies*. https://action.freespeechcoalition.com/age-verification-resources/global-age-verification-policies/

Frith, C. and Frith, U. (2005). Theory of mind. *Current Biology*, 15(17), 644–645.

Fung, L. K. (Ed.). (2021). *Neurodiversity: From phenomenology to neurobiology and enhancing technologies*. American Psychiatric Pub.

Garcia v. Character Technologies, Inc., No. 6:24-cv-01903-ACC-EJK (M.D. Fla. Oct. 22, 2024)

Gougeon, N. A. (2010). Sexuality and autism: A critical review of selected literature using a social relational model of disability. *American Journal of Sexuality Education, 5*(4), 328–361.

Greenspan, Stephen. (2020). Competency. In: E. Kelley (Ed.), *Representing people with autism spectrum disorder: A practical guide for criminal defense lawyers* (p. 15). American Bar Association.

Griffiths, D., Hingsburger, D., Hoath, J., & Ioannou, S. (2013). 'Counterfeit deviance' revisited. *Journal of Applied Research in Intellectual Disabilities, 26*(5), 471–480.

Grove, R., Hoekstra, R. A., Wierda, M., & Begeer, S. (2018). Special interests and subjective wellbeing in autistic adults. *Autism Research, 11*(5), 766–775.

Hassrick, E. M., Holmes, L. G., Sosnowy, C., Walton, J., & Carley, K. (2021). Benefits and risks: A systematic review of information and communication technology use by autistic people. *Autism in Adulthood, 3*(1), 72–84.

Hénault, I. (2005). Sexuality and Asperger syndrome: The need for socio-sexual education. In K. Stoddart (Ed.), *Children, youth and adults with Asperger syndrome: Integrating multiple perspectives* (pp. 110–122). Jessica Kingsley Publishers.

Hénault, I. (2006). *Asperger's syndrome and sexuality: From adolescence through adulthood.* Jessica Kingsley Publishers.

Hénault, I. (2009). Understanding relationships and sexuality in individuals with high-functioning ASD. In A. Scarpa, S. White & T. Attwood (Eds.), *CBT for children and adolescents with high-functioning autism spectrum disorders* (pp. 278–299). Guilford Press.

Higgs, T. & Carter, A. J. (2015). Autism spectrum disorder and sexual offending: Responsivity in forensic interventions. *Aggression and Violent Behavior, 22,* 112–119.

Higham, L., Piracha, I., & Crocombe, J. (2016), Asperger syndrome, internet and fantasy versus reality – a forensic case study. *Advances in Mental Health and Disabilities, 10*(6), 349–354. https://doi.org/10.1108/AMHID-07-2015-0034

Hoffman, B., Ware, J., & Shapiro, E. (2020). Assessing the threat of incel violence. *Studies in Conflict & Terrorism, 43*(7), 565–587.

Hooker, Matthew. (2016, February 23). The Relationship Between Digital Technology and the Interpersonal Communication Skills of Generation Y. Available at Hooker, Matthew, The Relationship Between Digital Technology and the Interpersonal Communication Skills of Generation Y (February 23, 2016). Available at https://ssrn.com/abstract=3057797.

Hruska, J., & Maresova, P. (2020). Use of social media platforms among adults in the United States – Behavior on social media. *Societies, 10*(1), 27.

Jouenne, E. (personal communication, April 24, 2023).

Kaser-Boyd, Nancy. (2020) Criminal responsibility. In: E. Kelley (Ed.), *Representing people with mental disabilities: A practical guide for criminal defense lawyers* (p. 24).

Koffer Miller, K. H., Becker, A., Cooper, D., & Shea, L. (2022). Justice system interactions among autistic individuals: A multiple methods analysis. *Crime & Delinquency, 68*(9), 1579–1603. https://doi.org/10.1177/00111287211054733

Lai, M. C., Lombardo, M. V., Ruigrok, A. N., Chakrabarti, B., Auyeung, B., Szatmari, P., ... & MRC AIMS Consortium. (2016). Quantifying and exploring camouflaging in men and women with autism. *Autism, 21*(6), 690–702.

Lapidot-Lefler, N. and Barak, A. (2012). Effects of anonymity, invisibility, and lack of eye-contact on toxic online disinhibition. *Computers in Human Behavior, 28*(2), 434–443.

Lapidot-Lefler, N., & Barak, A. (2015). The benign online disinhibition effect: Could situational factors induce self-disclosure and prosocial behaviors?. *Cyberpsychology: Journal of Psychosocial Research on Cyberspace, 9*(2).

Ledingham, R. & Mills, R. (2015). A preliminary study of autism and cybercrime in the context of international law enforcement. *Advances in Autism, 1*(1), 2–11.

Leung, P. W. S., Li, S. X., Holroyd, E. A., Tsang, C. S. O., & Wong, W. C. W. (2023). Online social media poses opportunities and risks in autistic youth: Implications for services from a qualitative study. *Frontiers in Psychiatry, 14*, 959846.

Liberatore, M., Levine, B. N., & Shields, C. (2010, November). Strengthening forensic investigations of child pornography on p2p networks. In *Proceedings of the 6th International Conference* (pp. 1–12).

Lim, A., Brewer, N., & Young, R. L. (2024). Revisiting the relationship between cybercrime, autistic traits, and autism. *Journal of Autism and Developmental Disorders, 53*, 1319–1330. https://doi.org/10.1007/s10803-021-05207-1

Loftin, R., Westphal, A., & Sperry, L. A. (2021). Sexuality and problem behaviors. In: F.R. Volkmar (Ed.), *Encyclopedia of autism spectrum disorders* (pp. 4320–4322). Springer. https://doi.org/10.1007/978-3-319-91280-6_102140

Louie, S. (2020, July 20). Why millennials love anime and hentai pornography. *Psychology Today.* www.psychologytoday.com/us/blog/minority-report/202007/why-millennials-love-anime-and-hentai-pornography

MacMillan, K., Berg, T., Just, M., & Stewart, M. F. (2022). Online safety experiences of autistic young people: An interpretive phenomenological analysis. *Research in Autism Spectrum Disorders, 96.* https://doi.org/10.1016/jrasd.2022.101995

MacMullin, J., Linsky, Y., and Weiss, J. (2016). Plugged in: Electronics use in youth and young adults with autism spectrum disorder. *Autism, 20*(1), 45–54. https://doi:10.177/1362361314566047

Madigan, S., Ly, A., Rash, C. L., Van Ouytsel, J., & Temple, J. R. (2018). Prevalence of multiple forms of sexting behavior among youth: A systematic review and meta-analysis. *JAMA Pediatrics, 172*(4), 327–335.

Mahoney, M. (2009). Asperger's syndrome and the criminal law: The special case of child pornography. Assisted by Aygun, S. & Polen, M., *Law Student Clerks.* Buffalo, NY: Mark J. Mahoney.

Mahoney, M. J. (2021). Defending men with autism accused of online sexual offenses. In *Handbook of autism spectrum disorder and the law* (pp. 269–306). Springer International Publishing.

Man, J., Siu, G. A., & Hutchings, A. (2023, November). Autism disclosures and cybercrime discourse on a large underground forum. In *2023 APWG Symposium on Electronic Crime Research eCrime* (pp. 1–14). IEEE.

Mandell, D. S., Lawer, L. J., Branch, K., Brodkin, E. S., Healey, K., Witalec, R., … & Gur, R. E. (2012). Prevalence and correlates of autism in a state psychiatric hospital. *Autism, 16*(6), 557–567.

Marttila, E., Koivula, A., & Räsänen, P. (2021). Cybercrime victimization and problematic social media use: Findings from a nationally representative panel study. *American Journal of Crime Justice*, 46(6), 862–881. doi: 10.1007/s12103-021-09665-2. Epub 2021 Nov 25. PMID: 34848939; PMCID: PMC8614072.

Massanari, A. (2017). Gamergate and the fappening: How Reddit's algorithm, governance, and culture support toxic technocultures. *New Media and Society*, 19(3). https://doi.org/10.1177/1461444815608807

Mazurek, M. O. (2013). Social media use among adults with autism spectrum disorders. *Computers in Human Behavior*, 29(4), 1709–1714.

Mesibov, G. B., Shea, V., & Adams, L. W. (2005). *Understanding Asperger syndrome and high functioning autism* (Vol. 1). Springer Science & Business Media.

Metro. (2024). Teenager hacked school's system because he was bored. *Metro*, Dec. 10, 2024. metro.co.uk/2024/12/10/teenager-hacked-schools-system-bored-22156731/.

Michael, Z. & Brewer, N. (2024). Detecting criminal intent in social interactions: The influence of autism and theory of mind. *Law and Human Behavior*, 49(1), 89–107.

Miller, K. H. K., Cooper, D. S., Song, W., & Shea, L. L. (2022). Self-reported service needs and barriers reported by autistic adults: Differences by gender identity. *Research in Autism Spectrum Disorders*, 92, 101916.

Milton, D., Gurbuz, E., & López, B. (2022). The 'double empathy problem': Ten years on. *Autism*, 26(8), 1901–1903.

Mitchell, K. J., Jones, L. M., Finkelhor, D., & Wolak, J. (2014). Trends in unwanted exposure to sexual material: Findings from the Youth Internet Safety Studies. Retrieved April, 15, 2015.

Mogavero, M. C. (2016). Autism, sexual offending, and the criminal justice system. *Journal of Intellectual Disabilities and Offending Behaviour*, 7(3), 116–126.

Morie, K. P., Jackson, S., Zhai, Z. W., Potenza, M. N., & Dritschel, B. (2019). Mood disorders in high-functioning autism: The importance of alexithymia and emotional regulation. *Journal of Autism and Developmental Disorders*, 49, 2935–2945.

Munderia, R. & Singh, R. (2019). The relationship between social skills and perceived smartphone usage. *Journal of Psychosocial Research*, 14(1), 201–210.

National Center for Missing & Exploited Children. (2023). CyberTipline Reports by Electronic Service Providers. 2024, www.missingkids.org/content/dam/missingkids/pdfs/2023-reports-by-esp.pdf.

National Institute of Justice. (2023, December 18). Five things about the role of the internet and social media in domestic radicalization. nij.ojp.gov:https://nij.ojp.gov/topics/articles/five-things-about-role-internet-and-social-media-domestic-radicalization

Neupane, A., Satvat, K., Saxena, N., Stavrinos, D., & Bishop, H. J. (2018, December). Do social disorders facilitate social engineering? A case study of autism and phishing attacks. In *Proceedings of the 34th Annual Computer Security Applications Conference* (pp. 467–477).

Nir, S. M. (2024, May 15). 'Chelsea' asked for nude pictures. Then the sextortion began. *The New York Times*.

Parti, K., Sanders, C. E., & Englander, E. K. (2023). Sexting at an early age: Patterns and poor health-related consequences of pressured sexting in middle and high school. *Journal of School Health*, 93(1), 73–81. doi: 10.1111/josh.13258. Epub 2022 Oct 17. PMID: 36251455; PMCID: PMC10092123.

Pataranutaporn, P., Liu, R., Finn, E., & Maes, P. (2023). *Influencing human–AI interaction by priming beliefs about AI can increase perceived trustworthiness, empathy, and effectiveness*. Nature Machine Intelligence, 5, 1076–1086. https://doi.org/10.1038/s42256-023-00720-7

Paul, H. A. (2015). *Asperger syndrome: Assessing and treating high functioning autism spectrum disorders*, edited by J. C. McPartland, A. Klin, & F. R. Volkmar: Guilford Press.

Payne, K. L., Russell, A., Mills, R., Maras, K., Rai, D., & Brosnan, M. (2019). Is there a relationship between cyber-dependent crime, autistic-like traits and autism? *Journal of Autism and Developmental Disorders*, 49, 4159–4169.

Pearson, A., Rees, J., & Forster, S. (2022). "This was just how this friendship worked": Experiences of interpersonal victimization among autistic adults. *Autism in Adulthood*, 4(2), 141–150.

Pryke-Hobbes, A., Davies, J., Heasman, B., Livesey, A., Walker, A., Pellicano, E., & Remington, A. (2023). The workplace masking experiences of autistic, non-autistic neurodivergent and neurotypical adults in the UK. *Plos One*, 18(9), e0290001.

Raymaker, D. M., Teo, A. R., Steckler, N. A., Lentz, B., Scharer, M., Delos Santos, A., & Nicolaidis, C. (2020). "Having all of your internal resources exhausted beyond measure and being left withno clean-up crew": Defining autistic burnout. *Autism in Adulthood*, 2(2), 132–143.

Recupero, P. R. (2008). Forensic evaluation of problematic Internet use. *Journal of the American Academy of Psychiatry and the Law Online*, 36(4), 505–514.

Ritzman, M. J. & Subramanian, R. (2024). Voices from a pandemic: Understanding how young adults on the autism spectrum use computer-mediated communication. *Autism*, 28(2), 381–389.

Romano, M., Truzoli, R., Osborne, L. A., & Reed, P. (2014). The relationship between autism quotient, anxiety, and internet addiction. *Research in Autism Spectrum Disorders*, 8(11), 1521–1526. https://doi.org/10.1016/j.chb.2020.106534

Roose, K. (2024, October 24). Can A.I. be blamed for a teen's suicide? *The New York Times*

Ruben, M. A., Stosic, M. D., Correale, J., & Blanch-Hartigan, D. (2021). Is technology enhancing or hindering interpersonal communication? A framework and preliminary results to examine the relationship between technology use and nonverbal decoding skill. *Frontiers in Psychology*, 11, 611670.

Ruvalcaba, Y. & Eaton, A. A. (2020). Nonconsensual pornography among U.S. adults: A sexual scripts framework on victimization, perpetration, and health correlates for women and men. *Psychology of Violence*, 10(1), 68–78. https://doi.org/10.1037/vio0000233

Ruzich, E., Allison, C., Smith, P. et al. (2015). Measuring autistic traits in the general population: A systematic review of the Autism-Spectrum Quotient (AQ) in a nonclinical population sample of 6,900 typical adult males and females. *Molecular Autism*, 6(2). https://doi.org/10.1186/2040-2392-6-2

Sallafranque-St-Louis, F. & Normand, C. L. (2017). From solitude to solicitation: How people with intellectual disability or autism spectrum disorder use the internet. *Cyberpsychology: Journal of Psychosocial Research on Cyberspace*, 11(1).

Saunders, J. B., Hao, W., Long, J., King, D. L., Mann, K., Fauth-Bühler, M., ... & Poznyak, V. (2017). Gaming disorder: Its delineation as an important condition for diagnosis, management, and prevention. *Journal of Behavioral Addictions*, 6(3), 271–279. https://doi.org/10.1556/2006.6.2017.039

Scrivens, R., Davies, G., & Frank, R. (2020). Measuring the evolution of radical right-wing posting behaviors online. *Deviant Behavior*, 41(2), 216–232.

Seigfried-Spellar, K. C., O'Quinn, C. L., & Treadway, K. N. (2015). Assessing the relationship between autistic traits and cyberdeviancy in a sample of college students. *Behaviour & Information Technology*, 34(5), 533–542.

Shane-Simpson, C., Brooks, P. J., Obeid, R., Denton, E., & Gillespie-Lynch, K. (2016). Associations between compulsive internet use and the autism spectrum. *Research in Autism Spectrum Disorders*, 23, 152–165. http://dx.doi.org/10.1016/j.rasd.2015.12.005

Shattuck, P. T., Narendorf, S. C., Cooper, B., Sterzing, P. R., Wagner, M., & Taylor, J. L. (2012). Postsecondary education and employment among youth with an autism spectrum disorder. *Pediatrics*, 129(6), 1042–1049. https://doi.org/10.1542/peds.2011-2864

Shea, L. & Burke, J. (2022). *Autism and the criminal justice system: Policy opportunities and challenges*. (Policy brief). The International Society for Autism Research. https://drexel.edu/autisminstitute/research/research-policy-analytics-center/autism-and-the-criminal-justice-system/INSAR-policy-brief/

Shirama, A., Kato, N., & Kashino, M. (2017). When do individuals with autism spectrum disorder show superiority in visual search? *Autism*, 21(8), 942–951.

Shiri, E., Goudarzi, G., Feyzi, F., & Khodaverdian, M. (2024). Investigating the role of the broad autism phenotype, social cognition, and sense of loneliness on Internet addiction in college students. *PCP*, 12(3), 263–274. http://jpcp.uswr.ac.ir/article-1-935-en.html

Shore, S. (2016). *If you've met one person with autism, you've met one person with autism*. www.wordpress.com.

Skirrow, P., Jackson, P., Perry, E., & Hare, J. (2014). I collect therefore I am-Autonoetic consciousness and hoarding in Asperger Syndrome. *Clinical Psychology &Psychotherapy*, 22, 3. https://doi.org/10.1002./cpp.1889

Slavny-Cross, R., Allison, C., Griffiths, S., & Baron-Cohen, S. (2022). Autism and the criminal justice system: An analysis of 93 cases. *Autism Research*, 15(5), 904–914.

Slavny-Cross, R., Allison, C., Griffiths, S., & Baron-Cohen, S. (2023). Are autistic people disadvantaged by the criminal justice system? A case comparison. *Autism*, 27(5), 1438–1448. https://doi.org/10.1177/13623613221140284

Speckhard, A. & Ellenberg, M. (2022). Self-reported psychiatric disorder and perceived psychologicalsymptom rates among involuntary celibates (incels) and their perceptions of mental health treatment. *Behavioral Sciences of Terrorism and Political Aggression*, 1–18.

Sperry, L. A., Stokes, M. A., Gavisk, M. E., & Gavisk, D. C. (2021). Stalking, autism, and the law. In: *Handbook of autism spectrum disorder and the law* (pp. 307–325). Springer International Publishing.

Stijelja, S. & Mishara, B. L. (2023). Psychosocial characteristics of involuntary celibates (incels): A reviewof empirical research and assessment of the potential implications of research on adult virginityand late sexual onset. *Sexuality & Culture*, 27(2), 715–734.

Stone, B., Saggers, B., Campbell, M. A., & Yates, C. (2025). Neurodivergent students' views on internet threats: A call for research. In *Students' online risk behaviors: Psychoeducational predictors, outcomes, and prevention* (pp. 45–86). IGI Global Scientific Publishing.

Stuart, J. & Scott, R. (2021).The Measure of Online Disinhibition (MOD): Assessing perceptions of reductions in restraint in the online environment. *Computers in Human Behavior*, 114, 106534. https://doi.org/10.1016/j.chb.2020.106534

Suler, J. (2004). The online disinhibition effect. *Cyberpsychology & Behavior*, 7(3), 321–326. https://doi.org/10.1089/1094931041291295

Suskind, R. (2014). *Life Animated: A Story of Sidekicks, Heroes and Autism*. Kingswell.

Tastenhoye, C. A., Ross, N. E., Dupré, J., Bodnar, T. V., & Friedman, S. H. (2022). Involuntary celibates and forensic psychiatry. *Journal of the American Academy of Psychiatry and the Law Online*, JAAPL. 210136–21. DOI: 10.29158/JAAPL.210136-21

Tastenhoye, C. A., Dupré, J., Ross, N. E., Bodnar, T. V., & Friedman, S. H. (2023). Incels: An introduction for mental health clinicians. *Journal of Psychiatric Practice®*, 29(5), 384–389.

Tateno, M., Tateno, Y., Shirasaka, T., Nanba, K., Shiraishi, E., Shimomura, R., & Kato, T. A. (2025). Depression, gaming disorder, and internet addiction in adolescents with autism spectrum disorder. *Behavioral Sciences*, 15(4), 423.

Thorne, J., Graham, S., & Barantini, P. (2025, March). Johnson, J. *Adolescence*. Netflix, Warp Films, It's All Made Up Productions, Matriarch Productions, Plan B Entertainment, One Shoe Films.

Time.com. (2011, December 6). Case of Scottish hacker illustrates divide between U.S. and U.K. extradition laws. *TIME*. https://world.time.com/2011/12/06/case-of-scottish-hacker-illustrates-divide-between-u-s-and-u-k-extradition-laws/

Tirkkonen, S. K. & Vespermann, D. (2023). Incels, autism, and hopelessness: Affective incorporation of online interaction as a challenge for phenomenological psychopathology. *Frontiers in Psychology*, 14, 1235929.

Trayvick, J., Barkley, S. B., McGowan, A., & Srivastava, A. (2024). Speech and language patterns in autism: Towards natural language processing as a research and clinical tool. *Psychiatry Research*, 340(116109).

U.S. Congress. (2025). S.146 – 119th Congress: TAKE IT DOWN Act. Congress.gov. www.congress.gov/bill/119th-congress/senate-bill/146

Van Brunt, B. J., Van Brunt, B. S., Taylor, C., Morgan, N., & Solomon, J. (2021). The rise of the incel mission-oriented attacker. *Violence and Gender*, 8(4), 163–174.

Van der Aa, C., Pollmann, M. M., Plaat, A., & van der Gaag, R. J. (2016). Computer-mediated communication in adults with high-functioning autism spectrum disorders and controls. *Research in Autism Spectrum Disorders, 23*(3), 15–27.

van der Kolk, B. A. (2014). *The body keeps the score by Bessel van der Kolk.* Penguin Books.

Venter, F., Morelli, J., & Erasmus, E. (2023). Understanding the lived music listening experiences of adults on the autism spectrum. *Psychology of Music, 51*(3), 971–985.

Ventura, F., Areias, G., Coroa, M., Araújo, A., Borges, J., Morais, S., & Madeira, N. (2022). Stalking behavior and high-functioning autism spectrum disorders–a case report. *The Journal of Forensic Psychiatry & Psychology, 33*(5), 639–645.

Visuri, I. (2019). A room of one's own: Autistic imagination as a stage for parasocial interaction and social learning. *Journal for the Cognitive Science of Religion, 5*(1), 100–124. https://doi.org/10.1558/jcsr.37518

Walsh, J. D. (2018, January 22). Dead wake. *New York Magazine.*

Wang, T., Garfield, M., Wisniewski, P., & Page, X. (2020, October). Benefits and challenges for social media users on the autism spectrum. In *Companion Publication of the 2020 Conference on Computer Supported Cooperative Work and Social Computing* (pp. 419–424).

Weber, S. (2018). *White supremacy's old gods.* Political Research Associates.

Welch, C., Senman, L., Loftin, R., Picciolini, C., Robison, J., Westphal, A., ... & Penner, M. (2023).Understanding the use of the term "Weaponized autism" in an alt-right social media platform. *Journal of Autism and Developmental Disorders, 53*(10), 4035–4046.

Wells, M. & Mitchell, K. J. (2014). Patterns of internet use and risk of online victimization for youth with and without disabilities. *The Journal of Special Education, 48*(3), 204–213. https://doi.org/10.1177/0022466913479141

West, M. J., Somer, E., & Eigsti, I. M. (2023). Immersive and maladaptive daydreaming and divergent thinking in autism spectrum disorders. *Imagination, Cognition and Personality, 42*(4), 372–398. https://doi.org/10.1177/02762366221129819

Whitney, T. (2023, July 5). Advocacy for the overlooked needs of autistic individuals in the US criminal justice system. *Autism Spectrum News.* autismspectrumnews.org/advocacy-for-the-overlooked-needs   =of=autistic-individuals-in the-US-criminal-justice-system/

Wijekoon, S., Robison, J., Welch, C., Westphal, A., Loftin, R., Perry, B., Rombos, V., Picciolini, C., Bosy, C., Senman, L., & Jachyra, P. (2024). Neurodivergence and the rabbit hole of extremism: Uncovering lived experience. *Autism in Adulthood.*

Williams, F. & Mann, R. E. (2010). The treatment of intellectually disabled sexual offenders in the national offender management service: The adapted sex offender treatment programmes. *Assessment and treatment of sexual offenders with intellectual disabilities: A handbook* (pp. 293–315).

Wittig, Karl. (2021). Inappropriate behaviors in adult autistics: We mean no harm. *Autism Spectrum News,* Sept. 23, 2021. autismspectrumnews.org/inappropriate-behaviors-in-adult-autistics-we-mean-no-harm/.

Woodbury-Smith, M., Loftin, R., Westphal, A., & Volkmar, F. (2022). Vulnerability to ideologically motivated violence among individuals with autism spectrum disorder. *Frontiers of Psychiatry, 13.* https://doi.org/10.3389/fpsyt.2022.873121

Wright, M. F. & Wachs, S. (2019). Does peer rejection moderate the associations among cyberbullying victimization, depression, and anxiety among adolescents with autism spectrum disorder? *Children, 6*(3), 41. https://doi.org/10.3390/children6030041

Wurzman, R. (2018, October). *How isolation fuels opioid addiction.* [Video] TED Conferences. www.ted.com/talks/rachel_wurzman

Yaffe-Bellamy, D. (2023, October 30). Sam Bankman-Fried trial: Founder of collapsed crypto firm has his own words turned against him. *The New York Times.*

Index

For Product Safety Concerns and Information please contact our EU
representative GPSR@taylorandfrancis.com
Taylor & Francis Verlag GmbH, Kaufingerstraße 24, 80331 München, Germany